D1601350

American Policy Making

American Policy Making

Welfare as Ritual

William M. Epstein

ROWMAN & LITTLEFIELD PUBLISHERS, INC.
Lanham • Boulder • New York • Oxford

ROWMAN & LITTLEFIELD PUBLISHERS, INC.
Published in the United States of America
by Rowman & Littlefield Publishers, Inc.
4720 Boston Way, Lanham, Maryland 20706
www.romanlittlefield.com

12 Hid's Copse Road
Cumnor Hill, Oxford OX2 9JJ, England

British Library Cataloguing in Publication Information available

Library of Congress Cataloging-in-Publication Data
Epstein, William M., 1944–
    American policy making: welfare as ritual/William M. Epstein.
        p. cm.
    Includes bibliographical references and index.
    ISBN 0-7425-1732-2 (alk. paper)—ISBN 0-7425-1733-0 (pbk.: alk. paper)
    1. Public welfare—Government policy—United States. 2. Social work—Government policy—United States. 3.United States—Social policy. 4. United States—Economic policy. 5. United States—Politics and government. I. Title.

HV95 .E69 2002
361.973—dc21   2001041925

The paper used in this publication meets the minimum requirements of American National Standard for Information Sciences—Permanence of Paper for Printed Library Materials, ANSI/NISO Z39.48–1992.

Contents

Preface		vii
Acknowledgments		xix
Introduction		1
Chapter 1	Political Theory, Ideology, and Social Welfare	25
Chapter 2	The Willow World of Virtue: Rationality and Effectiveness in the Personal Social Services	47
Chapter 3	The American Ethos 1: Two Civil Religions	91
Chapter 4	The American Ethos 2: America Speaks—The Polls and Policy Choice	111
Chapter 5	The American Ethos 3: Social Welfare Services as Rituals of the Civil Religion	135
Chapter 6	Two Romances: The Enlightenment and the Anti-Enlightenment	151
Chapter 7	Science, Limited Science, and Scientism	193
Conclusion	Hiding from the Jacobins	211
	Afterword	221
	References	223
	Index	237
	About the Author	249

Preface

American social policy making is profitably interpreted through the nation's social services, particularly its personal social services. Far from providing measures to relieve need, American social services play a role in denying claims on public resources, providing at best minimal protection and a meager security even for those who have worked for decades. The principal role of the social services is performed in affirming American values. These values are neither generous nor notably humane; they endorse the nation's economic and social differences. America's cultural stratification is widely popular, consistent with the nation's tradition of broad participation and its commitment to republican values but inconsistent with its sense of itself as a sharing, just society.

The social decision-making process contains few rational elements. Rather, it is profoundly ideological despite drawing its discourse from scientific theory. Indeed, political authority, failing to carry its rational virtues into social decision making, is only fashioned after scientific authority. The juxtaposition of the nation's enduring and consistent policy choices—its true values—with its global aspirations hints at the existence of two related but seemingly contradictory civil religions. Yet, logical contradictions are not necessarily political conundrums. The ceremonial civil religion of feast, holiday, and patriotic pomp translates the nation's policy preferences—its operative civil religion—into the transcendent language of chosenness. Political decisions that largely reflect the tacit but profound assumptions of group worth—the ascribed failings of character that constitute deservingness—are softened through the rituals of the civil religion into the timeless virtues of American destiny.

American social welfare policy is socially efficient (both inexpensive and compatible with existing social arrangements) and would be the pride of civilization if it were also effective. Yet broadly popular American social welfare policy fails to address widespread need. In part, the acceptance of inadequate social policy is facilitated by the corrective myths of the social sciences, the little lies of program evaluations that social welfare arrangements are actually effective or at least promising leads, important beginnings, and steps in the right direction. Mythmaking is a central role of the social sciences, performed more in agreement with the nation's operative civil religion than out of a more noble commitment to the Enlightenment that inspires the rhetoric of its ceremonies.

It might be wise, especially while it is flush with economic success, for the United States to experiment with a better way of doing its social business in order to carry the nation through inevitable bad times. Neither the current system of human services nor the more restricted provisions of social welfare policy have prevented or handled the enormous amount of deprivation among Americans, especially those with lower incomes. Indeed, until the economic progress of recent years, about 40 percent of the population had been losing ground between 1973 and 1996, while the next 20 or 30 percent have barely been keeping up. Yet the nation appears to have accepted with little protest the increasing concentration of wealth and income at the top. As a result, the current range of policy options is narrow.

The better way of doing its social business might involve a more sincere pursuit of Enlightenment ideals through public policy—greater social and economic equality among citizens and the routine production of more reliable information to inform the intelligence of democracy. Yet even cautious steps in this direction require greater public spending, an extremely unpopular choice. The United States has characteristically resisted redistributive policy impulses except when economic booms lift poorer groups and the good fortune justifies national braggadocio, as though greater equality was intended from the outset. Moreover, the immense centrifugal forces of this highly homogenized culture have routinely undermined rational authority, notably the investigative freedom of the social sciences along with the university itself.

Any challenge to the orthodoxy of social welfare (on the one hand, providing even fewer social services and less security for poor and working people; on the other, doing more) corners the dog of social resistance if it fails to offer plausible proof or at least comforting assurances of its effectiveness. The general wisdom in pressing for a novel idea, especially if it is to replace a popular one, rests on two principles. First, the novelty needs to demonstrate that it achieves favored goals better than the old idea—the car as superior to the horse, penicillin over wild herbs, democracy over the divine right of kings, the computer over the typewriter. Second, its relative advantage must also confer a social advantage, that is, prestige, status, or power. Yet a strategy to resolve the dilemma of the contemporary American welfare state—the popularity of its frank inadequacies—cannot adopt this strategy. After listening to arguments for greater economic and social equality, a strong governing consensus of

Americans has rejected alternative visions of society; the existing conditions of American society appear to be more comfortable than promised changes. Even from the narrower perspective of efficiency, the patience to try on welfare styles or even to test different welfare policies in microcosm is limited by cost and practicality, while the rational attempts of the social sciences to do so in the past have been uniformly compromised by powerful political stakes and crippling methodological pitfalls.

The alternative to the winning strategy of substituting better for good is to loosen the society's grip on its institutions to stimulate the exploration of uncertain futures. Exploration is encouraged by the observation that social problems as well as resistance to change are more the products of human choice and tradition than monuments to an ineluctable physics of social life. In contrast, exploration is impeded by the absence of pressure to extend the coverage or to increase the benefits of the American welfare state. Social need has been increasing in the United States for decades, yet the political voice for a welfare response has been largely mute. If anything, there is a sizable constituency that would roll back the scope of even its largest and most popular programs—Old Age, Survivors, and Disability Insurance (OASDI) and Medicare—in the name of actuarial prudence while limiting the general role of the public sector in many other policy areas, including health, cash assistance, personal social services, and education. Worse for the prospects of greater equality, political candidates for national office are running and winning on historical sentimentality, the long-discredited planks of returning responsibility for the reform of personal deviance back once again to the philanthropic sector, business, and local government.

Highlighting the problems perpetuated by a meager social policy, deflating the pretenses of existing policy to rational authority, and perhaps, too, giving heart to the poorly paid and needy to campaign for their own claims might increase the nation's political appetite for more ambitious social welfare policies. There are some who already willingly support generosity in spite of their own economic success; hopefully, too, inevitable economic difficulties, growing inequalities, and incessant penury will energize rather than silence others. But impulses toward greater equality are frequently frightened off by premature claims of success that in the end discredit the search for alternatives. Rather than prophecy, gnosticism, and a mawkish reverence for tradition, the society is better off in the long run with a seasoned sense of the inhumane conundrums of Romanticism, learning perhaps to patiently devote resources to the search for politically viable and programmatically sound social welfare programs.

The social welfare industry, including a large number of disciplines, workers, and social institutions, has typically been a tame and late participant either in developing public consciousness of a social problem or in pursuing effective responses. Except in protection of its own unfortunately narrow organizational and financial interests, the business of welfare is a conflicted and hypocritical advocate for those in need or even for the general welfare of the nation. Reflecting the dominant social ethos that sanctions its operations, the social welfare enterprise is inattentive and often contemptuous of those who depend on its provisions.

The first step toward a solution is not a solution itself but the stimulation of the political will to acknowledge a problem. In this case the problem is not simply the deprivations of many citizens but the absence of social institutions sensitive to their needs and a misguided set of political priorities. The morality of a social problem is conjectural, but its political consequences are less so, especially if the mute inequalities of American life burst the courtly channels of social discourse.

Still and all, the United States may have largely solved its social problems. Its political system may simply be realizing the sense of American citizens that its problems are minimal: a few addicts and street people, a small number of dependent children, and a few citizens with other, but-for-the-grace-of-God problems. American rewards and punishments (in the form of socioeconomic stratification) are probably consistent with American intentions. Indeed, the happy state of American affairs seems quite plausible as the nation's economy is reaching record low unemployment for a record labor force, while the American people seem to be the wealthiest, best-served population the world has known. Indeed, the wonderments of America's high culture tempt comparison with classic civilizations. Unless this perception is refuted or the American people tire of their materialistic consumerism, no change is possible. Indeed, the increasing acceptance of the current social and economic regime suggests a form of governance and society that will become timelessly enshrined as the American experience.

Despite the efforts of political science, the determinants of social decision making remain largely unproven; society does make choices, but they do not appear to be consistent with the nation's ceremonial religion or predictable extensions of standing social theory. Societal change apparently takes place, but aside from the bland observation that technological innovation is somehow implicated, these changes also defy prediction. The tie between ideology and action is tenuous at best: whether one is the cause of the other, or whether both are expressions of more fundamental forces, or even whether avowed justifications are the true motives of competitive groups. Political choice is mystical, largely unexplained except after the fact. Out of the immense complexity, variety, and possibilities of reality, some one thing is institutionalized and then seems to exert an independent influence.

Nineteenth-century Romanticism raised mysticism to the level of explanation. Unfortunately, it defied reason but abetted the social tendencies of rebarbative, fractured cultures. The supremacy of the human will, not human reason, emerged from a conviction that reality was no more than sensory perception and therefore amenable to a reperception, a remolding, as an act of human will. Perception became all as though the epistemological problem of man's sensory limitations could be reversed: stimuli leading to perceptions of reality turned on its head as perception creating reality. With little social restraint on the notion of absolute idealism (or perhaps as absolute idealism became a convenience for a frustrated age), objective reality was rejected by the anti-Enlightenment as an unnecessary restraint on human ambition. The will was a causative agent with nearly limitless possibilities.

Nonetheless, allowing the assumptions of their own systems, the Romantics may not have been any less internally correct than Enlightenment figures, just less useful and suggestive of quite different social visions. As polar ideologies, each has been available as inspiration for political rivals through contemporary times. Each is a battalion flag for politicized social experience. Yet it is more than simply coincidence or a question of poor literary skill that, with few exceptions, the major figures of both Romanticism and postmodernism (really neo-Romanticism) routinely produced works of almost impenetrable density. Indeed, postmodernists have been dismissed for knowingly obfuscating intellectual discourse (Sokal and Bricmont 1999; Vattimo 1991; Norris 1990). Fichte, Hegel, Schelling, Marx's economics, and Kierkegaard prefigure Baudrillard, Derrida, and Foucault in both style and substance. Each developed self-absorbed, unique "ego" languages that demanded the student's total absorption and unquestioning belief in the author's revealed truth. Each also verges on dogmatism, the faith that some undefined cultural determinant trumps reason.

While modern American liberals claim lineage to the Enlightenment, their social programs far more closely parallel Romantic thought. Indeed, many continuing social problems stem from an ideological confusion that demands a political discourse in the terms of the Enlightenment but actually adheres to Romantic impulses and ideals. The politics of the nation reverberate with the Fourth of July fireworks of democratic decision making and social equality but in the end produce an imagery of extreme individualism through feckless rituals of state interventions that cannot possibly realize those goals. To the contrary, the embedded parsimony of social welfare provisions for poor and lower-status Americans and the corrective myths of the social sciences—the broad refusal of the nation's intellectuals to acknowledge the failure of these programs—figure in a mystical cultural decision to deny remedy for social inequalities.

Nonetheless, Romantic thinking probably accurately describes the state of politics in liberal democracies—"how small a part conscious choice and realistic thinking play in human action" (Aiken 1956, 204, paraphrasing Nietzsche). However, the absence of rationality in social decision making is not necessarily desirable; existence does not recommend itself. American socioeconomic stratification triumphs in the politics of the United States through the excessive claims of Romanticism's extreme individualism: superior intellect, superior character, superior civic virtue, and, as a very dark and frequently tacit subtheme, superior biology. Frequent inattention to social need in the twentieth century and its episodic slaughters have been customarily justified in the name of some Romantic ideal of ethnic purity, cultural destiny, class justice, and, with greater frequency, economic necessity.

In addition to democracy and decency, the arguments against Romanticism in political life are also profoundly sectarian, reflecting the ancient fears of social and ethnic minorities troubled by mystical civic ideals that sustained mass impulses to override the law. An orderly society that installs pragmatic processes to protect justice usually offers a more secure future than a reliance on the hysterical ignorance of absolute idealism and collective subjectivity. The efflorescence in America of some of the world's despised minorities may well testify to the possibilities of structural, enlightened reform: broad entitlements in support of a more informed and equal citizenry and a richer popular culture. Yet Lindblom's simple faith in full understanding pursued through factional research is inadequate. Understanding even as a necessarily limited or relative ideal still may require a degree of investment in information and greater equality that eclipses temporal political tolerances.

Human Services and Personal Social Services

Human services constitute the broadest category of planned care; they include health care and public health provisions, education, and social welfare services for any population in either the public or the private sector.[1] The personal social services constitute a limited category of human services that are better explained in terms of custom and professional attention than by definitive categorization. Many allied semiprofessions, such as public administration and planning, counseling, social work, and clinical psychology, provide the personal social services. Personal social services can be adjunctive to health care and education, but they provide benefits that address a multitude of personal and social problems such as poverty, mental and emotional disorders, unemployment, crime and delinquency, drug and alcohol addiction, and so forth. The personal social services address these problems either by providing greater equality directly through the replication of customary social institutions (e.g., foster care for children without families) and through programmatic strategies of cure, prevention, or rehabilitation that are intended to

change personal behavior and remedy the consequences of prior deprivation and imprudent willfulness.

Publicly financed income security programs targeted on the nonpoor
are expressions of social values as much as public assistance personal
social services for the poor. Yet the concrete benefits and the generally
economic styles of analysis for cash programs have disproportionately
emphasized their rationalistic content as though concreteness immu-
nized them against ideological interpretation. Still, the emptiness of the
personal social services that provide less countable benefits, if benefits at
all, better disclose the unanchored immaterialism of social preferences
and the pervasively political, as opposed to the rational, determinants of
social decision making. While the personal social services constitute a
small portion of the human services, the social decision-making process
that creates and maintains them discloses the national preferences that
determine the human services generally. Indeed, those preferences seem
to be cultural fixtures, telling institutions that are, in a literary sense, the
national character.

The personal social services, while not particularly powerful, well
funded, or effective, are institutions of American life. Indeed, their enduring ineffectiveness belies their importance and the degree to which their
roles, especially in failure, profoundly mirror American social preferences. The seemingly eternal disjuncture between the legislated and the
stated goals of the personal social services, on the one hand, and their
actual performance, on the other, may explain much about the way the
United States socializes its people and addresses its cultural flaws. Any
social change, and certainly any planned attempt to promulgate policy in
anticipation of problems, is facilitated by an appreciation for the contingencies of the American ethos.

The puzzle of the personal social services begins with the observation that they rarely, if ever, meet their avowed goals. Nevertheless,
they are annually refunded with only cursory attention to their effectiveness and only superficial demands for a credible scholarship of their
functions. Naturally, logically, almost by definition, culture writes itself
into all its institutions. Yet the solipsism that isolates personal experience from the dictatorial forces of socialization is central to the myth of
self-determination. Notably powerful in America, metaphors of individuality and personal autonomy may explain the nation's attachment
to an extreme credo of personal as opposed to social responsibility.
Among modern industrialized nations, the United States pays the least
attention to the needs of its lower-income citizens (Gilens 1990, 205).

The partisan role of the personal social services in dramatizing the
dominant ethos of the culture becomes even clearer in reference to care
that is provided for marginal, poor, and lower-status groups. Along with

some small degree of help, they invariably carry along society's hope, if not coercive insistence, for behavioral conformity. There is much to be learned about American society and its social policy-making process from the reluctant provision of public and private charity for services whose tacit importance relates only tangentially to their direct service missions. Rather than serious assaults on need, the social services and notably the personal social services are political theaters for a performance of American values: by and large, winners own their good fortune and losers their hardships. In this sense, social services are profoundly ideological metaphors for the American myth.

It is no surprise that throughout a society that cherishes material possessions and economic success, market differences are carried over into the provision of human services whether supplied publicly or purchased through private markets where the wealthy obviously outbid competitors for scarce resources. The inequalities of American culture are perpetuated through the human services: like seats at a ballpark or theater, the quality, access, and amount of care closely reflect social status and economic capacity. This would not mean much if the service inequalities were superficial and unrelated to social problems themselves. However, social problems are not independent of social stratification. That is, the social decisions about who gets what and how much—the inequalities themselves—may be important determinants of social problems.

The study of America's social decision-making process through the social services investigates the powerful reasons, that is, the ideologies, that justify social outcomes. Thus, the focus of the study relates far more importantly to issues of American stratification than simply to the problems of indigent people. The debate over public assistance for the poor is usually fierce, truly out of proportion to the tiny segment of the federal budget allocated to Food Stamps and Aid to Families with Dependent Children (AFDC), which is now known as Temporary Assistance to Needy Families (TANF) and to the even smaller amounts allocated to other social services intended for marginal and poor populations. However, the rules of American society are being discussed, and not simply the conditions of relief for the less than 5 percent of the population that receives support, often for short periods of time. The debate over provisions for the poor is a proxy battle for the main event—the fairness of social and economic conditions in the United States.

Even more important than as a subject in its own right, the political role of the personal social services provides an unusual instance of a nearly pure ceremonial social institution seemingly devoid of any production function in achieving its avowed goals. These ceremonies largely support political institutions in shaping and maintaining social boundaries and the preferences that endorse them. The purity of rituals increases as they address issues of poverty and personal deviance; as the recipients of services become less compelling political actors, their benefits naturally decline, while the services tend to increasingly address the rules of the game and all that goes into legitimizing them.

Even when purchased by relatively wealthy people in competitive markets, many personal social services, notably psychotherapy, are dominated by roles that are more meaningful in continuing and justifying social preferences than in achieving any of their assigned purposes. In the end, political rituals may, to a far greater degree than commonly accepted, be a necessary dimension and perhaps the largest dimension of many other social institutions, even business. Indeed, commercial firms play such substantial political roles to promote their perceived conveniences, notably the virtues of the free market, and to boast of their good corporate citizenship and their contributions to social progress that it is very difficult to separate the economic productivity of a business corporation from its pursuit of political favor and public esteem. Both the market position and the political influence of a business reflect the success of its ritualistic value in promoting broadly embedded social mores.

Every social institution and every social policy decision to address an explicit social goal also perform ritualistic roles. At a minimum, they endorse and promote the social preferences that gave rise to their programmatic manifestations. Yet even in the case of the clearest instances of a social policy production function, perhaps the OASDI program and its role in income security, it is not so very obvious that the programs are necessary to achieve their goals. Indeed, the Social Security program largely routinizes intrafamilial sharing in the form of intergenerational support while continuing into old age the market standing of American workers and their sense of moral superiority to those with less attachment to the labor force. The emphasis on deservingness is even carried over to the regressive taxes of OASDI and Medicare and its denial of adequate benefits. With little forgiveness for economic failure, the social insurances enshrine the rigidities of American society, maintaining many elderly, retired workers in very straitened circumstances. As much as protection against the vagaries of old age, the social insurances are active partisans of American social preferences. Indeed, there is little that is insurance about OASDI and Medicare, since benefits are neither a right of contract nor secured as a function of contributions and much that is welfare in the form of a transfer of moneys between current and former workers. Just like its stigmatizing mirror images—the AFDC program and its reincarnation in 1996 as TANF—the benefits and the eligibility rules of OASDI and Medicare are set politically, but again, not as a judicable right of contract.

Large as it is in the social insurances, the ceremonial proportion increases dramatically in public assistance programs for poor people, especially those intended for apparently healthy citizens without long and recent attachment to the labor force. The comparison of OASDI with AFDC and even more so with TANF highlights the ceremonies of social preference that burden private and public programs for marginal populations. Even the largest program to feed the poor, Food Stamps, does not simply supply cash to those who need to purchase food. It enacts a totemic belief in the improvidence of the poor by imposing the demeaning ritual of vouchers—recipients are publicly degraded for their immorality each time they purchase food.

Plan of the Book

The introduction provides a backdrop to the crucial conflict between rationality and politics in social decision making. Chapter 1 sets out the role of ceremony in social decision making as a process that is political, not rational, especially as it addresses problematic social conditions through social services. Rationality rarely informs social discourse, which would be immensely improved if the impulse toward democracy was frankly acknowledged as a confession of ignorance. Instead, perhaps in denial of near-universal uncertainty, self-interest is the principal contingency of political truth. As a consequence, social policy is made through the complex interactions of groups and individuals in pursuit of their own subjective desires with only rare and incomplete attempts to objectively establish causality, program outcomes, and the effects of policy options. The struggle over limited resources between partisans confident in their virtue irresistibly distorts the highly circumscribed theories of the social and natural sciences into political ideologies complete with decisive metaphors of compelling myths. The ceremonial roles of the personal social services play out these myths.

Chapter 2 lays out the failure of the personal social services to achieve any production function. Their pervasive ineffectiveness establishes the probity of looking for the meaning of social welfare arrangements outside of their explicit program goals. That is, the personal social services do not persist as rational attempts to address their defining social problems. Rather, they are symbols of cultural belief, ideological touchstones, dramas for public instruction, and, in the end, ceremonies of the nation's civil religion.

Chapters 3 and 4 argue that there are actually two American civil religions, a ceremonial civil religion that proselytizes the ritual beliefs of the nation and the operative civil religion of the nation's determinative values. The ceremonial functions of the personal social services are played out in behalf of the puritanical, individualistic, pervasively conservative, and sometimes cruel preferences of the nation's operative civil religion. A prevailing conservative political preference in America may explain the population's passivity in the face of enormous and growing inequalities, the riddle of people accepting their diminished fortunes quietly.

Numerous methodological and interpretive pitfalls largely vitiate the usefulness of survey research in identifying the values of the civil religion. Indeed, the actual choices of social welfare policies may be better indicators of the nation's ethos than its reported attitudes. Chapter 5 analyzes a variety of social welfare programs as ritual and ceremony.

Chapter 6 gives deeper ideological meaning to the play of political ritual by translating the rhetoric of contemporary political dialectics (its pursuit of Enlightenment ideals into the reality of its social institutions (the embrace of Romantic individualism). While the United States took over the vanity of exceptionalism from European admirers—the fantasy of political pragmatism as a noble experiment—the nation's social welfare decision making more closely approximates the reactionary subjectivity of nineteenth-century Romantic thought most recently revived as postmodernism. Moreover, in spite of a distinguishable Enlightenment in the United States, expressed by the nation's constitutional patriarchs, social policy making, then and now, has been largely the product of enthusiasm, intuition, superstition, revelation, and tradition, that is, widely shared popular beliefs and preferences. Revivalism and an extraordinary attachment to an all-embracing subjectivism are at the heart of the American style of religion and its social decision-making process.

The Enlightenment argued for a "science of man" modeled after the natural sciences, notably Newtonian physics, although it never reached a truly operational form until the second half of the twentieth century. Rather, "moral science" remained only a mood of Enlightenment thought expressed in its profound respect for the probity of skeptical criticism as a natural right based upon the autonomy of the intellect more than in the development of any specific objective methodology. The philosophes wrote history and philosophy; they rarely engaged in science. Aside from a nascent push for education—both schooling and preparation for citizenship—and broad principles for government and social reform, they never developed a coherent program to realize their hopes for progress through the application of reason. Implementation was left for succeeding centuries.

Chapter 7 applies the romances of the American ideological legacy to the problem of providing credible information for social welfare policy making. In practice, contemporary social science, expressed through bounded rationality and "rational choice theory," actually distorts and subverts the Enlightenment's central mood of skepticism and its hopes for a science of human affairs. Indeed, neither the social sciences nor obviously the social decision-making process has developed a successful practice of limited rationality. The social sciences, rather than engaging in skeptical criticism, develop the corrective myths that justify the stringencies of contemporary social welfare policy. Particularly as they concern themselves with social welfare decision making, the social sciences promulgate a malleable Romantic notion of man, providing credulous witness to the operative American civil religion in defiance of any objective or coherent practice of rationality, that is, science.

If the Enlightenment experiment is to succeed beyond the startling material plenty of the United States, it still needs to nurture rationality in social decision making. Yet the feasibility of implementing a true, limited rationality is more complex than Voltaire's simple instruction to "tend one's own garden." Power does not yield readily to truth. The grand tyranny of collective imperatives, notably Hegel's World-Spirit, remains a true approximation of social consciousness, the way societies in fact operate. Still, the effort to dispel anointing subjectivities—to ground policy at least in its knowable effects—lies at the heart of social progress.

Note

1. The subdivision of human services has importance only to the extent that the different categories serve analytic purposes for the receipt of benefits, training of personnel, research, and so on. Different categories of services convey different meanings; education and public health care are more or less universally available and speak to a general civic goal of egalitarian citizenship. Health care and the social services, and particularly the personal social services, provide a very different view of America, illuminating the ways that society preserves economic differences and social hierarchies, carrying them over into public policy. (Note: Public financing of health care is largely intended to increase access to the private health care system. Nevertheless, many Americans, perhaps one-sixth of the population, have no coverage at all and cannot afford to indemnify themselves. They remain outside of the public and private insurance systems and are not eligible for either Medicaid or benefits through the Veterans Administration. Many have made sense of the strange exclusions of the American health care system in terms of its social preferences and not by reference to need. Indeed, reforming both health care and Social Security in the United States in order to provide greater equality and sufficiency perhaps awaits a resolution of the nation's social stratification.)

Acknowledgments

I wish to pay debts. This book represents the current state of an intellectual lifetime whose awakening began when I was young and progressed through the profundities of those who marveled at the frequency of the "slip between the cup and the lip." While civilization has defined its majesty in appreciation of the rational, even realizing it occasionally with a variety of technological wonders, life is run by a becrazed farmer, milking the horses and riding the cows. The ideological force with which the nation covers its flaccid bosom with a gauzy rationality is almost a burlesque of its long political performance. It would indeed be comedy but for the many who are harmed.

This bad-tempered conclusion has been nourished by the brilliant contributions of many, some of whom I read and understood, some of whom I read without comprehending a syllable, and some of whom I distorted in order to come up with original insights. One day my body chemistry will change sufficiently so that I can understand what the absolute idealists of nineteenth-century Germany, including Marx the economist and Hegel the obscurantist, were talking about without consulting intermediaries whose interpretations I take on faith. The absolute idealists seem to have had something to say although I mourn that many were inspired to action by their vapors.

Through the portal of Emerson, the New World's first maven of spontaneity, who probably never edited a word he wrote, American society has built a shrine to individualism that is so shorn of social peace and compassion as to rape pleasure from success and passion from procreation. This of course could never have been authorized without the keen novelties of social scientists who insist that their wizardry points to the founts of all progress. It is delightful that they disagree with each other so fiercely. But for the recent growth of population, their infinite schools would contain only a seer, three reluctant students, a consort of negotiated gender, race, age, and ethnicity, and a computer person. The value of numeracy has been exaggerated beyond good taste. Science in the social sciences is still a goal. Come to think of it, humanity in the humanities lives in the same airless cellar. There is always hope, of course, mainly because it is such an inexpensive commodity.

Friends, colleagues, and correspondents helped greatly with early drafts: Carol Case, Stephen DeBelle, Robert Dippner, Paul Epstein, Ronald Farrell, Chris Khamis, Richard Lewontin, Colin Loader, Brij Mohan, Robert Morris, Cyril Pasterk, Lisa Rapp-Paglicci, Jonathan Reader, Jerry Rubin, Linda Santangelo, Ashok Singh, and David Stoesz. Their intelligent comments and patience frequently overcame my stubbornness. Nevertheless, any errors that do remain are the result of bad luck, bad information, the printer's carelessness, misinterpretations by the reader, and life's multitude of oppressive distractions. The author is blameless and refuses to shoulder the slightest responsibility for the epiphanies or the hives that lead readers to abandon children and spouses for the bohemian pleasures of Passaic, New Jersey, or to become resident mourners at Graceland.

The University of California, Santa Barbara graciously opened its library to me, and the librarians at the University of Nevada, Las Vegas made every effort to accommodate my requests. This book was completed during a sabbatical granted by UNLV.

Short portions of chapter 2 describing the pitfalls of the Illinois family preservation experiment and the scholarly tradition in social services are drawn from my book *Welfare in America* (Madison: University of Wisconsin Press, 1997) and are reprinted by permission of the University of Wisconsin Press. The figure in chapter 1, slightly modified, originally appeared in my chapter "Critical Analyses," in *Handbook of Social Work Research Methods*, ed. B. Thyer (Thousand Oaks, Calif.: Sage, 2001), and is reprinted with permission.

Introduction

The United States is the world's wealthiest nation, wealthier now than it has ever been and better insulated from economic turmoil than any other modern society. Yet its indifference to the hardships of many of its citizens, perhaps even more than half of its population, is a solemn curiosity, especially in light of an intricate and pervasive system of social welfare services. However, the social insurances, public assistance programs, and personal social services ostensibly designed to address suffering and poverty are so superficial and poorly funded that they rarely achieve their goals.

Social services for the poor constitute one of the principal stages on which social factions compete over the stratification of American society. At the same time that many social services provide some degree of concrete care, the social service agencies themselves perform political displays of probity, decorum, and worthiness for the rest of society that assess the relative cultural standing—the moral and social worth—of service recipients. As Handler argues "welfare policy . . . is not addressed to the poor—it is addressed to us" (1995, 8–9); the society at large, not the service recipients, is the true audience for the lessons of the social services that set boundaries around desirable social behavior. Indeed, the ideological role of social service agencies, typically reinforcing regnant social values and implementing the dictates of social efficiency, dominates their service roles.

The obedience of social service agencies to political power may go far to explain the persistence of the social welfare industry despite its obvious inability to achieve its service missions. It may also begin to explain the success of the sham interventions of the welfare state such as psychotherapy, counseling, case management, and job training, the politically popular entertainments that suppress attention to the nation's unmet needs and continuing social problems. In the end, the social services, as well as their

1

academic intellectual life, are institutionalized forms of resistance to serious social reform or analysis.

The social welfare industry encompasses the policy and programmatic activities that attend to social problems. It employs millions of people and spends hundreds of billions of dollars each year.[1] Broadly construed, social welfare refers to all of society's provisions for its protection, health, comfort, and benefit. It encompasses the fullest range of public sector and private sector arrangements. In its modern, restricted usage, welfare is understood as charity for which customarily poor and low-status recipients have some legal claim in the public sector and none in the private sector. During the past few decades, this narrow sense of public welfare has dominated American social policy; public responsibility has been consistently constricted and shifted back to the traditional philanthropic sector, as well as to newly formed profit-making agencies. Repenting the nation's brief and forlorn experiments with greater equality, the 1996 welfare reforms reestablish America's traditional social ethos in celebration of growing inequalities and the decisive influence of the commercial sector (Brown 1999; Davies 1996).

The American Welfare State

In 1996, five program responsibilities accounted for almost three-quarters of the federal budget: defense 17 percent; social security Old Age Survivors and Disability Insurance (OASDI) 22.2 percent; Medicare (I) 12.3 percent; Medicaid 5.9 percent; and net interest 15.5 percent. All other programs to benefit the low-income population (including both the working and the nonworking poor)—Food Stamps, Aid to Families with Dependent Children (AFDC), Supplemental Security Income (SSI), Earned Income Tax Credit, and others—accounted for only about 10 percent of federal outlays in 1996 (Ways and Means Committee 1998, 1354–55). The federal government has the authority to regulate almost every aspect of national life. In practice, however, the mandate is enacted sparingly; administrative regulatory agencies are protective of the industries they oversee, and the specific interventions of the welfare state intended to handle deviance, poverty, income security, health, and even education provide only minimal benefits and coverage.[2]

The stunted role of the American welfare state is not an accident of historical development; rather, it legislates the intentions of the American people. In spite of the nation's phenomenal wealth, 13.3 percent of the population remained poor in 1997, up from a low of 11.1 percent in 1973. One-quarter of blacks and Hispanics were poor in the same year. The American poverty line is very low, adjusted since its inception in the 1960s for inflation but ignoring the general rise in the standard of living. Thus, in 1997 the threshold poverty income for a parent and two children was only $12,931. Surprisingly, large numbers of the poor work either full- or part-time, but their wages are unable to lift them above the low poverty levels (Rawlings 1998).

American income inequality is very large and continues to grow. In 1998, the mean family income of the lowest fifth was $7,828; the highest fifth, $97,181; and the top 5 percent, $171,613. The top fifth earned 12.4 times as much as the bottom fifth in 1998 but only 7.0 times as much in 1972 (U.S. Census Bureau 1999, table F-3C).[3] The enormous income inequality is overshadowed by differences in wealth. In 1962, the top 1 percent of income earners owned 21.9 percent of the nation's net worth, while in 1989 they owned 25.3 percent (Slemrod 1994). In a different tabulation, Mishel, Bernstein, and Schmitt (1999) report that the top 1 percent owned 55.5 percent of the nation's wealth. In 1995, the wealthiest 10 percent owned fully 88.4 percent of the nation's net assets, up 2.4 percent from 1989 (Mishel, Bernstein, and Schmitt 1999). In addition to insufficient income, many Americans lack adequate housing, health and mental health coverage, and basic education. Two million Americans are in jail and prison. There are continuing concerns with drug and alcohol misuse, teenage pregnancies and births, and employment and underemployment, along with many other apparent problems (Miringoff and Miringoff 1999).[4]

In 1993, only Japan among the modern industrial states (members of the Organization for Economic Co-operation and Development [OECD]) spent less than the United States on its welfare arrangements. The average OECD nation allocated 18.6 percent of its gross domestic product to social spending, whereas the United States allocated only 9.8 percent (Goodin et al. 1999). Not surprisingly, even basic welfare programs in the United States provide meager benefits. In 1996, the OASDI and Medicare retirement benefit for a worker and spouse was only $1,186 per month, and for the low-income worker and spouse, $759 per month; the maximum family benefit was only $1,666 per month. The median 1997 state payment of AFDC (now Temporary Assistance to Needy Families [TANF]) and Food Stamps for one parent with two children was $692 per month, only 62 percent of the poverty line. Foster care payments were typically under $400 per month. The benefits of the SSI program left the permanently and totally disabled in poverty. Rent subsidies were rare. Medicaid paid only a small portion of actual costs. Moreover, the many programs targeted on low-income populations were grossly underfunded, highly restrictive, and typically covered only a portion of even those who were eligible (all data from Ways and Means Committee 1998).[5]

The charitable sector does not pick up the slack. Although the amount of money raised by the nonprofit sector appears huge ($460 billion in 1996), little of it is spent to address poverty or deprivation generally;

most is spent on hospitals, research, and education (Salamon 1999, 34). Expenditures for health and education—donations for research, hospital construction, colleges, and so forth—constitute fully 83 percent of the nonprofit sector's annual budget. Social services account for only 10 percent, and these programs typically are not targeted on the needy. In spite of its vaunted humanitarian gestures, the nonprofit sector probably has less of a redistributive function than the public sector. Indeed, paying for hospital care and education with public tax dollars would probably draw more from wealthier groups and give services more to the needy than the operations of the charitable sector. The charitable sector is best understood as the heart of America's civil society occupied by the voluntary organizations and the donations that sustain basic communal institutions. Like the American people themselves, the nonprofit sector is rarely a force for reform or change. To the contrary, it institutionalizes the fundamental orthodoxy of dominant social attitudes, infrequently acting in behalf of those in need.[6] Benevolence as played out in the nonprofit sector customarily demonstrates the middle classes' self-service rather any large impulse to humanitarian relief. Indeed, the nonprofit sector's social service organizations, besides subsidized schools and hospitals, that come closest to addressing economic deprivation and its attendant conditions typically draw more than 50 percent of their budgets from the public sector (Smith and Lipsky 1993).

The United States chooses to define the threshold of economic need at absolute, low levels, with a concern for basic subsistence, not social participation, greater equality, or individual fulfillment. In contrast, poverty can be seen as defined relative to the customary conditions of a society. Thus Townsend defines poverty relative to social expectations that allow all people "to play the roles, participate in the relationships, and follow the customary behavior which is expected of them by virtue of their membership of society" (Citro and Michael 1995, 22). Then, too, poverty beyond simply economic insufficiency is profitably understood as a general cultural phenomenon, implying the want of proper participation in fundamental social institutions that are necessary for full citizenship and socialization. If inadequate socialization is accepted as the root of social problems, then even the noneconomic poor become the focus of public attention for their lack of nurturing parental experiences, education, communal participation, and so forth.

The exquisite tracking of the material conditions of Americans through numerous surveys fails to get at the core of social problems. No condition is ipso facto problematic. Payments for the poor are inadequate if, in some sense, the society decides that these individuals deserve more. But even the very low benefits of the American welfare state can be perceived as generous if the poor are considered morally defective, deviant, and criminal and if the assumption is made that the payments are critical incentives for their rehabilitation. Especially in the absence of widespread threats to subsistence and survival in the United States, deprivation is fundamentally ideological. Thus, the pressing analytic quest is to dis cover the determinants of choice, especially when national resources are sufficient to handle almost any degree of material deprivation.

It is obvious that the American welfare state defines need narrowly. Moreover, American provisions seem inadequate even against the nation's own restrictive sense of deprivation and moral worth.[7] Yet the common idiom of contemporary social problems ignores the profoundly political nature of poverty and social need. There is, after all, a popular and long-standing insistence in the United States that social problems result from characterological and subcultural failures; people have problems because of their own improvidence, ignorance, sloth, inattention, and moral shortcomings; they voluntarily participate in oppositional and dysfunctional subcultures that abet their immorality. This highly individualistic tradition of responsibility shifts the analysis of need from the demography of social conditions to an accounting of moral and ethical factors of society. Yet the survey of souls, let alone their appraisal, frustrates the empirical capacities of the social sciences, inviting an ideological evaluation of social choice.

The American preference for characterological and subcultural social explanations over structural ones remains ideological, reflecting both the absence of any rational test of their premises and the long-standing and wide satisfaction with the inadequacies of the welfare state. The American welfare state is the product of consensual, open democracy, a projection of the society's effective political voices and the assessment of its members. Policy is power rather than truth or even dispassionate, considered estimates of need.

Rationality and Method

If social need is to be defined rationally and transcend the politics of cultural choice, then it entails two obligations: the first, to prove that certain objective conditions, whether moral or structural, are the causes of defined outcomes such as crime, mental and physical disease, political turmoil, and so forth; the second, to demonstrate that the outcomes or conditions are socially problematic. If the proven relationships are to be truly rational, then the methodological task implies randomized controlled trials.[8] At least in the social services, but also more broadly among the social sciences themselves, the attempts to implement scientifically credible methodologies, discussed in following chapters, have turned out to be burlesques of science.

The capacities of the social sciences may be inadequate either to design or to implement the controls necessary to test the effects of naturally occurring social conditions and of the interventions (the social services) designed to address specific problems. Yet remarkably, across the range of their involvement with social policy, the social sciences have routinely failed to evaluate social welfare programs by applying available, scientifically credible methodologies. As a result, their effectiveness is at best indeterminate, although a substantial body of information suggests their failure and possible harm. Moreover, the theories of human behavior that inspire their creation remain largely unevaluated. There is not one study that is scientifically credible and attests to the effectiveness of psychotherapy, manpower programs for the poor, compensatory programs for children, rehabilitation programs for offenders, social work's various effusions, drug and alcohol treatment, substance abuse prevention, child welfare programs, and many others. Indeed, there is hardly a single causal relationship of any importance to social welfare—for example, the relationship of cash welfare and work participation—that is rationally established (Epstein 1997).

The social services have been near-uniform failures, their only successes resulting from modest income replacement through concrete provisions such as OASDHI, and then only for a favored majority of those lucky enough to have spent most of their lives in the workforce. Yet even in the case of OASDI and Medicare, a considerable amount of research speculates over the welfare of beneficiaries. At best, social services for lower-status Americans loan out a beggar's tin cup with a few rattling coins, along with perhaps some surveillance of presumed miscreants. At even minimal levels of modern decency, the social services fail to handle material want, emotional deprivation, the absence of parents and family, educational failure, unemployment, crime, addiction, homelessness, permanent physical and mental disability, or even the presumed civic and personal sins of the depraved. Preaching offers a very safe tenure, the pious boundaries of public virtue, firewalls of civic self-righteousness, created by vilifying the alleged sinner, which may be the point of the social services to begin with.

In consideration of the many decades of social welfare programs, it is pathetic that the only examples of success identified by one of the most comprehensive reviews—*Programs That Work*, published by the prestigious Russell Sage Foundation—are relatively new, small-scale experiments whose achievements, if any, are tributes to the unique, unrepresentative, and rare abilities of staff and the special capacities of highly screened service populations. No credible evidence is provided by any of these experimental demonstrations that their routinized forms would be able to match their performance as demonstration projects. Few even offer credible evidence that they have achieved their goals. To the contrary, a large body of evidence points to the unusual demonstration effects achieved by programs under glass, that is, by small-scale tests of social welfare interventions that employ highly motivated, extremely competent staffs, enroll unusually motivated service recipients, and carefully monitor program activities. Moreover, evidence of bias in social research, the ability of researchers to confirm their programmatic preconceptions of effectiveness despite their ostensible commitments to objectivity and coherence, is far more compelling than any evidence that the social services have addressed their defining social problems (Rosenthal and Rubin 1978). The stakes in the success of social services as political forms create a powerful incentive to distort their actual performance in the creation of corrective myths. The huge body of social welfare research constitutes overwhelming evidence of man the mythmaker, even hinting at a biological, species-specific genius for self-deception. Compassion and rationality are only occasional shards that the society leaves behind in remembrance of its social sciences.

The routine misrepresentation of research has created a situation in which the political effects of distorted social science, especially as they create illusions of effectiveness, perniciously deflect social attention away from continuing, unmet social needs. The effects of psychotherapy and counseling, which are the prevailing strategies of many personal social services, are notably unknown. The literature, such as it is, is even weaker in the other areas of social concern, including crime, juvenile delinquency, addiction, mental and emotional health, and so forth.

Furthermore, procedural remedies such as affirmative action must fail against the reality of the substantive deprivations of family, community, and education that produce tragic incapacities. As a trope of concern, affirmative action encourages social complacency by appearing to handle the effects of discrimination. Its inevitable inability to close the social and economic gaps between blacks and whites through employment and educational preferences creates smug evidence to support ascriptive assumptions of minority inferiority. Indeed, the failure of affirmative action, just like the material failures of the social services, suggests the refusal or inability—shortcomings of character or intellect—of minorities to avail themselves of opportunities. In this way, insubstantial social welfare programs and misused procedural remedies such as affirmative action are the final score, the spoils, of a political competition between the very few wishing to redress social inequities and the many wishing to justify deprivation.

The social sciences have also failed to document the importance of basic social institutions, even those as apparently central as the family. Thus, Harris (1995) reinterpreted decades of murky family studies to argue that the peer group and not the family played the dominant role in socializing children. Even less is understood about the relationship between social problems and communities, work, and schooling. Nonetheless, social attitudes are both formed and firm in all these areas.

Moreover, the selection of rational goals may be an insurmountable task. Without reference to the rational values that are threatened by objective conditions—the criteria of social problems—it is obviously impossible to rationally define a social problem. Notwithstanding centuries of philosophy's smorgasbord of "highest goods," cultures seem quite content with their own embedded, traditional, implicit processes to choose goals for social policy. More to the political point, culture tends to make policy choices that coincide with powerful interests, and not necessarily elite ones, more than they evidence any deeper concern with the general good or the nature of man, assuming for the moment that these can be understood in any but subjective terms.

Whatever the relative virtues of subjectivity and objectivity in policy making, the record seems greatly shifted toward the subjective, that is, the political. American society and probably all cultures freely rely upon subjective notions of social problems. A social problem is a condition or conditions that influential groups of people perceive to warrant attention; the response to these perceived conditions is proportionate to their perceived threat to cherished social institutions and the stakes of powerful groups. Therefore, rational (scientifically coherent) policy making rarely, if ever, occurs. Looked at another way, society does not and perhaps cannot guide its deliberations with scientifically credible information in either selecting rational goals or designing rational social welfare interventions to achieve them. The traditional invocation of science as a totem in the United States—the toney and sacred image of its phenomenal material wealth—belies any broad cultural commitment to objectivity, coherence, or rationality in social policy.

Therefore, the wisdom to accept or reject prevailing social conditions remains conjectural. The social sciences have failed rationally either to trace American deprivation as a cause and not just a correlate of problematic outcomes or to describe the moral contingencies of those who engage in socially problematic behaviors. The mutual adjustment of political factions remains fiercely ideological, unanchored by any tested insights into the causes of social conditions. Consequent to the absence of rational information and to the presence of profound stakes in particular outcomes, social policy making can only be political.

Civic Ideals

Political processes are natural expressions of their societies' rules and customs that are often summed up in a civic ideal. In the United States, consensual liberal republicanism is the dominant civil ideal that controls public discourse. Differences over the meanings of these concepts provide the subtext for most analyses of American history. The size of the de jure voting franchise in the United States has consistently expanded throughout the past few centuries, yet the effective republican base of decision making, the de facto franchise, has been shrinking, with smaller and smaller percentages of eligible voters participating in elections. Liberalism itself has two very different meanings, although its classical libertarian sense as protection from government has dominated American social policy. Adam Smith's elegant argument—the classical form of liberalism that Berlin (1969) terms negative liberty—inspires conservatives to justify the ascendancy of laissez-faire public strategies, a near-inviolable law of private property, and a series of protected rights from possible governmental abuse. In contrast, modern liberalism—Berlin's positive liberty—accepts much of negative liberty but also limits the inviolability of private property to justify the welfare state's regulation of commerce along with its communal corrections for injustice and inequality.

Nevertheless, the contemporary retrenchment of the welfare state, often justified by the ascribed unworthiness of lower-status Americans, suggests that the two ideologies that dominate contemporary political discourse in the United States are both conservative doctrines. The first is the typical conservative preference for the market to provide the organic structure of society. The second, an epigone of modern or welfare state liberalism, is a form of conservative thought that nominates other social institutions (the church, the family, the charitable sector, the neighborhood but not government) for this central role. It is a bogus liberalism that moans for a world with a tamed marketplace of civic virtue that never existed. Its fulsome humanitarianism displaces concrete, financial obligations to those in need by insisting—again without evidence—that the size of government and therefore the amount of public redistribution can be decreased and still benefit those in need. In this regard, the New Democrats sound very much like the old social conservatives.[9] Both forms of conservatism minimize the collective obligations of society to correct the decisions of the market through redistributive taxation and public spending; both pursue the implementation of their favored private sector institutions through the coercive force of public policy; and both inevitably fall willing victims to the problems of classical liberalism—the excessive influence of both the marketplace and private wealth in social policy making.

The Enlightenment enterprise offers emotionally satisfying goals and perhaps even valuable banners for social decision making, but it has not yet inspired a pervasive cultural commitment to rational information. The processes of modern democracy remain deeply Romantic, intruding on every institutional expression of culture. Indeed, the dominance of the Romantic style—a fatalistic attachment to the subjective—may be the principal impediment to cultural progress in the United States. Without recognition in the policy-making discourse of the distance to be traveled to rationality, let alone to basic human rights, there is little hope of change. In spite of formal public doctrines of broad equality, ascriptive civic beliefs have been consistently decisive in limiting the scope of consensual liberal republicanism in the United States (Smith 1997). Negative stereotypes of minorities, women, immigrants, and others have been successfully invoked throughout American history to deny rights and relief to a variety of citizens. Today's ascriptive assumptions of unworthiness deny expansive social welfare to a new underclass of the poor, notably the homeless, unwed young mothers, the mentally ill, and addicts, that conservative dialectics easily expand to stigmatize much greater numbers of citizens— all low-income people, including the huge number of the working poor (Gans 1995).

The conditions of society are customarily measured as population distributions and comparisons across a variety of social values: some members of the society are poor, some are ill, some are employed, whites do better than blacks and Latinos, and so forth. These common distributions assume a sense of equality that teases at a judgment of fairness. Yet neither socioeconomic immobility nor the lopsided stratifications of the United States have enticed the American national will, customarily the construction of a surprisingly broad consensus in the United States, to experiment broadly with greater equality.

The nation remains committed to a civic Calvinism—Emerson's individualism, but shorn of his antagonism to commerce—that imposes personal responsibility on an enormous range of social behaviors, with only rare tolerance for the possibility of exculpating social forces. This metaprinciple that guides American social policy is not rationally chosen and may well be unwisely conceived. Nevertheless, civic Calvinism is nearly ubiquitous, even accepted by the poor in defiance of their apparent economic self-interest: "The winners are convinced of their virtue and the losers suspect their economic failure must be their own fault" (Kuttner 1999). This perverse acceptance of culpability challenges the notion of Enlightenment progress and the glorious conceit of the Left that the poor are unwitting victims of elite conspiracies.

The inadequacies of American public welfare appear to be structured by the presumed moral inferiority of welfare recipients and low-income people generally. The civil religion is committed to a puritanical dogma of social salvation through labor and toil in which wealth is proportionate to virtue and deprivation is a valuable spur to self-reliance and prudence. Yet its precepts seem blithely unfazed by the contradictions of a welfare system in which the same needy child, as one example, receives very different subsidies depending on whether her parent died at work, abandoned her, or is simply poor, unattached, and not working (Ways and Means Committee 1998).

If individualism and a generalized Christianity were the decisive principles of American welfare, then certainly America's welfare population would be handled more decently; after all, the most worthy American citizens—children and the disabled—when they must fall back on public support are treated with little regard for their comfort, future productivity, or individual dignity. In defiance of civic Calvinism, American social welfare policy routinely harms those who are not morally depraved. Most of those who receive public subsidies and do not work—children and the totally disabled who are impoverished—obviously cannot and should not work. Two-thirds of those who receive AFDC (now TANF) are children, while many, if not most, adults in the program are too ill to work but not ill enough to qualify for SSI. All recipients of SSI are clearly disabled, although a very small fraction, about 4 percent, still make heroic efforts to normalize themselves through work in spite of crippling disease and mental disability; their total payments are still under the poverty line. Children in foster care and protective services are also presumably relieved from work at least until they graduate from high school or reach the age of eighteen. Yet public policy provides obviously inadequate welfare payments for dependent children, the ill, and the disabled that suggest their moral "less eligibility." Indeed, there is not a single public assistance program for the aged, children, or the disabled that elevates them even to the deprivation of America's poverty line.

It seems likely that individualism is only a cushioned excuse for social neglect and that civic Calvinism structures the hierarchy of public deprivation within the constraints of social welfare parsimony. Social efficiency, the principle of getting away as cheaply as possible and in socially compatible forms that preserve existing social relations and sensibilities, seems to explain social policy in the United States better than any lofty pretense to moral worth and individual dignity. The politically weak lose out financially while enduring the scorn of the winners. In fact, the nation does as little as possible, consistent with contemporary social preferences, to address the deprivations of its citizens. Throughout its history and continuing today, these preferences have been persistently cruel, self-absorbed, and, alas, widely popular. The nation's neglect seems limited only by fear of insurrection, communicable disease, pervasive crime, the intrusion of the indecorous into public places, and other frank threats to its tranquillity, comfort, safety, and self-regard.

The popularity of an individualistic civil religion, along with the probability that social efficiency motivates policy choice, also discredits the fashionable theory of the "autonomous state" in which well-intentioned elites fulfill a tutelary role through government, imposing wise policy on the mulish, superstitious, tradition-bound masses. The theory of the autonomous state has much in common with the *patron* mentality of peasant Latin America and the oracular pretensions of the highborn and wealthy to serve the public good but, of course, never their own private, sectarian interests. Charitability and civic virtue commonly mask the more mundane ambitions for money, power, and prestige. Nevertheless, popular opinion, notably concerning public assistance for the poor, has consistently supported harsh public policy, as well as the current form of representative government in the United States. It is still not at all certain that some unseen alchemy of this consensus has "spontaneously" transformed private motives into public benefits.

Too much has been made of the rare differences or the lag in perceptions between early advocates, late supporters, and opponents of social policy. The occasional attitudinal disparities between elites and the common people have fueled the paranoia of elusive antidemocratic conspiracies by corporations, developers, capitalists, one-worlders, and Area 51 alien abductors. The evidence of support for a more generous welfare state comes from tortured, distorted surveys. Indeed, opposition to the traditional minimalism of social policy in the United States has occurred more intensely at the margins of society among modernity's pop-military anarchists, who desire even less public welfare and more local government, if government at all, than among principled, sophisticated visionaries pressing for an enlarged cooperative state.

The viable spectrum of policy choice in the United States is narrow. American social welfare policy has consistently yielded to the right, without any profound or politically intense diversions. Even the reforms of the 1930s, notably the Social Security Act and its various amendments, were not evidence of great communality, sharing, or departures from the principles of civic Calvinism or social efficiency. They simply recognized the changing demographics of the nation and made modest moves toward a national system of domestic services (which were largely recanted by the welfare act of 1996). The social insurances are intergenerational public transfers that largely routinize intrafamilial sharing. However, they are not truly insurance programs that assure specific benefits as a contractual right; rather, they are elaborately disguised welfare programs dependent on legislative intent and susceptible to negotiation between current workers and retirees. Instead of a generous system of forgiveness, the Social Security Act's two-tiered approach to services and security and its highly structured payment schedules implement the work ethic, the hierarchy of labor, individualism, and even the ascriptive assumptions of the inferiority of the poor and blacks (Lubove 1968). The Social Security Act failed to attack American stratification or to provide a decent minimum. Later on, poverty won the War on Poverty, and a guaranteed, universal floor under income was beaten under Nixon and again under Carter, reflecting the stolid opposition of Americans to greater social and economic equality.

Rationality versus Politics

Rationality rarely influences social decision making. Even though typically justified in the language of scientific theory, social policy lacks the credibility of science, and consequently its authority. Social policy is rationalistic, that is, culturally coherent ("isomorphic" with social preferences following Meyer and Rowan 1978) and ideological, not logical and objective. Ideology abstracts scientific social theory from the limiting contingencies of its tests of truth, creating myths of cultural belief. By severing social theory from its precise meaning, social ideology certifies as a point of political convenience its own underlying assumptions about the nature of social problems and social interventions. Ideology attends to the ceremonies of power by freeing itself from the constraints of a true production function in addressing social problems.

The mood of a scientific community is incompatible with ideology. Scientific theory is modest, democratic (at least within the community of scientists), deferential to objective proof but not to social authority; ideology is doctrinaire and authoritarian. Both the products and the conduct of science, by conferring enormous economic and social advantages, often undercut established political power and cultural orthodoxy. Recommended first by its market prowess, the instrumentalities of the scientific community—democracy, equality, openness— become models for social decision making. In contrast, ideology is constantly tempted to control science and propagate its own more malleable truths.

The most penetrating criticism of the social decision-making process, especially among highly technological societies that have replaced Mother Earth as the abiding goddess of richness and plenty with effigies of science, is that its tenets are essentially ideological. Debunking the myths of scientistic, rationalistic convenience is a profoundly political act that questions the value of current social arrangements. Still, the subjective nature of social decision making does not entail the acceptance of subjectivity, a confusion that subverts much of the postmodern fashion in social logic. Indeed, the recognition that social problems are embedded in social belief rather than in the firmament or man's biology employs the tools of social science to open the box of ideological self-certification. Unfortunately, social science and perhaps even science itself have become as obedient as any other social institution to the social will.

The social decision-making process is therefore neither predictable nor logically and temporally consecutive. It does not follow the steps of rational discovery nor lead to a cascade of coherent, purposive tasks in resolving identified social problems. Social policy is neither engineering nor patterned experimentation; it is infrequently even intelligence guided by experience. Rather, social policy making is profoundly political, a process of socializing reality to political convenience that is grounded in group and individual preferences, with only the most casual and occasional reference to credible information.

Social decision making is constrained from the beginning by received preferences and tradition. In contrast with the typical assumptions of high school civics, Lindblom notably refuses to define a specific, graduated, time-ordered series of policy-making steps, deferring instead to the structure of decision making—the formalities of public policy—and the ambiguous force of social attitudes (Lindblom and Woodhouse 1993). He suggests that social policy making responds to a number of special considerations (the unique role of business, impaired capacities, and inequalities) but not in predictable ways. Yet these special considerations are themselves seemingly the products, correlates, or causes of America's social ethos. They do not sanction themselves, and it is difficult, if not impossible, to discern the role of leadership, even in the heroic guise of charisma. Leadership may be the routine response to underlying consent; it may form it; or, in the deafening complexity of social forces, it may simply enact the summary myths of social reality.

Political perceptions are tested against the nation's civic religion of individualism and personal responsibility. Its civic ceremonies and rituals, including the social services, express the nation's fundamental ideological assumptions about ethnicity, class, region, social status, background, education, and other assumptions that are frequently ungenerous, cruel, and denigrating. In even more reduced form, American republicanism tacitly screens its social policies through the dictates of social efficiency, that is, political parsimony and social compatibility.

In this way, contemporary social welfare policy is sanctioned by the ascribed immorality of an American underclass rather than by any credible proof of individual incapacity, social causation, or actual irresponsibility. The presumed deficiencies of failed citizens are the bulwarks of inequality and socioeconomic immobility. Little of the dispute over social outcomes—not even the measurement of income and social stagnation at the core of the issue—is grounded in credible information.

Politics, Ideology, and Social Services

Social policy is a course of action sanctioned by society. The sanction has largely remained political throughout history, with only the briefest interludes of rational or, better said, near-rational or protorational reflection. Nietzsche's nihilism—culture's imperative to control all of its institutions—best describes policy making even in societies that boast of Enlightenment rationality. American society and culture generally have staunchly refused to apply rational methods except to the most narrowly limited and broadly accepted social goals such as engineering, medicine, weaponry, and gambling casinos. Certainly, the failures both of social welfare services and of the literature pierce any subterfuge of achieving Enlightenment goals. Rather, the endurance of social services despite their disappointing performance suggests that they are actually sanctioned to fail, at least as responses to social problems. Instead, they are mandated symbols of central social preferences.

The American preference for the decisions of a private sector dominated by the market rather than the church, the family, or the community
seems to be both historically pervasive and politically strategic. However,
it may be neither just, well-informed, nor wise. American deprivation
disproportionately affects blacks, Latinos, Native Americans, women,
and recent immigrants, creating diversities that seem to coincide with the
ascriptive assumptions of its fateful folklore. Politically these groups are
weak and suffer stereotypes of intellectual and moral inferiority that
depreciate their claims to greater policy attention.

The business of welfare in the United States, whether conceived as
philanthropy in the private sector or welfare policy in the public sector,
has not resolved social and personal problems: poverty, drug and alcohol abuse, illegitimacy, criminality and violence, suicide, failed socialization, marital disharmony, and so forth. To the contrary, the long-standing
satisfaction with obviously weak social welfare programs suggests that
the welfare business is more a political ritual of mock concern than a sincere attempt to resolve social and personal problems, particularly among
poorer citizens. The hypocrisy is relieved by a social service literature
that persistently creates evidence to sustain the corrective myths of
social welfare.

The rituals are enacted through social welfare agencies. It is rare for
either a public or private social welfare agency to take even a planful, let
alone objective or rational, approach to services by estimating and identifying need, then designing specific services that it monitors and evaluates
objectively against performance criteria of success. Rather, the process is
political, in highly ritualistic deference to community power.

A new service or need is initially pressed on social welfare agencies by
a constituency of staff, untrained volunteers, board members, and influential citizens to establish a trial period of operation. Its acceptance into
the customary array of community services depends on its conformity
with important cultural values: the degree to which elite groups concur
with its goals and derive status from supporting a popular, emerging
cause; public reactions to the idea of the service; the degree to which the
program maintains fiscal and administrative control, a flow of recipients,
and a modest waiting list; the degree to which existing service patterns
that express cherished communal norms remain undisturbed. In the
United States, these values are propagated through services that empha-
size a sense of individual responsibility in denial of commensurate communal obligations. It is important recognize that services are not
evaluated against their specific production functions to reduce social
problems; first, appropriate methods are too costly or unavailable to be
applied to discern the actual effects of the program; second, the literature
of the social services has not produced credible program evaluations.[10]

The values of the community are expressed quite specifically in the selection of service recipients, the conditions of the care they receive, and generally through the justification and interpretation of the agency's role that its auspices—the boards of private agencies and the legislatures and administrations that charter public agencies—provide to the community. Most community services, especially those with any sort of psychothera-peutic or counseling content, act as churches of the civil religion, secular expressions of a generalized Christianity. They select a clientele that has failed (sinned); put these individuals through a process of "rational induction" and insight that allegedly offers the opportunity to take responsibility for their own actions (to confess their sin); exhort them to change (preaching the word of God) on grounds that they will fulfill noble social roles as parents, colleagues, neighbors, workers, spouses, or others; and reinforce their reformed behaviors (forgiveness and ulti-mately salvation). The recipients' decisions to conform to socially accept-able behavior are rewarded occasionally by a modest amount of short-term, concrete care, but more frequently with little more than churchly goodwill and a pat on the back. Virtue is its own reward.

The workers (apostles) are embarked upon personally satisfying careers (saintly missions) to help people help themselves (conversion). At the end of their careers, the community and the agency pay their respects at retirement dinners, through awards of professional recognition, and eventually with obituaries that laud the achievements of the workers (the miracles of saints).

The services supposedly provide opportunities for miscreants and deviants to change. Their failure to do so is interpreted clearly as their continuing defiance (unrepentant sin), with the consequence of relieving the society of the moral obligation for assistance except to maintain its altruistic efforts. However, continued service reflects back more on the community's enduring faith in civic virtue (a financial martyrdom to its mission to save sinners) than on the service recipients' needs or actual sit-uations.

In this catechism of civic virtue and vice, the agency's actual perform-ance in meeting its avowed goals is relatively unimportant, a distant sec-ond from the principal goal of setting social boundaries by isolating and frequently punishing service recipients for violating the social ethos. The community's sense of righteousness ostensibly motivates the judgments, although the direct result of unworthiness is to reduce pressure for public relief. The budgetary parsimony of social efficiency (a wise corrective for sin) is more graphically served than any fictive ability to count saved souls.[11]

In just this way, the United States has enacted a network of services for those with emotional and mental problems, the long-term unemployed, welfare recipients, unmarried mothers, criminals and juvenile delinquents, battered women, foster children, and so forth. It is rare, and even in these cases largely symbolic, for any service to go past preaching to actually provide substantial relief from hardship or to put up the requisite resources to change environments or to make the efforts to describe and evaluate its own actual performance.

American Opinion

Americans' attitudes create and enforce social welfare policy, with hardly any of those attitudes containing much more than ascriptive assumptions (positive as well as negative) about the poor and social conditions. Indeed, sixty-five years of national surveys largely establish the conformity of attitudes between the mass of the American people and their social policies, most often in defiance of any objective truth or rationality. The interpretation of both differences and conformities among groups with different political power remains an intractable methodological problem of disentangling leadership, self-interest, and best interest—the issue of whether citizens are manipulated and propagandized or freely consent to the policy choices of their representatives. Nevertheless, in view of the long-standing consistency between the masses, on the one hand, and actual social policy and the attitudes of elites, on the other, the statement of the popular will commands respect, if not agreement, as to what is in the best interests of citizens.

The effectiveness of the social services as institutions of dominant social values measures the society's achievement of its professed goals. The persistent failure to either address issues of inequality or their own far more narrow program goals suggests social intent; the failures themselves are the intended social policies and probably account for the political value of the programs as rituals of social learning. Social problems endure alongside a stable offering of superficial, disingenuous, underfunded social services in a nation that can easily afford far more generous arrangements for the deprivations of its citizens. If it had the will, the society would devise a structural ideology to justify surrogates for the failures of social institutions: families and homelike places for children without them, schools for the uneducated, decent communities for those who live in urban jungles, jobs for the unemployed, and, yes, lifelong character-enhancing, citizenship-building experiences through the philosophizing benefits of counseling, nature walks, arts and crafts classes, Scouts, and community theater. Society's refusal is ideologically committed but not rationally bound to convenient assumptions that social failure is the product of flawed character—immorality—and not the misfortunes caused naturally by imperfect social institutions.

Thus, ignorance, ambiguous research, denigrating ascriptive assumptions, and the consistent conservative preferences of American politics challenge the proposition that the United States is pursuing Enlightenment goals of rational social policy and greater socioeconomic equality. Instead, the nation is taking an uncharted course into the future based on the most Romantic grand fallacies—the assumption that human behavior and social institutions are perfectible through an epiphany of truth and a disciplined will. Yet rational inquiry has been incapable of dispelling the fiction of social efficiency; to the contrary, it has been seduced into the production of corrective myths. Functional analysis and social engineering have been barren in cultivating a social analog for the drugs of medicine or the bridges, motors, and computers of science and engineering. Even Frederick Winslow Taylor, the apotheosis of management science, did less to define business rationality than to justify the ascendancy of management over labor, a political imposition that perversely went far to stimulate union formation. Invoking corrective myths to justify minimal social welfare arrangements in protection of established inequalities, American social policy sanctifies a civil religion that quietly acquiesces social efficiency.

The Social Service Imagination

Except as a compliant trustee of dominant social values, the social service imagination has fled the business of welfare without leaving even a telltale of insight or courage. The relationship between professing good intentions and actually being effective—between moral imperatives and enforceable claims—is weak, perhaps even antagonistic. There do not appear to be inexpensive social welfare remedies for social problems. Nevertheless, in imitation of medicine and engineering, the welfare industry has staked out professional claims along the sight lines of science. In fact, however, it has more closely followed cultural precedent, like law and the clergy. Indeed, scientific practice, although theoretically possible at times, is an elusive standard in the live context of social services. As a result, the persistence of most social welfare programs and the occupations that staff them may be better explained by their reinforcement and conformity with social values—their symbolism as social charitability and the political ceremonies they perform in preaching the creed of individual responsibility—than by any true technological ability to reliably achieve predetermined goals, that is, by their social welfare production functions. There is little evidence that advanced specialization in any of the academic disciplines of the social services (notably public administration and management, counseling, criminal justice, social work, and psychology) or close identification with their professional organizations has stimulated solutions for social and personal problems. There is also little evidence that volunteerism or eclectic general preparation is any more effective.

Only a small portion of the roles mandated by either the expansive or narrow definition of social welfare is conducted by professionally trained workers, that is, by people with university degrees from formal programs. The majority of work in the human services, even outside of education and health, is performed by people without much specific training in the human services or the social sciences. Moreover, many social service workers, and frequently the direct caregivers, have little formal schooling at all.

The professionalization of social services has routinized neglect. Professional human service disciplines maintain their historic role as incantations of the dominant social ethos and regnant political ideologies, routinely failing to advance the interests of needy groups even when they constitute a huge proportion of the society's members. Yet the relatively small number and restricted roles of professional workers understate the cultural importance of the social services, particularly the personal social services. Their very weaknesses enact the ethos of the nation—its attitudes toward less successful and more needy Americans—through the profound ceremonies of professional social services that create and disseminate the justifications for social denial and social rewards. Professionalized personal social service, like a morality play, a documentary, or a situation comedy, is better understood as one of the educational entertainments of the nation's ethos than as an independent professional activity with a serious and measurable role to prevent and treat social problems.

While no less self-important but certainly better informed than the professionalized social services, the social sciences have stumbled into similar pitfalls of political acquiescence and faulty, biased research. Nevertheless, the general lack of any disciplinarian edge argues for a dissolution of practice franchises in creating an open field—and more open minds and purses—to address social problems. Mills's (1959) sociological imagination already controls the intellectual life of generic social service practice. Unfortunately, the Romantic reconciliation of biography and history—the personal with the traditional—inevitably favors the regnant social ethos, producing social myth through processes that adjust personal aspiration to governing realities. Rarely has the sociological imagination created the independent estimates of sociological reality that Mills's oppositional heart craved. Nevertheless, myth by itself is not coincidental with more profound processes of social integration. Rather, the social service imagination turns on social choice: the selection of problems for social attention, beneficiaries of social interventions, and methods to pursue social goals. Predictably, this imagination has been put to work in justification of established privileges and economic distributions when social conditions threaten the culture's institutions.

The failure of the social welfare enterprise begins with its sectarian refusal to credibly evaluate its programs. Nevertheless, it is often possible to apply randomized, controlled designs, especially when services are offered in a clinical setting, as is the case for psychotherapy and counseling, manpower training, intensive casework, and so forth. Although the ability to evaluate programs is ready to hand, they have rarely been applied outside of clinical medicine.

However, systematic and controlled comparisons of structural alternatives are nearly impossible even in theory, since the United States cannot be divided into controlled and experimental subentities to test the effects of political motives, economic conditions, or social organization. Therefore, the deeper that any analysis probes, the less certain its argument becomes. As each level is peeled away from questions of programmatic adequacy, explanations become more uncertain, increasingly relying on literary coherence, surmise, and political self-interest, and less often on rational, that is, scientific credibility. Social dialectics rarely rise to even protorational levels and usually only after social discourse has so narrowed the operative issue that policy questions can be decided through empirical evaluation. It must be so, creating profound doubt about the Enlightenment's hope for rational social discourse.

While the absence of a credible scholarship is the principal reason that the business of social services cannot graduate from immaturity into a true profession (nor the social sciences into a true scientific form), their deeper failure emerges from obedience to established social goals, the staunch denial of alternative political claims. This denial is expressed ideologically as a preference for liberal individualism and programmatically as a preference to address social problems as issues of individual deviance through psychotherapeutic and other personal strategies of intervention.

It may well be that the culture of the United States is such a compelling, binding force that true dissent is nearly impossible by any group that depends on public funding and broad private approval. But if this is true, then the failure of social service is all the more profound, and the desirability of change, especially in light of growing social need, is all the more necessary. Unfortunately, an effective political response may be tragically deferred as social perceptions lag behind growing deprivation. One hopes that the recognition of the extent of social service failure will hasten the political recognition of need and perhaps minimize the number of sacrifices to complacency.

In spite of the whimsy of personal autonomy that has engendered restrictive public policies, the reality of modern society, with its inherent financial insecurities for enormous numbers of Americans, probably undercuts the economic and social independence of the family and the individual along with broader notions of civic equality. As a result, liberal individualism (a society of equal freeholders, opportunity on the frontier, the entrepreneur as hero, unbounded competition) becomes a pernicious sham. Political success within the constraints of America's consensual liberal republicanism depends more on the mechanics of affability than the substance of need. The humanitarian social imagination is challenged to achieve political success for broadly egalitarian policies even while it accepts the personal drama of Mills's notion of producing popular myth. Yet reducing the critical imagination to grubbing after the petty worms of social efficiency seems unworthy of the mature intellect and all the expense and bother of social research.

There are, after all, only three alternative strategies for social policy: continuing current social policy and perpetuating its inadequacies, doing less, or doing more. There is no compelling theoretical reason, no rational basis, for any choice among the three, although continuing on the current course has the greatest attraction simply because it is already politically successful; to paraphrase Hume, it bribes indolence. Yet it appears unlikely that social efficiency will ever solve the embedded problems of society. Doing less seems barbaric and probably risks activating the deprived, a true threat to the many who appear to be content with current policy. Therefore, if social policy is to relieve those who suffer personal problems and who face social barriers to a full life in the United States, then the nation might profitably consider a strategy of greater generosity, especially if the forecasts of huge federal budget surpluses and robust economic growth prove to be accurate.

The social service imagination is challenged by the inadequacy of current policy and the cruelty of further retrenchments to devise a political justification, including serviceable myths, that reduce inequalities by addressing the many institutional deficits of American life—its failed families, communities, educational systems, job markets, and the rest. The imagination to resolve the conundrums of effective social policy is a general task for the nation that has been unwisely franchised to the social sciences and the social service disciplines. There are livelier possibilities provided by alternative educational paths and less formalized professional commitments. Yet without political support, no solution is possible, and therefore the process of pursuing a generous alternative might start with the political problem of constituency.

Greater Equality: A More Satisfying Social Myth

Both the scientific mood and the egalitarian promise of the Enlightenment are reasonable inspirations for a modern society's civic ideal. They require a bit of updating by the experience of the past few centuries, but the Enlightenment provides the essence of fairness and human compassion. Consensual liberal republicanism is already realized in America's high culture, which, unfortunately, is restricted to too few and, too frequently, the children of privilege and wealth. But this could be simply corrected by appropriate taxing policies that sop up money from the top and invest it in central cultural institutions to enable greater numbers of citizens to flourish. Heavier taxes might even prod the privileged to use their remaining money more wisely and thus promote greater economic productivity. The doors of the high culture should be opened to multitudes. This would be greatly facilitated by intense public education along with all the adjunctive bangles of family and community support.

These are not novel ideas. Indeed, they are the elements of the natural experiment conducted every day by moneyed citizens who lavish attention, education, and an immense array of other cultural advantages upon their own children. As adults, these children have created the most astonishing economy and the richest high culture the world has ever witnessed. Replicating this level of investment in many more people would certainly cost plenty, at least for a few generations. Still, investments in basic social institutions are far more sensible and probably wiser uses for surplus capital than the pointless RVs, behemoth autos, mink-hair pants, empty manorial houses, truffles, ostruga caviar, and the rest of the expensive drapery, adornments, and indulgences of American wealth.

Social progress probably requires a Nietzschean miracle in "overcoming" the inertia of tradition, but this time hopefully one of rationality. There have been triumphs of reason over cultural fatalism. But even apparent technological successes such as the Tennessee Valley Authority and other dam projects, nuclear power plants, insecticide, economic development, amplified music, antibiotics, and Las Vegas have had perverse, unintended consequences such as erosion and flood control problems, biological perils, environmental and noise pollution, hyperconcentration of power and wealth, iatrogenic disease, compulsive gambling and corporate depravity. Nevertheless, rationality may be a fruitful epiphany even with only the hope of limited application.

Notes

1. The 1998 Occupational Outlook Handbook lists 923,300 people employed in "Individual and Miscellaneous Social Services"; social workers, counselors, psychologists, human service workers, and recreation workers total 1,461,000. Many more employees not contained in these categories, perhaps millions, also work in public and private social service agencies as clerks and secretaries, support technicians, social scientists, managers, and so forth. In a very broad sense of social welfare, Salamon's (1999) "Selected Social Welfare Functions" includes $425 billion spent by the federal government (1994), $225 billion spent by local and state governments, and $460 billion spent by nonprofit organizations. In addition, an enormous amount of money (some double-counted, but much arising from indi-

vidual spending that is not counted in the previous categories of government and nonprofit spending) is spent on social services through profit-making organizations, particularly for vocational, recreational, and day care services. The nonprofit sector alone contains about 1,600,000 organizations. In short, the human service industry is vast, probably consuming well over $1 trillion annually outside of medical services, while the social service sector and its subsector, the personal social services, account for many hundreds of billions of dollars each year. Whether the focus is relatively narrow or broad, the social service industry accounts for a substantial portion of the American economy.

2. In contrast with most other social welfare categories, local and state government account for 93 percent of public expenditures on education (Salamon 1999, 52).

3. The income disparity is reflected in growing Gini ratios: .376 in 1947, .348 in 1968, .430 in 1998 (U.S. Census Bureau 1999, table F-4).

4. American social conditions are routinely tracked by a variety of government agencies, notably the United States Census Bureau and the United States Department of Labor, as well as by numerous research organizations, including the Center on Budget and Policy Priorities, the Brookings Institution, the Economic Policy Institute, and many others. The argument is less over conditions than over whether to do anything about them.

5. Greater detail on individual programs is provided as they are discussed throughout, but particularly in chapter 4.

6. The opposition of traditional voluntary organizations—the bulk of the nonprofit sector—to change is legendary. See Patterson 1981; Jencks 1992; Marris and Rein 1967; Smith and Lipsky 1993; and Titmuss 1971, among a library of additional criticism.

7. Citro and Michael (1995, a National Academy of Science report) recognize the inadequacy of welfare payments and call for almost a 20 percent increase in payments, along with the implementation of a relative threshold.

8. Randomized placebo-controlled trials are necessary to establish the scientific credibility of a social service's effectiveness. The necessity for randomization and careful control is greater in the social sciences than in the natural sciences, presumably because physical matter lacks the human's consciousness of the research environment. Randomized placebo-controlled trials are necessary protections against alternative explanations for outcomes: maturation, seasonality, "spontaneous" remission, and placebo and other demonstration effects. In addition, standard procedures of measurement objectivity and reliability are necessary to protect against a host of experimenter and research biases, notably confirmation bias—the tendency of the researcher to allow her love of hypothesis to overwhelm her commitment to science and probably through Orne's (1962) "demand characteristics." The wide respect for these principles of classical experimentation and the rational authority they confer on findings has not translated into actual research. Nevertheless, randomized placebo-controlled trials set the standard for instrumental rationality. The fact that they have not been adequately

applied in the social services does not either diminish their inherent logic nor require an adjusted definition of rationality. See Epstein 1993b; Meinert 1986.

9. For example, the 1996 welfare reforms are consistent with Olasky's (1992) preference for the religious sector over the public sector, personal responsibility over social responsibility.

10. A portion of this paragraph is drawn from Epstein 1992.

11. Even a step further, the social service system could be seen as aborting the constitutional separation of church and state and fiercely pursuing the apostolic creed of its civil religion but without specific reference to denominations or God. Perhaps if the United States did away with the separation of church and state, social services would be more clearly revealed for what they are.

Chapter 1

Political Theory, Ideology, and Social Welfare

Theory becomes ideology to the extent to which its political utility, that is, its symbolic authority, extends beyond the rational sanction of its verified propositions. The subtle transformation of the limited and specific authority of scientific theory into a generalized justification for sectarian claims is a natural outgrowth of social competition. The dialectical interplay of ideology is intimately bound up with the organization of power. By reassuring supporters in order to maximize their cohesion and by extending an invitation to potential allies, ideology endorses the organizational strategies of political rivals.

The Enlightenment held out a hope for the practice of reason (i.e., science) to ground social authority in a compelling objectivity. Yet the reality of modern society constrains the pursuit of rational information. Even the compromised rationality of the social sciences, limited by goals that are defined through the political process and employed instrumentally to evaluate social interventions, may be illusory. Acultural authority— asylum from social tradition—may not exist except as a temporary grant of immunity from the culture to one of its institutions and for usually enumerated objectives such as technological and medical innovation. In this sense, social welfare and social policy generally are not neutral searches for humanistic goals and effective interventions but concrete realizations of the culture's preferences, its ethos. The social policy-making process is detached from idealized moral imperatives in pursuing the claims of political actors.

Ideology justifies particular policies. It conveniently blends political interests with cultural lore to vindicate the ambitions of competitors in securing greater amounts of money, status, power, security, territory, and other scarcities. As distinct from the testable propositions of scientific theory, ideology asserts a pattern of beliefs concerning the nature of society. Since it is largely impossible to test fundamental propositions about social cause, even the most precise and graphic ideologies swing free of actual verification, always vulnerable to dogma as social dialectics heat up. Consequently, social policy is a course of action that is sanctioned through the political decision-making processes of society. It builds consensus through negotiation, persuasion, and control rather than rationally through compelling, scientific proof of value and outcome.

While some areas of social policy may enjoy a modicum of rational content, social welfare policy is rarely informed with even coherent information, let alone scientifically credible estimates of causal relationships. Consequently, the problem of effectiveness bedevils all social services. There are no scientifically credible studies that testify to the effectiveness of any of the social services, notably the personal social services; to the contrary, the more credible research tends to suggest their ineffectiveness and possible harm.

Deprived of demonstrable production functions, the political roles, that is, the ceremonial functions of the social services explain their persistence. Social services by and large do not have the resources to address social problems; at best they provide some thin surveillance of problematic populations and at times a modest amount of concrete relief. Their funding, however, is sufficient to transmit ideology, reinforce prevalent social values, set boundaries of acceptable social behavior, test emerging forms of social education and social symbols of preference, and propagate social values by celebrating conformity and stigmatizing deviance.

The typical social service agency evangelizes the dominant social ideology. Its concrete services, such as they are, are offered to recipients in the manner of city missions that bribe alcoholics with meals to sit through their sermons of religious insight and conversion. Customarily stressing personal responsibility, the themes of the preaching focus on the wayward souls of derelicts rather than the compulsions of their disease. Yet the alcoholics are only the apparent targets of the sermons; after all, even if they remain awake during the exhortation, they are hardly, if ever, converted to abstinence. Rather, the rest of society is the intended congregation for the sermon. Indeed, the symbolic dramas of social services, with the recipient usually playing the part of villain, rascal, degenerate, or miscreant, define the limits of appropriate behavior—the penalties for deviance and the rewards for virtuous conformity—while providing socially efficient reassurances that the nation's problems are being attended to in approved ways.

Although its expression in specific policies may be protean, any social welfare theory makes a relatively small number of strategic choices in defining its core assumptions about the determinants of human behavior that also explain the emergence and perpetuation of problematic social conditions. These theories of cause typically differ in two major ways: over the type of proof they employ to verify propositions about reality and over the nature of reality itself, that is, their explanations of human

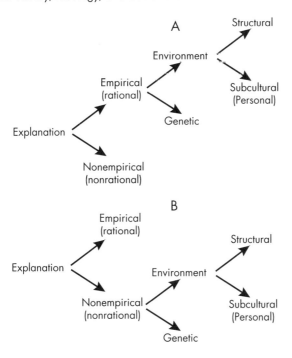

Figure 1.1 *The Nature of Explanation*

behavior and social problems. In the first instance, following figure 1.1, propositions can be tested through coherent empirical means (the canons of science) or through nonrational forms of truth (faith, tradition, subjective experience, superstition, fatalism, and religion, even civil religion) that in the end constitute social politics. Second, theories of human behavior adjudicate between the relative influence of the environment and of genetics (the nature-nurture controversy), as well as among the environmental factors themselves—the social structures or subcultural and characterological influences—that explain human behavior.

In the United States, these choices have been made to explain and fix responsibility for social failure and success, apparently belying more fundamental concerns with political cohesion, social integration, and even profit. Indeed, personal responsibility—the struggle over worthiness in American social dialectics—is the pillar of the nation's ethos and even a discreeet camouflage for more vulgar motives such as parsimony and social stability. The degree of responsibility that any individual bears for his or her economic, psychological, and social standing has direct bearing on whether to fulfill personal needs or to accept them as the unfortunate but necessary consequences of unwise, immoral, undesirable but uncoerced personal choices. Still, the pressing, if frequently tacit, imperative

for civic order tests ideology in the sobering reality of social consent, soft-
ening the harshness of social efficiency at the heart of America's civil religion with occasional cushions of social welfare.

The First Branching

At the first branching, causal propositions about social behavior profess
to be true either nonrationally or empirically. Empirical validation,
notably through credible scientific methodology, has been accepted by
most contemporary political theories as the definitive test of their truth.
Political rivals typically claim that their preferred policies are coextensive
with the nation's loftiest traditions and goals, that the policies are valuable means to those ends, and, perhaps expressing the status of science
and technology in modern society, that the effects of the policies, as well
as their fundamental causal propositions and visions, are measurable and
testable.

Yet true rational goals have never been demonstrated. Without invoking another summa bonum, there is no way to adjudicate among Ben-
tham's utilitarianism, Pareto optima, and an intuitive choice of a
particular rule for progress such as Rawls's theory of justice. The collective
and individual definitions of utility fail empirical rationality; they are necessarily metaphysical. Pareto optima measured as relative economic and
social distance contradict Pareto optima measured as absolute distance; a
system cannot get bigger for everyone (everyone better off) while preserving both the relative and the absolute distances among different socioeconomic classes (no one worse off). Justice and any other nonutilitarian rule
(although they all seem to be pressed on utilitarian grounds) are intuitions. In the end, claims for a higher rationality are accepted without
rational proof when they are also instances of cultural preference.

Indeed, a philosophic system mostly requires internal consistency
after allowing itself a mulligan or two for its initial assumptions (the
metaphysics or incompleteness of any system). Thus, empiricism is
applied instrumentally to means, that is, to the supposedly rational
tools—the social policies—of society in pursuit of its goals. The social
goals themselves are typically derived from some sort of political process
and the workings of tradition. However, the degree to which the goals are
met by any policy is frequently amenable, at least in principle, to empirical testing. By and large, the social sciences have been ostensibly elaborated to fulfill at least the function of policy evaluation.

Thus, without an ability to define rational goals, social decision making is restricted from the outset to an instrumental rationality at most.
Instrumental rationality implies randomized placebo-controlled trials,
experimental demonstrations of cause and effect, in order to provide scientifically credible information for policy making. Even Lindblom's clas-

sic contention that social decision making muddles through with only rare instances of rational information is testable (Lindblom 1959). Decision making is instrumentally rational to the extent to which it has developed scientifically credible information. Certainly, political decisions about social services, which are probably characteristic of most other policy choices, have never been informed with scientifically credible policy information. It simply does not exist. None of the many studies of theory and programmatic effectiveness have credibly established causal relationships. They are uniformly defective experiments; as a result, decision making that relies on their credibility summons the authority of science as a ceremony of reputation instead of legitimizing conclusions with credible information. Indeed, the fundamental criticism of the social sciences portrays them as hypocrites that justify a practice of a limited rationality but surreptitiously perform a political role—a sheep in wolf's clothing or, as some would have it, a sheep in sheep's clothing.

Yet the effects of social policies, notably welfare policies, are frequently impossible to verify scientifically as a practical matter, since credible tests are often inconvenient, politically threatening, and illegal. It is both illegal and unethical to withhold care from a control group when the services are mandated by law and a less formal sense of humane necessity, as in the case of child protection. Rational information is also immensely expensive; randomized trials require great investments to achieve representative samples, adequate controls (placebo, nonservice, standard treatment, and the variations of experimental treatments), reliable and valid measures, sufficient follow-up assessments, and neutral measurement. Large social experiments cost hundreds of millions of dollars, but even for the best of them, it is not evident that the value of the information was worth the cost.

In addition, controlled experimentation may be strategically impossible; the United States cannot be divided into any sort of comparable subdivisions that control for the effects of economic factors such as interest rates, of political factors such as forms of participation, or of social factors such as migration. For these reasons, economics, as one example, cannot grow into a true experimental science. Rationality is also impaired in principle; uncertainty, notably when it is created by the unpredictable perturbations caused by measurement, enters a particularly powerful wild card into any policy consideration, since policy changes affect social systems in unknowable ways. The unpredictability of measurement may be less of a concern in physics, where quarks presumably lack consciousness and motive, but in human affairs the unpredictable responses of sentient people to experimental conditions, including their unacknowledged demand characteristics, enormously complicate analysis.

In contrast with classical experimentation, the possibility of substituting panel data for experimental data has not been able to adequately address the problems of self-selection; groups of respondents by dint of the very choices they make are not adequate controls for each other. Creating controlled equivalence through statistical manipulation instead of randomization creates provocative pilot investigations but not definitive tests. Demographic analyses of one sort or another also fail to prove cause. Rather, they tend to assume cause in spite of the post hoc nature of their data and their correlational analyses.

The typical social welfare intervention is not evaluated either through field information that measures or explains its outcomes or through experimental and laboratory tests of its core theories. General propositions about human behavior—the causes of social failure and success—have not been credibly tested. It is maddening that after decades of the modern debate over public cash welfare programs, echoing back through the centuries of poor relief, the fundamental relationship between welfare and labor force participation is still undefined (Epstein 1997). The numerous studies and experiments—notably, the negative income tax experiments of the 1960s and 1970s, along with the frequently recondite literature of labor supply economics—have simply failed to produce credible estimates of the effects of cash relief of one sort or another on labor supply. Their technical flaws and, lamentably, the political tropism of the researchers undercut the authority of the research. Not coincidentally, the literature routinely cites research, but usually without recognition of its imperfections, in support of a variety of public policy initiatives.

Ignorance can be politically useful. The realization that a social service is ineffective accumulates slowly and anecdotally as the defining problem persists in the form of visible irritations—target behaviors that do not change, as well as persistent injustice and inequalities. This has been the experience with drug and alcohol rehabilitation, programs for juvenile delinquents, school busing, remedial education programs, sex education, psychotherapy for psychotics, women's shelters, and public foster care for children, to name a few. The broad recognition of their failures develops despite reports of positive outcomes by social welfare professionals and social scientists. However, the perception of ineffectiveness is accepted, and other programs are instituted only when the service's symbolic utility becomes obsolete. The recognition of programmatic failure does not by itself lead to the replacement of a social service unless it is paired with a political decision to address the underlying problem. Yet low-level social priorities—a preference to ignore the claims of particular groups of people—may well be satisfied by ineffective social services that perform political rituals in support of dominant political preferences. As a consequence, social service agencies that successfully deflect through their ceremonial roles the claims of particular recipients may be perversely rewarded with funding that is ostensibly allocated for definable production functions, that is, explicit social needs. The funding is adequate to maintain the political role of the service agency but grossly insufficient to address the deprivations of service recipients.

The extent of institutionalized hypocrisy is not surprising as society may cherish an organizational imperative for continuity and order more than any rational goal, sense of justice and equality, or inherent impulse toward progress. Societal change, as LaPiere (1954, 1965) insists, is acultural if not actually anticultural and emerges not through planned consent but rather through inherent social contradictions and competitions over money, status, power, and the rest. The legitimacy of realizing social cohesion through the social services and more broadly through social policy is a consequence of political perspective, the clarifying democratic processes of self-interest. Those who consent to political priorities approve of them, and those who are denied, who resent the penalties of their political unimportance, contend for change. In this sense, then, the socioeconomic stratification of the United States is simply a condition of society but not necessarily a problem. The preferences of its citizens, their choice of ideology, sanction its spread, determining whether inequality is viewed as a social problem or as legitimate diversity.

As a consequence of rational indeterminacy and the ineluctable cultural pressures to create social myth, the authority of political theory is customarily exaggerated. Empirical accountability has largely been confined to medicine, engineering, and the natural sciences. The rituals of science—its sociological meaning as a vehicle of status and belief—dress up politics, reaffirming faith more often than testing reality and conferring rational authority. Occasionally, credible data, such as on the effects of DDT or nuclear waste, intrude on policy deliberations; more often, policy data consist of best estimates by beholden experts whose consistent findings are often secured through the homogeneity of their institutional commitments rather than by neutral and objective experimental replications. Factional research is not science even while it may constitute a sensible discourse for representative government.

Without a rational core of verified and verifiable statements of social cause, political theory becomes bald ideology, failing even as protoscience. The claim of rationality in social policy—the insistence that particular policies are not simply group preferences but are objective truths—is itself frequently asserted dogmatically in denial of political influence in the practice of the social sciences. Yet reflecting the prestige of science, contemporary ideology also embraces, but only as a convention of discourse, the canons of scientific proof in testing political theory.

Nonrational forms of validation encompass the faith-based justifications of religion, revealed truth, superstition, and tradition, which indeed may be largely synonymous. Political decision making is a nonrational form; indeed, it is the opposite of rational decision making and operates through social consensus with only rare reference to rational goals or rational means. Political processes derive goals from implicit self-interest and satisfaction and evaluate the means for achieving them both as symbols of their sustaining ideologies—banners of sectarian preferences— and as actual production functions. Some policies *appear* to be effective, but this is customarily a deception of political convenience and often one related to symbolic value—the degree to which the interests of powerful individuals and groups are promoted by the appearance of a policy's effectiveness. In this way, boys and girls clubs, women's shelters, Scouts, Head Start, the Peace Corps, services for unwed mothers, psychotherapy, and boot camps for juvenile delinquents, as examples, are popular symbols of the culture's civic values, but none have been adequately evaluated to test whether they actually promote socialization, protection from further abuse, job preparation, international harmony and economic development, emotional serenity, sanity, and education. Indeed, the policy-making process invokes tradition, custom, precedent, contemporary beliefs, and even divine concern, but it rarely pursues good information to sanction its decisions. When some partial but good information does exist (e.g., the death of the snail darter, the hothouse effects of carbon dioxide), it is most often transformed into the symbolic agent of an underlying theory (e.g., environmental protection, whose tenets are, again, more ideological than profound). Thus, policy authority resides in political power, the product of leadership and force, acquiring legitimacy through the mythic workings of ideology rather than through rational proof.

Democratic decision making is a strategy to spread the risk of ignorance. By its very nature (the political sovereignty of citizen subjectivity), democracy is political, relying on nonrational elements embedded in social habit and expressed in summary form in the nation's civil religions. The psychological discomfort of thoroughgoing uncertainty—a consequence of ignorance—is probably the motive force behind ideology and its myths of truth and authority. In the end, democracy may provide the greatest benefit to society, but this proposition is practically untestable (two equivalent nations cannot be created, with one as the democratic experiment and the other as the perhaps autocratic control, while the starting line for natural comparisons among different cultures are never equal) and may even be untestable in principle.

The Second Branching

At its second branching, contemporary social theory selects between genetic and environmental explanations of human behavior, again, on grounds that the choice is rational (i.e., informed by scientifically credible evidence). While much is known about genetic processes, little is known about their influence on behavior. At best, assumptions about genetic determination of social actions are premature, incomplete, and wistful; at worst, they tendentiously deny greater social equality. The scholarship of genetics estimates the degree to which a variety of human behaviors, such as schizophrenia, crime, and intelligence, are determined by inheritance. Yet heritability scores, essentially measures of correlation between the proximity of relationship (i.e., unrelated individuals, cousins, siblings, and identical twins) and behavioral similarity, rarely translate into rational guides for social policy, even while they may be mystified into the sacred justifications of particular policy choices. Genetic inheritance remains a factor, even an essential one, that influences human behavior, but its determinative role has not been specified with reference to the actual limitations and potentials—the interplay—of genes and environment.

The horrors of genetic social policy enthusiasms (genocide, sterilization, slavery, rigid class and caste systems, and the rest of eugenic authoritarianism) have spooked the current political debate in the United States. Nevertheless, genetic explanations are the periodically reprised ghosts that haunt policy debates.

The *science* of genetics rarely informs social dialectics. Rather, the ideology of genetics (e.g., sociobiology, evolutionary psychology, behavioral genetics) performs this role. Genetic ideologies have been invoked to justify social and economic stratification and customarily with a eugenic subtheme in protecting the purity, freedom, and dominance of the alleged sources of human progress. In this guise, genetic ideology is an essentially conservative argument attractive to status quo winners. The severe rational limitations on the quality of proof have not deterred the unfortunate proclivity of American opinion toward ascriptive assumptions of inferiority. In this way, the current debate over the test score gap between blacks and whites is broken into two polar camps, with one searching for environmental determinants and the other seemingly content with genetic, that is, racial explanations (Jencks and Phillips 1998; Hunt 1999).

In any case, it would seem to follow that if genes determine behavior, then individuals are not responsible for their actions. Consequently, the American ethos would seem obliged toward generosity, on the one hand, or toward brutal isolation and sterilization, on the other. Yet the logic of genetic superiority works through stereotypy to delegitimize political rivals. The biologically ascendant, who are usually also those in power, claim scientific authority (extracultural permission) to deny equality to the biologically inferior, who are invariably members of other races, castes, and ethnicities, and to assert their own continuing access to greater resources, status, prestige, and control. Genetic ideology ignores the impossibility of separating genes from the environment.

Genetic ideology, giving succor to the basest impulses of civilization, typically produces a very intolerant and abusive social policy. Through the distortion of science, it has certified the subordination of a variety of groups, barring them from the common protections of society and justifying their persecution and subjugation as threats to the culture. Without rational proof of determination, the genetic sanction for social policy is the ideological consequence of political motives, beckoning to the material ambitions and psychological frailties of its advocates.

Surreptitious genetic assumptions about the inferiority of a variety of groups probably power the virulence of the contemporary social debate over the environmental factors that determine behavior. Logically this should not occur, since biological incapacity would seem to exculpate character flaws. Yet ideological imperatives interpret flawed character and dysfunctional subcommunity as evidence of genetic inferiority. Indeed, the desire to create a political partnership between genetic explanations, on the one hand, and subcultural and characterological explanations, on the other, may account for the popularity of *The Bell Curve* (Herrnstein and Murray 1994) and the earlier works of Spencer, Pierson, Shockley, Jensen, Rushton, and many others.[1]

The Third Branching

At the third branching, environmental theories of social outcomes take two basic forms: structural and subcultural (which is actually a form of characterological explanation). Structural arguments trace the genesis of human imperfections to the flaws in cultural institutions. In this way, discriminatory practices, broken families, economic poverty, depraved communities, unemployment, deviant peer groups, inadequate schools, and so forth produce problematic individuals and dysfunctional subcultures. Structural explanations dramatize the individual as relatively weak in the grips of compelling cultural forces; in this way, deviant behavior becomes a social responsibility, especially when the flaws of institution are tolerated by the society. Thus, structuralists tend to look toward government to redress social problems.[2]

In contrast, subcultural and characterological explanations of social problems place strong emphasis on the individual's own responsibility for his or her plight—the freely chosen, attitudinal defects of character that cause individual and group failure. Subcultural adaptations are the collective results of shared values, voluntary decisions to support compatible lifestyles. People are poor because they choose to be lazy, dissolute, and undisciplined; they opt for a criminal life and freely join gangs, electing to live in opposition to the law; promiscuous young women choose to have babies out of wedlock; drunks and drug addicts are morally weak, retreating from responsibility into narcosis; divorce results from parental immaturity; inadequate schooling is the product of undisciplined, inattentive children and their uncaring parents and not the result of an involuntary psychological "disease" such as attention deficit disorder. Productive subcultures are the communal accumulation of pro-ductive, responsible members. Deviant subcultures are the result of morally flawed individuals.[3]

The test of subcultural influence—whether subcultural patterns persist after the structural impediments are removed—is impossible to apply except as a grand experiment but one lacking a control group. Many of the experiments of the social sciences tried to do just this. However, the proxies for structural enrichment—the Henry Higginses of contemporary personal social services—were invariably inadequate, and the structural situation changed little. They were more studies of tepid minimalism (socially efficient interventions) than true approximations of social insti-tutions. Indeed, this is the broader context of most evaluations of social services.

The Mix

The final decision in constructing a theory or ideology of social explana-tion identifies the mix of specific subcultural and structural elements that are critical determinants of behavior. Ideology can combine many differ-ent pure strains of thought. Political explanation is not so much a question of internal consistency as much as a Solomonic apportionment of the ide-ological baby to satisfy competitors. The frank irrationality of political ide-ology turns on the division of spoils among competitors. With little regard for rational outcomes, the long-term consequences of just about any social condition are ignored in accommodating to constituent pressures.

The richest portion of the social sciences' scholarship, often contribut-ing more to literature than to science, speaks through its schools of thought to one or another of the theoretical possibilities for explaining human behavior. Again, however, the vast expanse of the learning is ide-ological because the literature routinely fails to achieve rational proofs. Some portions of the social sciences may have reached this level, explain-ing simple learning among rats and pigeons, and so forth. However, little, if anything, of *general* theoretical value has been provided to confer rationality on social welfare policy making. The jots of rationality are typ-ically isolated from their specific and limited relationships and promoted as political metaphors, almost as synecdoches: whales and spotted owls for the environment, blue-collar workers for lower-status employees, the computer for technology, motherhood for tradition, science for authority. Each political figure of speech is understood with some precision within its narrow application, but none of the institutions for which they stand have transcended an implicit cultural meaning. Whales and mothers are scientifically known largely as biological entities; computers have been finely engineered; lower-paid workers are understood rationally in terms of the tasks they perform, if even that. Yet their interactions as institutions and agents with the rest of society—their specific economic, ecological, social, and psychological effects—are still unexplained. Nonetheless, as political symbols they express the motives and interests of different groups, or, better said, of different roles that affect individual and group behaviors.

The Social Policy-Making Process

As a consequence of "impaired capacities," Lindblom's elegant euphemism for the limitations of rationality, social decision making is not rational (Lindblom and Woodhouse 1993). Particularly in reference to the problems that are the focus of social services, it frequently is not even culturally coherent. Despite the great expanse of the social sciences and their reach for rational authority, scientific theory has not matured in any relevant area of social welfare policy (e.g., criminology, welfare services, youth care, drug treatment and rehabilitation, mental and emotional health, the economic effects of welfare). Rather, tatters of science are stitched together into costumes of political preference for the cultural competition over resources. These factional studies of political rivals are uniformly flawed; consequently, the devices of social dialectics are typically deployed to puncture the rational pretenses of opponents. Even when a consensus exists on the criteria that would settle a debate, for example, the labor supply effects of a guaranteed income, the methodological pitfalls of subsequent tests frustrate definitive conclusions. The hope that truth will emerge from the constant discrediting of questionable information in open democratic debate seems rather a recipe for consensus; despite bad information, a governable constituency eventually develops to apportion perceived risks relative to power.

Simon's "satisficing" is similar to Lindblom's sense of the policy process, but it is even less hospitable to the possibility of rational information. Yet the rational traditional is very persistent in detailing the possibilities of greater rationality in the policy-making processes of society. However, neither the rationalists (the multitude of sophisticated quantitative social scientists, especially in economics and sociology) nor the protorationalists in the applied social policy fields (e.g., Rivlin 1993; Simon 1983; Coleman 1990) have ever succeeded in fashioning systems that compelled any sort of diminution of the political. First, they have been unable to define truly rational information methodologies that are both practical and pragmatic, or to successfully demonstrate the value of their compromised methodologies, or to defend the costs of rational information against the value of the proposed insights. Most problematically, they have not gotten past the normative problem of whose benefit is to be served. The Rand Corporation approach, perhaps well matched to weapons analysis, requires tightly closed systems amenable to operations research. But operations research becomes progressively unreliable the further a policy problem moves away from the models of an internal combustion engine, an assembly line, or a bridge, that is, as critical information becomes less available.

It is very difficult to abandon rationality as a compelling inspiration for policy making. After acknowledging the many problems of achieving even an instrumental practice of rationality in policy making, Dahl and Lindblom ([1953] 1992), in their classic work, argue strenuously that rationality, in spite of its many practical imperfections, is still possible although in a limited form; greater rationality is always desirable; and sufficient rationality is occasionally achieved. "Rational social action" can be taken with knowledge about the consequences of alternative policy options and an ability to "control others whose responses are needed to bring about the desired state of affairs"(Dahl and Lindblom 1992). Amenable to scientific investigation, control processes can be made objective and predictable. Nevertheless, Dahl and Lindblom enumerate limitations on the practice of rationality that are not simply tactical impediments to the application of credible scientific methods. Rather, inherent incapacities to handle complexity, along with characteristic refusals to engage with the objective world (projection, denial, sublimation, narcissism, and the rest), sabotage the impulse to transcend the political; the ontology of the species prevents true rationality. Dahl and Lindblom cede much ground to the political in social decision making while arguing tenaciously for the possibility of rationality and, usually tacitly, for its role in achieving social progress.

Unfortunately, their evidence for rational victories in social policy is thin, customarily reducing to the success of engineering projects, such as dams for flood control and electrical power. Their examples customarily enjoy a large popular consensus, narrow goals, and reliance on civil engineering. Notably now, after many decades of experience with flood control on the Mississippi and water conservation on the Colorado, it is not so evident that these projects were irredeemably wise; many difficulties remain in achieving even their targeted technical goals (e.g., flood prevention downriver on the Mississippi, soil depletionconservation, and so forth). It is tempting to interpret these projects' successes as the result of fortuitous trial and error that needs to be discounted by consideration of all the other similarly planned projects that failed. For every vaunted success by the Tennessee Valley Authority or the Army Corps of Engineers, there are innumerable failures and serious unintended consequences of rational programming to be recalled from the experiences of the New Deal and subsequent federal administrations: the War on Poverty failed miserably; the United States still lacks an adequate, universal health care system (let alone an appropriate method to manage the existing system, notwithstanding the efforts of the Rand Corporation); inflation and unemployment were not managed well in the 1970s and 1980s; the deficit was not closed by economic planning; American child poverty exceeds 20 percent; ozone depletion, environmental degradation, Third World underdevelopment, crime, emotional impairment, and so forth continue with little interuption.

In consideration of the routine failure of rationality, its few apparent successes may perhaps be more accurately reinterpreted as accidents of representative politics that create symbols of cultural security for super-stitious popular devotion in the manner of the intermittent rainstorm that reinforces the tribal rain dance. As much as the literature maintains a hope for rationality, it contains a thoroughly documented warning: planned change—the essence of rational policy making—is a profoundly intuitive exercise in sorting through personal and social advantage more than it is a systematic analysis of rational means and ends. To forget the patterns of culture and its sanctioned policies is to invite defeat at the hands of the very people who are the intended beneficiaries of the change.

Dahl and Lindblom hold out for a judgment that even the imperfect application of rationality to social policy making has been valuable. But they ignore their own advice, failing to apply rational analysis to their own case examples in proof that chosen policies have been superior to their alternatives, that they were the best possible courses of action even within the context of limited options. At no point do they or the rest of the social sciences come to grips with the grave deformities of the underlying proofs that are pressed forward as rational testimony. Rather, the field's literature substantiates Lindblom's formulation of policy making as a muddle of uncertain information and not his hope for greater rationality.

Second, Dahl and Lindblom also fail through any of their vignettes to improve upon purely political interpretations of social choice, that is, the likelihood that policies are chosen not for their ability to maximize pro-fessed social goals but because they conform with power. Even when social goals clearly entail a production function (roads, bridges, electrical power, postal service), the basic civil engineering is far more rational than the processes to select goals and the methods to achieve them. For exam-ple, a road is a highly rational construction, but the social choice that encourages travel by automobile rather than by train is problematic. In this case, the political decision has overridden every point of rational choice—goals and means—except the final one to produce the best type of the chosen means. Yet even here the final application of rationality is constrained politically by investment decisions related to cost.

In the more immediate case of the human services, especially outside of medicine but often there as well, a production function has not been engineered. Services do not enjoy any credible proof of instrumental

rationality, in practice or in theory, in the field or under optimal laboratory conditions. Moreover, political utility probably accounts for their
persistence better than the painful reach for social progress through
rational policy making. In any event, it is very difficult to find a
respectable place in any hierarchy of the rational for even the best of the
social services policy research. A political analysis of the way that ostensibly rational research symbolizes and engenders the dominant social ethos
is more convincing than the research's claims to have established credible
relationships among key variables, that is, the policy's achievement of
explicit social goals.

The failure to achieve rationality necessarily leaves politics—the subjective and collective processes of decision making that are enmeshed in
cultural experience—to explain the choice of social policy.[4] The challenge
remains to define the pillars of the social decision-making process instead
of simply describing the time-ordered events that precede social choice
but may be neither its necessary nor its sufficient conditions. The political
task, which has built the experience to date, requires the identification of
the processes and outcomes that conform with cultural preference. For
methodological reasons as well as for their institutional motives, the
social sciences have not adequately identified the political *determinants* of
social choice (neither actors, motives, nor imperatives of culture and
species) but only a series of seemingly important issues, the fault lines of
political conflict and analysis. Indeed, Dahl and Lindblom may well have
been inspired to elaborate their notions of control processes by watching
the social sciences acquiesce political power.

Social decision making is a mysterious composition of the felt but only
partially apprehended experiences of individuals and groups that defines
the goals and motives, the totems and taboos, the rewards and punishments of contemporary society. The social process to achieve a governable consensus negotiates the symbols and ceremonies of preference and
self-interest with only rare deference to objective consideration of alternatives. Yet the pursuit of social agreement has been endlessly complicated
by numerous interpersonal and organizational differences, along with
the bewildering richness of contemporary possibilities. Partisan interests
have been defined with eidetic clarity, and the footprints of social choice
with the graphic precision of an Arthur Murray dance chart. However,
few, if any, objective explanations reliably predict either the conduct of
policy processes or policy choices themselves. Theories of social decision
making, such as they are, customarily reiterate the political truism that
power explains social choice but with little ability to explain power itself
beyond a tabloid newspaper's appreciation for the virtues of ascendancy—animal attractiveness, money, influence, and intellect.[5] More generally, no theory of the middle range, let alone theory with grander reach,
has substantiated a rational decision-making practice for democracy.

Rather, the baroque intensities of the social sciences reflect the political universe of discourse and the ideological banners of apparent group self-interest.

As one example of the failure of social science's attempt at rational technique, the predictive ability of opinion polling in electoral politics increases once the determinants of the contest are defined. However, polling has a poor ability to predict the determinants themselves or even the way the electorate interprets and evaluates most concrete events. The accuracy of polls improves as the date of election nears, but naturally their value decline as opponents have less time for corrective campaigning while the effectiveness of the corrective steps themselves are taken without the benefit of any rational assurance. There is even more difficulty in predicting the next great political crisis: the economy, the point of inequality that produces mass grievances, and social eruptions of dissatisfaction over crime, education, family behavior, natural catastrophes, international rivalry and war, famine, pestilence, and others.[6] Constantly exacerbated by the measurement uncertainty of continued polling, the problems of reliability in self-reported information beggar the ambitions of opinion surveys for interpretive value.[7]

In addition to the techniques of political negotiation—the mutual adjustment of competitors (Lindblom 1965)—Lindblom and Woodhouse (1993), as one example, propose three special considerations that affect American policy making: (1) business has a special role in America's policy deliberations that also reflects both (2) embedded socioeconomic inequalities and (3) citizens' impaired capacities to probe objective conditions, the consequences of policy alternatives, or even social motive and their own self-interest.[8] But this formulation, characteristic of the typically intuitive processes of the contemporary discourse over social decision making, while acknowledging the impossibility of defining a time-ordered, logically consecutive process, still preserves the fundamental enigma, the Crack of Doom, of cultural experience. Despite a keen eye for detail and process, Lindblom is as mute as any in providing reasons— the cultural imperatives—that create his three considerations or the conditions of successful competition. That the powerful win is probably tautological; the demonstration of the unique reasons for power and political change remains a challenge.

The barriers to rationality in policy making may be insurmountable; wisdom may reside in political mood, a cultural form of reassurance, rather than in social leadership or the very partial and imperfect attempts to transcend culture. Still, there are profoundly accepted social preferences that do become embedded policies—America's social institutions. However, their true effects, their actual superiority to alternative institutional arrangements and the reasons for their attractiveness, remain speculative. Indeed, deprived of rationality, the literature of social decision making behaves more like the arts than the sciences, with its truths and insights offered up as the spectral proofs of their virtues.

The scholarship of social decision making customarily describes limited, sequential, iterative processes: initial instigators lead to explorations; initial explorations eventuate in a working definition of the problem—the planning or research task—that is amenable to a variety of alternative solutions; policy options are subsequently compared against resources and social preferences, with the best fit being implemented; the implemented policy is then evaluated and fed back into the decision-making system. Thus, progressive social learning occurs by trial and error if not actually Rivlin's 1993 patterned experimentation. The process is orderly, informed, controlled, socially responsive, open, comforting, democratic, and sensible. It is also probably imaginary.

Rationalistic descriptions of policy making are less approximations of reality than myths, comforting illusions of reasonableness and security that obscure the terrifying uncertainties of social existence through a civil religion that provides decisive metaphors of fairness, righteousness, and historical continuity in adjusting aspiration to the political reality of scarce resources. Yet every point of policy consideration is caught in the cultural web. Time-ordered consecutivity is imposed on perception, giving the impression of order and suggesting that cultural choice is a malleable contingency of rational reflection. In contrast, strongly held social values, such as a preference for market solutions over government action, define the terrain of possible choice, preceding and shaping the political response to any event. Moreover, consecutive learning rarely takes place, since few policies are actually understood beyond their conformity with contemporary tastes. Political victors have naturally small appetites for exploring the objective conditions of their success and consequently place little emphasis on research that might benefit rivals. Received preferences and the reigning social system constrain every option in every planning and policy system except in the rare instances when society must discard its comfortable old shoes because of catastrophe or bunions. Nevertheless, social science's formulations of policy making insist on at least a partial or limited rationality in their own methods of analysis, if not also in the objects of their study (social decision-making processes).

In spite of characteristically failing in practice to sustain its purpose, social science theory, with its ostensible commitment to an objective reality, contrasts sharply with the philosophic nihilism of postmodernism. The scholarship of postmodernism may be valuable as a reminder of the enduring pervasiveness of political influence. However, it offers no proofs for the virtue of its own political preferences nor any ability to explain the development of power. Postmodernism is largely the product of literary criticism, with its weakness for fiction as reality and perhaps, too, as strategy for investigation. Its political commitments, Marxist and otherwise, are in no way logically entailed by the stale insight of post-modernism that power rules. But at least on this score, the social sciences have provided more credible descriptions or at least less ideologically beholden ones of how rule is exercised. Foucault is no anthropologist but rather an intellectual provocateur who constructs a plausible explanation of events but alas without truly deconstructing plausible alternatives.

On their part, social scientists, even while recognizing the conun-drums of rationality, still argue for their disciplines' "nuanced" insights for social planning, policy analysis, and political leadership. Yet they press the subtleties of erudition as mystical protection against the failures of rationality, a sly attempt to sidestep rigorous social accountability by substituting the safely implicit for the objective, the reasonable for the rational, and the ineffable for science. In fact, the scholarship of social pol-icy making has not conducted rational demonstrations of the necessity of any political factor, the influences of cultural patterns, nor the true effects of alternative courses of action. The best of the studies of leadership, insti-tutional influence, demography and economic conditions, communica-tion, and received values are engaging commentary and perhaps even exemplify an informal personal wisdom. They may be infinitely sublime, justifying extensive permission for the social sciences to script the lore and legends of modern society. Yet without the methods of science, their quivering awe of culture lacks the rational authority to explain reality. Deprived of rational tools and rational purposes, the analytic tasks of social decision making do little more than identify the seemingly perma-nent issues of governance and the possibilities for political action. Policy studies become portals into the dialectics of political discourse.

In Sum, a Civil Religion

The social policy-making process is political, not rational, especially as it addresses problematic conditions through social services. Policy is made through the complex interactions of groups and individuals in pursuit of their own subjective self-interests summated as the tenets of a civil reli-gion, with only rare and incomplete attempts to objectively establish causality, program outcomes, and the attractiveness of alternative poli-cies. Rationality itself, the application of science to social problems and the policy-making process, is converted into a ceremony of power sym-bolizing society's cherished regard for technological prowess.

It is rather simple to falsify this conclusion by identifying triumphs of rationality in social decision making: on the one hand, scientifically cred-ible information, and on the other hand, actual policies that are imple-mented on rational grounds. Particularly relative to social welfare, there are no scientifically credible studies that establish critical causal relations, that test the effectiveness of social welfare programs, or that compare the benefits and costs of policy options. The literature of psychotherapy, public welfare, and the rest of the research covering social services and social welfare has not produced a single study that conforms to rigorous scientific standards. There are few that even exemplify a *reasonable* expression of rationality, failing to provide a coherent estimate of program effects or causal relationships. The very best of these exercises (the negative income tax experiments, particularly in Seattle and Denver, the Manpower Demonstration Research Corporation's studies of work and welfare, the evaluation of intensive family preservation services conducted in Illinois) deviate greatly from the standards of credible science by compromising randomized controlled trials. In the end, there is not one credible evaluation that testifies to the success of any social service intervention, while there are considerable grounds for conjecture that social services are routinely ineffective and possibly even harmful. Rationality may be an impossible goal outside of the very restrictive assumptions of science and engineering.

Policy making, either the public legislative and administrative processes or the workings of civil and private society, does not call upon rational information. To the contrary, the society customarily subverts rational research through funding and design limitations and more subtly through the tacit but very powerful ambitions of researchers and social service institutions that lead to their acquiescence with dominant goals and values. In this way, the call for a "nuanced" practice of social science in deference to the grave flaws of its accumulated literature is inspired by social success more than by a respect for objective reality.

Without rational information or rational processes, social decision making relies on political sanctions to authorize its policies; self-interest and power, not truth or the good, motivate competition over scarce resources. Nevertheless, the perfusion of philosophic nihilism is not cause for psychological nihilism even while the facts of alternative social policies are unknown. Some societies appear hospitable to productive, humane, and pacific citizens, and some do not; life's satisfactions are possible even without deep insight and knowledge. The reduction of policy making to its political determinants contributes to social modesty, a reminder that institutionalized arrangements are not the inevitable consequences of the universe or of its creator's will. Benign social institutions remain a challenge for the imagination of the culture.

Notes

1. Murray's reported regret for the book's genetic claims was more stylistic than intellectual; he never recanted the statement of black inferiority, only the editorial decision to include the argument in a book that might have made its points without inflammatory allusions that needlessly detracted from its central argument to

deny resources to the poor. Apparently, he felt that the book's characterological arguments did not need genetic support to justify a diminished role for public welfare.

2. A structural logic is one of the defining tenets of modern liberalism. It is the essential assumption of Berlin's (1969) positive liberty. Gans, Myrdal, Wootton, the socialists and Fabians, Marx, J. S. Mill, and more recently Walzer and Sandel, among many others, find common ground in the assumption that manipulations of social structures will achieve a better society by improving human behavior. Oscar Lewis's (1961, 1966) dramatic descriptions and condemnations of dysfunctional subcultures have been appropriated by subculturalists in support of their position. Yet Lewis, in a manner repeated by Wilson (1987), was detailing the unfortunate effects of poverty, as a structure of society, on the subculture of the poor. Both Lewis and Wilson disapproved of poverty, in contrast to the subculturalists, who disapprove of the poor.

3. The subcultural and characterological ideology at the center of contemporary conservative thought—the prominence of individual responsibility—traces back to the nineteenth-century absolute idealists, who rejected science and Enlightenment goals generally (see chapter 6). Modern conservatives such as Murray, but also including many associated with the religious right as well as free-market libertarians such as Hayek and Friedman, are also being joined by social scientists such as Mayer (1997), who moralize issues of social cause: she succeeded on her own efforts, and others should also; individual behavior results from uncoerced individual choice.

4. Alternative nonrational possibilities (predestination, divine intervention, superstition, and control by space aliens) also defy testing and are thus unknowable and irrelevant; culture is at least in principle objectifiable, although in fact it may not be.

5. Moreover, the accuracy of forecasts degrades with time, suggesting a declining utility for any rationality that may exist. If today's political weather is the best estimate of tomorrow's, then a political weather service is not going to make much profit. Rather, any value of weather forecasting rests with much longer range abilities. The craft of opinion polling may be cherished more for the comfort, language, apparent coherence, and reassurance of the concrete that it provides esurient candidates than for any rational capacity to actually predict voter preference.

6. O, that it were possible to have control sets of candidates, one set running with current factors, one set competing in an experimental condition that entered a wild card such as a severe recession, and another set perhaps running under campaign finance reform, heavy voter registration, and other electoral modifications.

7. In tribute to Heisenberg uncertainty and the concern with measurement perturbation that it inspired, polling itself may change polled responses in unpredictable ways as respondents learn to react differently to being questioned by changing perceptions of the media, that is, the survey and the survey situation. A

person responding to, say, a phone interview today has been trained for decades by television to play out a fairly sophisticated role that may entail an enormous amount of response falsification to report the socially acceptable.

8. Note the constant departure from the formal rules of *public* policy making, which is customarily seen as an extension, an ultimate codification, of the more important social processes outside of government, among people in their civic, family, and commercial interactions that eventuate in law. The basic intention in a democracy is for private policy to precede public policy, even acknowledging a gentle tutelary role for government. Tyranny is usually the product of a public policy that operates without nongovernmental consent, as in Romania under the Cousesceaus and Haiti under Duvalier.

Chapter 2

The Willow World of Virtue: Rationality and Effectiveness in the Personal Social Services

While some areas of social policy may enjoy a dollop of rational content, social welfare policy is rarely informed with even coherent information, let alone scientifically credible estimates of causal relationships. The effectiveness of social services is not routinely or accurately measured. Despite the Italian opera of good works and altruism, the ability of the social services to resolve social and personal problems does not explain their persistence. Rather, the corrective myth as the thematic expression of social efficiency disciplines the intellectual life of the social services, converting the objective pursuit of social melioration into the symbolic appeasement of political preferences. This interplay is prevalent in all the social services but most clearly in the personal social services.

The common, indeed characteristic, distortion of science in the evalua- tions of social services inhibits the maturation of social theory and pre- vents the social services from developing true production functions. Social science theories rarely enjoy any direct empirical validation; their usefulness is generally tested through their predictions, realized in the social services. Notably, the effectiveness of the social services tests the specific theoretical assertions about social cause and effect that justify the services in the first place. Social services embody, actually operationalize, broader social scientific propositions concerning the causes of social problems and their resolution. Without true tests of these assertions, statements about social reality necessarily remain ideological, that is, the subjectivities of political rivals in competition over economic, political, and social resources.

There have been no credible tests of social services and, therefore, no definitive tests of theory. At best, grievously flawed approximations of science serve as flash points for public debate even while frustrating Enlightenment hopes for coherent, scientifically credible information to inform social decision making. Social science falls far short of a "science of man." Instead, Romantic notions of heroic self-creation, implicit in the

47

corrective myth, dominate the logic of social policy while obscuring its extreme individualism in the communal lab coats, journals, and rhetoric of science.

Psychotherapeutic interventions inspire much of the contemporary personal social services. Relying largely on one form of rational induction or another, psychotherapy is the apotheosis of social efficiency, promising to address the effects of grave, long-term deprivations with relatively inexpensive, short-term, and culturally compatible cures. There is no scientifically credible evidence that psychotherapy has ever been effective with any class of patients in any setting. In contrast, the social services that are surrogates for missing or failed social institutions—child foster care is the quintessential example of surrogate care, but also public assistance and Old Age Survivors and Disability Insurance (OASDI) and Medicure are surrogates for income—are customarily provided at such meager levels that they achieve none of their goals and simply maintain recipients in frequently inadequate and abusive situations. In the end, neither the theory nor the practice of social welfare has been credibly substantiated. Changing patterns of service are occasioned by impulsive political moods that customarily avoid the obvious inadequacies of care, running from one cheap, poorly considered promise to another, a process ever young with hope but ancient with neglect. Indeed, the institutionalized meaning of American social services has far more to do with their performance as political ceremonies—ritualizations of embedded social beliefs in the social and characterological inferiority of lower-status and marginal populations—than as serious attempts to remedy personal and social dysfunctions.

Theory: The Nurture Assumption

On the authority of supposedly credible research, particularly in developmental psychology but also in behavioral genetics (sometimes referred to as evolutionary psychology), Harris (1995, 1998) challenged the apparent wisdom of the social sciences. Against the bedrock American assumption of the importance of the family, she argued that the family's influence over the socialization of its children had been greatly exaggerated; instead, child and adolescent peer groups were principally responsible for the development of the adult's personality. However, the subsequent controversy in the popular press and in the scholarly literature exposes the degree to which the social sciences have been unable to rationally develop theory. Indeed, Harris's reliance on behavioral genetics, particularly the Minnesota Study of Twins (MST), to establish a large inherited determinant of adult personality hints at an intellectual dialogue in the social sciences bereft of an ability to mirror the authority of the natural sciences despite an increasingly sophisticated quantitative discourse. If either the standing assumption of the centrality of the family or Harris's challenge was grounded in rational proof, then the debate would have been far more limited and specific. The social sciences provide the language, the terms, of social discussion. Class, ego, upward mobility, aggregate demand, status, and so forth may in fact have no greater analytic or taxonomic power than belly button descriptors: innies and outies. Yet social science's categories ennoble and give graphic form to the political debate expressing, if not actually shaping, contemporary discourse. Social science theory—with the Harris controversy offered as a characteristic example—is routinely an erudite reflection of social stakes more than an estimate of social reality sufficient to create adequate interventions. Rather than seriously searching for cause, it seems more likely that the social sciences manufacture and store ideologies for social dialectics like slapdash clapboard bungalows at a summer resort, waiting to be rented out for a short while.

Harris's essay and its reception feed into the social dialectics that consider shifts of social organization as conscious decisions, in this case from the family to the peer group, which is a more diffuse, less formal, institution of socialization. Perhaps the shift is inevitable for Marxists as the next great social step in the ultimate atomization of society by the demands of the market for mobile, unconstrained labor. Perhaps in less tendentious terms, it simply acknowledges the realities of modern living and its requirements for caretaking surrogates for the family. Yet Harris's authority is certainly not rational. Indeed, her building blocks for "group socialization theory" (GST) have not been hardened through credible experimentation. GST performs a characteristic function of the social sciences, scripting social dramas more than uncovering social truths.

On the basis of an exhaustive reanalysis of existing research, much of it in behavioral genetics, Harris concluded that "within the range of families that have been studied, parental behaviors have no effect on the psychological characteristics their children will have as adults" (Harris 1995, 458). The argument supports Maccoby and Martin (1983) and others, explaining adult personality as largely heritable (40 to 50 percent of the variance). Parenting (the shared environment, the home) contributes less than 10 percent, while measurement error, unexplained variance, and factors outside of the home (the nonshared environment) account for at least 40 percent. "Thus, about two-thirds of the reliable variance in measured personality traits is due to genetic influence" (Bouchard 1994). Harris claims that the "quite reliable" research from behavioral genetics, in near-complete rejection of the conventional wisdom, has pinned down the unimportance of the home in socializing children and developing their adult personalities (McGue et al. 1993; Pederson et al. 1992; Plomin, Chipuer, and Neiderhiser 1994; Plomin 1990; Goldsmith 1993a).

Harris goes on to test whether the unexplained variance can be accounted for by conditions within the family: child-driven effects, relationship-driven effects, parent-driven effects, and family context effects. Rejecting all these explanations, Harris backs into a residual theory of context-specific socialization emphasizing the power of the peer group, especially in adolescence, to mold adult personality. However, while she demonstrates that existing studies fail to pin down the influence of the family, often because of their methodological shortcomings, literally none of the cited research can sustain her estimates of influence on the adult personality, again, largely because of their methodological infractions. In this regard, Harris's work is typical of social science theory development, promoting studies that endorse her theory as more definitive than those that disconfirm theory.

Behavioral Genetics and Harris's Essay

MST takes advantage of an extraordinary natural experiment to estimate the genetic contribution—heritability—to intelligence, adult personality, and other behaviors.[1] Behavioral similarities among identical twins who were separated in infancy and reared apart in allegedly dissimilar environments presumably can be attributed to genetic inheritance as opposed to the environment, that is, learning; in the absence of any demonstration of similarity in their childhood situations, "all resemblance between reared-apart twins owes to genetic factors only" (Bouchard and McGue 1990, 278). On average, similarity among fraternal twins in gene-influenced traits is expected to be one-half of that in identical twins, since they share one-half of common genes, again, on average. Adoption studies generally make the assumption that the heritability of gene-influenced traits is proportional to genetic relationship. In addition to estimates of the heritability of intelligence and personality, MST claims to have provided estimates of the degree to which other behaviors are genetically determined: vocational interests (Moloney, Bouchard, and Segal 1991); EEG performance (Stassen, Lykken, and Bomben 1988); information processing and special mental abilities (McGue 1988); risk of divorce (McGue and Lykken 1992); temperament (Goldsmith 1993b); television viewing in early childhood (Plomin et al. 1990); inhibited and uninhibited behavior (Robinson et al. 1992); and many others. The studies flowing out of MST together with similar experiments, notably in Colorado and Sweden, constitute the heart of the field of behavioral genetics. Behavioral genetics is a respected academic discipline whose core studies appear in prestigious, peer-reviewed journals and whose books are published by prominent presses.

MST recruited forty-four pairs of identical twins and twenty-seven pairs of fraternal twins, all of whom were reared apart. "The twins' age of separation [from each other] ranged from birth to 4.5 years, with a median of 0.2 years. Separation time (number of years from separation to first contact) ranged from 0 to 64 years, with a median of 33.8 years" (Tellegen et al. 1988, 1033). The twins reared apart were compared with 217 pairs of identical twins and 114 pairs of fraternal twins reared together who were recruited from an earlier study. At the time of the study, the twins reared apart were on average about twenty years older than those reared together.

The degree to which the behaviors (personality, IQ scores, and others) of identical twins reared apart fail to correlate with their environments suggests the size of the genetic contribution. In turn, the degree to which their behaviors correlate with measures of their youthful environment dampens the explanatory power of their identical genes. Indeed, the "equal environments" hypothesis has been a major challenge to the credibility of behavioral genetics. As a point of skepticism, the equal environments hypothesis holds that the environments of fraternal twins systematically differ from the environments of identical twins, and these environmental factors, rather than genetic inheritance, explain the differences between the groups. Similarly, in the studies of identical twins reared apart, the equal environments hypothesis holds that probably because of similar standards and practices of the adoption agencies, the relevant environments of the twins were actually more similar than assumed or tested; therefore, without accounting for these similarities, genetic explanations exaggerate the contributions of inheritance to the behavioral similarities among identical twins reared apart. Moreover, the equal environments challenge to the credibility of behavioral genetics quite properly focuses attention on the techniques and instruments that the field employs to measure nongenetic factors.

MST endlessly measured the dependent variables, notably adult personality and IQ. The assumption that identical twins share identical genes, at least at conception, controls for one of the two independent variables. The problem remains with the second major independent variable, the degree to which the environments of twins were similar or dissimilar. If the factors of the child's environment that presumably contribute to adult personality cannot be measured reliably, then MST has proportionately little ability to explain the occurrence of adult behaviors such as personality and IQ. Bourchard and McGue state:

A major assumption underlying the present analyses is that twins were separated early in life and placed in rearing environments that are *uncorrelated with respect to factors influencing the development of personality*. The existence of selective placement could bias both genetic and environmental comparisons, by providing an environmental means by which biologically related, but separately reared individuals would resemble one another, and by providing a genetic means by which biologically unrelated, but reared-together individuals would resemble one another. (Bouchard and McGue 1990, emphasis added)

In the end, Bouchard and McGue (1990) report that only between "1% and 9% of the variance in adult personality *may* be due to differences in rearing environment" (286–87). Tellegen et al. (1988) report that "the [personality] correlations for the [identical twins reared together and apart] are overall highly similar . . . .49 and .52 respectively. . . . On average, about 50% of measured personality diversity can be attributed to genetic diversity" (1035). Yet the similarity of their personalities is only remarkable to the extent that their environments are dissimilar. Indeed, without environmental dissimilarity between pairs of identical twins and the ability to prove that identical twins and fraternal twins "are equally similar in the environmental influences" on personality, the question of heritability remains unanswered (Loehlin 1992, 11).

MST takes considerable pains to consider and refute the possibility that "environmental similarities in rearing environments explain . . . the similarity" of identical twins reared apart (Bouchard et al. 1990, 225). The MST relies on Moos and Moos's Family Environment Scale (FES) to measure the rearing situations of the twins. On the basis of FES measurement, Bouchard et al. (1990) report very low correlations between the adoptive environments of identical twins reared apart, with the result that similarities in the twins' environments probably explain no more than 3 percent of their IQ scores. Nonetheless, the environments of identical twins raised apart were probably not as uncorrelated as Bouchard et al. (1990) suggest. Indeed, the simple problem of faulty recall may account for many of the differences in their reports of their youthful homes. Moreover, the amount of similarity in reports of early environments between identical twins raised together may result from a process of reaching common agreement through youth and adulthood more than from any objective reality.

The FES is a problematic interview instrument that relied entirely on recall to measure events many years later, in some cases after the passage of decades (Moos and Moos 1986). Moreover, the biometric properties of FES are inadequate for the tasks that it was put to by MST. Indeed, Moos and Moos (1994) report reliabilities between .68 and .86 for scale items on the basis of a two-month test-retest conducted among only forty-seven subjects. The four-month test-retest, this time with a sample of thirty-seven, produced reliabilities between .54 and .91. The reliabilities of five of the ten subscales decreased markedly, suggesting a rapid and important decline in recall; the reliability of one scale improved by more than 10 percent; four changed only slightly. In any event, the true reliability test should have involved interrater comparisons and over a much longer period for a group of subjects more apparently similar to MST subjects.

Furthermore the FES does not seem to discriminate well between normal and distressed families, producing small differences in all of the subscale mean scores (Moos and Moos 1994, table 4, 21). Average "family incongruence scores" seem quite similar for normal and distressed families; indeed, the average difference in incongruence between normal and distressed families is less than 0.2 on scales that vary from 0.0 to 9.0 (table 2., 19, and appendix B). Although psychiatric staff agreed with their patients' FES ratings (Moos and Moos 1994, 28), Moos and Moos concede, "Overall, however, families vary in how closely individual family members agree about the characteristics of their family. In some families, individuals are in close agreement . . . but in others there is considerable disagreement" (19).

FES' problematic reliability artificially increases the variability between the reported environments of identical twins reared apart and thereby artificially inflates the prominence of heritability as an explanation of similarities in the twins' adult personalities, IQ scores, and other behaviors. Moreover, FES is designed only to assess the *perceived* emotional environment of families—conflict, cohesion, expressiveness, and so forth—and thus fails even in its intentions of measuring anything approaching objective environmental conditions. Moos and Moos (1994) even seem to be suggesting the use of FES as a diagnostic tool, not simply as a descriptive measure of family conditions. In short, FES is not reliable; it discriminates poorly among family environments, and it measures only perceptions, not environmental realities or possibly even stable emotional conditions.

Employing the FES to measure the "underlying" environment, Bouchard and McGue (1990) confirm heritabilities of .51 that support previous estimates of the genetic determination of personality (Tellegen et al. 1988). Yet their review of the FES fails to dispel skepticism toward its weaknesses. The problem of recall persists as a prominent alternative to heritability in accounting for the much larger standard deviations of the twins' self-reports compared with the responses of the normal families reported by Moos and Moos (1994). Indeed, Bouchard and McGue's (1990) report of more children (and consequently less time lag in recall) in the normal sample would seem to further substantiate this possibility.[2]

The possibility of greater similarity in the environments of twins raised apart than indicated by the FES is further amplified by the practices of adoption agencies to provide similar family environments for their wards; adoption agencies are, after all, specifically designed to cull out unacceptable potential parents and homes. Moreover, the possibility of unaccounted characteristics of adoptive environments that may confound a genetic interpretation of personality is further heightened by the lack of randomization of subjects to assure environmental variation among twin pairs, a procedure that is impossible for ethical and legal reasons. In these ways, misreported and unaccounted factors in the environments of the different twin groups pose a consistent threat to the validity of the twin studies.

Loehlin (1992) is less sanguine than MST about the heritability of personality, pointing to a number of threats to the methods of behavioral genetics: "We have found that an assumption of some degree of nonadditivity in the genetic variance or an assumption of unequal resemblance of identical and fraternal twins' environments must be added to a simple model of genes and unshared environment in order to fit the data" (47). Yet Loehlin's sources for measuring the environment are no more reliable than MST and perhaps even as subjective, relying on parents' perceptions of nurturing rather than the adult recall of the twins themselves.

In a study that sidesteps the challenges to the FES and other similar instruments that measure the environment, Plomin and Bergemen (1991), amplifying Plomin's (1990) comments, insist that the reported measures of the environment by twin groups themselves indicate heritability, that is, the degree to which genetic similarities account for similar responses. Indeed, the study takes advantage of its own adversity.

Plomin and Bergeman (1991) summarize research that applies the logic of behavioral genetics to reported measures of the environment. The variation in reports of the home environments between each twin of identical and fraternal pairs, as well as between adoptive and nonadoptive siblings, is taken to signify the extent to which genetic differences account for variations in those reports. The reported differences are assumed to vary systematically as a result of the degree of shared genes. However, this procedure stands the logic of behavioral genetics on its head, since the instruments for measuring the twins' environment are crucial to assess whether the objective conditions of the different environments—the degree of their similarity—offer alternative explanations for the twins' and siblings' behaviors. To the extent to which the twins' responses can be explained genetically, they fail as useful research instruments. The research interest in responses-to-environment as indicators of genetic influence converts a leaky pot into a planter, tacitly restoring the respectability of unreliable measures as valuable behaviors to study. Yet the research seems to assume that which it is attempting to explain, relying on the genetic determination of behavior to assess the influence of genetics on particular behaviors. In this way, the assumptions of the research preserve the logic of behavioral genetics by explaining the variability of measures and lessening the problems of measurement unreliability and recall. Yet the inability to reliably measure the environment persists as a problem throughout behavioral genetics.

Other problems tarnish their analyses. Plomin and Bergeman (1991) consistently confuse measures of the environment with the environment itself, accepting support for their methodological assumptions without independently validating the objective environments of their subjects. "The most surprising of these results is that the reared-apart twins rated different families similarly, and that this was the case to a greater extent for [identical] than for [fraternal] twins" (Plomin and Bergeman 1991, 376). Also, "although [identical] twins were found to be treated more similarly by their parents for some measures, the bottom line was that . . . differences [with fraternal twins] . . . do not relate to twin differences in behavior" (376). And again, "The correlations for identical twins reared apart from early in life are particularly impressive because these individuals were reared in different families" (Plomin 1990, 133).

However, the category of "different families" has no analytic importance unless it actually refers to different environmental conditions that are conceptually relevant. In this case, the precise wording ("different families") obscures the actual referent (different environments), raising an eyebrow toward the researchers' motives. Yet there were few independent corroborations of the environmental measures, and therefore there were proportionately few reasons to conclude that different families represented different environments. The Home Observation for the Measurement of the Environment (HOME) scale, which was applied "objectively" (i.e., it did not rely on the report of children) in the Colorado Adoption Project, produces surprisingly high similarities in the environments of adoptive and nonadoptive siblings, suggesting that the differently reported environments of twins reared apart may not be so different but that their recall, especially after many years, may be a very chancy basis for any conclusion. Furthermore, any reliance on Rowe (1981, 1983) to conclude that "identical twin correlations were significantly greater than fraternal twin correlations for measure of parental warmth" needs to come to grips with his procedure for collecting information: "The instructions [on the data questionnaire] emphasized the importance of completing the forms independently and, if the twins chose to compare responses, not changing a response because a co-twin had responded differently" (Rowe 1981, 204).

Not a word of self-doubt appears in the research to address the possibility that identical twins more than fraternal twins might collude in their responses. Even in light of a universal love for one's own hypothesis, respectable science systematically withstands the seduction of dubiously crafted findings with systematic skepticism. Yet statistical adjustments to test the five "nontrivial assumptions" of behavioral genetics methodologies (Loehlin 1992) are far more common than experimental protections and probing investigations.

Additionally, the field of behavioral genetics ignores the vagary of human perception, the source of its numerous report biases. The list of biases might well begin with what appears to be the insurmountable problems of recall but might also go on to consider the probability that their samples, given recruitment constraints, were demographically and environmentally more similar than the researchers care to concede (thus possibly violating the equal environments assumption twice: in comparing twins raised apart by exaggerating their differences and in comparing identical and fraternal twins reared together by understating their similarities). It also seems plausible that the possibly restricted range of environments (even without consideration of unusually abusive conditions) considered in behavioral genetics may in the end explain very little about the effects of customary social conditions; indeed, the study of twins may not be a general case of the population.[3]

The research agenda of behavioral genetics seems to defy scientific neutrality in its hasty application of imperfect methods. While the MST authors and many behavioral geneticists are exquisitely sensitive to racist social policy, their research is taken up with little caution and less restraint by policy analysts with very different social preferences. The policy recommendations in Herrnstein and Murray are instructive, and the huge popularity of their book speaks to more than a general interest in the scholarly debate over behavioral determinants. *The Bell Curve* (1994) argues that inheritance largely determines intelligence and personality—the human behaviors at the core of social productivity—and that the casual ties have been scientifically demonstrated by behavioral genetics. Their sense of the ideal modern community looks like an attempt at postindustrial feudalism, a renovated Platonic republic.[4] Genes-as-destiny justifies the socioeconomic stratification of American society and the public's pronounced disinterest in greater social and economic equality.

However, at its present state of development, behavioral genetics provides little rational support for any social policy, let alone unimpeachable proof of its narrow conclusions. Indeed, its use by Herrnstein and Murray, along with many others, including Harris, is a telling example of the conversion of the specific, operationalized authority of science into a generally applicable metaphor at the core of ideology. Yet even if all the field's assertions are granted, and heritability scores are as high as claimed, behavioral geneticists have still not detailed the contingencies of deriving behaviors from genes. As Plomin acknowledges, the field has not explained how genes and environment interact—the processes by which intelligence and personality are developed—and until this occurs, the findings have little meaning for social policy.

Nevertheless, the terms of social policy discourse seem to have been overly influenced by appreciation for the natural order. Yet it is not clear that personality and intelligence need constitute so great a justification for the good society. Social harmony and social integration (let alone Darwinian survival itself), which are probably as important as scientific and economic innovation in social progress, depend on a considerably greater number of social and personal skills—perhaps Goleman's (1995) "emotional intelligence," along with the numerous traits of decency, responsibility, and caring—than behavioral genetics, as ideology seems ready to concede. Indeed, greater scholarly skepticism within the behavioral genetics community might dampen the popularity of market solutions and restrictive government.

Still and all, behavioral genetics cannot sustain its claim that 50 percent of personality is heritable. As a consequence, all of Harris's estimates of the other determinants of personality take on greater importance, with simple ignorance winning out hugely in the end. Perhaps less than 40 percent of personality can be explained by genes, the family, and factors outside of the home, notably the adolescent peer group. The rest, probably more than 60 percent, remains unexplained. This level of uncertainty should preclude any conclusion, especially since the basic processes of human socialization are so poorly understood. In spite of more than one hundred years of serious investigation, socialization and social decision making remain profound mysteries. While Harris expands her preference for a theory of group socialization, she fails to handle alternative explanations, namely, the perfusion of a consistent and powerful culture throughout all its institutions. Indeed, the homogeneity of values throughout American society probably coordinates each one of its core institutions—the family, the community, the school, the workplace, the peer group, as well as influential American values.

Heritability itself, like many of the other major constructs of the social sciences, may be untestable, cut off from even the possibility of definitive proof by ethical, legal, and practical constraints on prospective experimentation. Individual freedoms, even for orphans and foster children, cannot be arbitrarily restricted for purposes of science. In turn, natural experiments, especially after a hiatus of decades, become victims of frail recall. Moreover, the technical problems of instrumentation and meaning (e.g., the relevant environmental influences) may be intractable without a more sophisticated basic science of social and psychological influence; appropriate tests await appropriate instruments, while the experience of the FES is not hopeful.

In these ways, Harris's unverified theory defies definitive tests: children cannot be randomized to families and peer groups of different types, and the influences of family or of culture itself cannot be divorced from peer group influences without depriving children of some basic institutional experience. Yet GST transforms the science of behavioral genetics, bounded and restricted by its imperfect procedures and assumptions, into social ideology. By graduating intellectual fashion and speculation to the level of rational authority, GST arrogates the rational authority of science for broadly ideological purposes. Shorn of their methodological contingencies, the factional studies of behavioral genetics become the decisive metaphors of social value that endorse American social and economic inequality.

Genetic determination cultivates a sense of futility in addressing social differences, promoting the soothing realization that the society may be in as good shape as possible, that it is indeed the best of all possible worlds. Harris puts the corrective myth to work in fulfilling her ambitions for group socialization. To the extent that any change is possible, it will take place through supervision of peer groups, providing a bit of renewed hope for the therapeutic philanthropy of group social services, a socially efficient method of treating people compared with the costs for treating people individually or with the enormous resources required to repair the social system itself.

The Canard of Behavioral Genetics

Two overriding conceptual flaws dwarf the technical pitfalls of behavioral genetics and cut to its polemical role in social policy dialectics. In the first case, heritability is only a measure of association between behavioral traits (phenotypes) and presumptive causal factors (e.g., genotypes); thus, heritability does not estimate the degree to which genes independently cause traits. Appropriate experimental designs are required to establish the actual, causal, relationships—the norms of reaction—among factors: genotype, phenotype, and environment (Lewontin 1974). While MST claims to constitute a unique natural experiment in testing the causal relations among these factors, it produced highly constrained, "local" data, if this much, that do not stand as evidence for more general, functional statements about the contributions of genes to specified behaviors. General conclusions based on restricted measures of the environment (and in all probability relatively similar environments of separately reared identical twins) probably underestimate the amount of interaction among the factors that would occur over a wider and more representative range.

The twin studies and behavioral genetics generally have not approximated the rigor of genetic research with fruit flies, as one example. Importantly, research on fruit flies suggests a considerably greater amount of interaction among genetic and environmental factors than behavioral geneticists seem willing to concede for human behaviors. However, the ideology of behavioral genetics as applied to humans is cut off from rigorous testing by legal and ethical considerations that prevent arbitrarily assigning people with similar genotypes to varied environments for research. In the end, MST conducted a post hoc analysis—not a natural experiment—of individuals with similar genotypes who were probably assigned to largely similar environments by adoption agencies.

Perhaps, then, there is less to marvel at in the similar outcomes of the identical twins than in the fact that there were so many differences. Nevertheless, without tight experimental designs that are still impossible with humans, associative analyses fail to certify causal relations.

The force of behavioral genetics, created through an enormous descendent literature that includes Harris among the swollen ranks of social conservatives, promotes a futility of policy intervention—a reluctance to intercede in social conditions—that feeds off of its second major conceptual problem. The fact of genetic influence does not imply that a trait is proportionately immutable. Heritability is not destiny; if it were, the treatment of genetic diseases, possibly including schizophrenia, would be impossible. Indeed, even conceding a large amount of genetic influence over intelligence, it is remarkable the degree to which adoption raises the IQ scores of children and insulin compensates for diabetes.[5] Yet behavioral genetics is employed to justify social inequality, debasing efforts to create greater parity among citizens as ignorant utopianism. Behavioral genetics has *not* described the interaction between genes and the environment that predicts any important human attribute. It has, however, inspired conservative dogma.

The social sciences are torn between the political demands of the culture for compatible ideology and their own aspirations to develop an objective authority. The actual role of the social services and the quality of its attempts to define outcomes evaluate the degree to which social science has transcended cultural imperatives. In this way, the literature of the social sciences, particularly the evaluations of their inspired interventions, tests both their scientific achievements and their institutional meaning in policy making.

Practice: Psychotherapy

Psychotherapy is extraordinarily popular, touching perhaps as many as one-third of Americans at some point during their lives (VanderBos 1996). Elaborating subcultural and characterological ideologies, psychotherapy is the nuclear intervention of many personal social services. Psychotherapy promises to cure, prevent, and treat individual deviance through relatively short-term, office-bound processes of rational induction (a discourse between a trained professional and a miscreant about problems, goals, resistance, childhood trauma, and so forth); these are also the decisive metaphors of the corrective myth. The many forms of psychotherapy all claim to be socially efficient. Psychotherapeutic practice, often conducted through for-profit arrangements recalling the prevalent solo-practitioner style of medical practice prior to the 1970s, is the common professional motive for careers in social work and the personal social services.

With only a few well-spaced demurrers, the field's researchers have created an enormous bibliographic tribute to the efficacy of psychotherapy. Anthologized and indexed in countless professional journals and texts in counseling, clinical and consulting psychology, social work, educational psychology, management, planning, and the like, the scrolls of practice uniformly claim not merely a practice wisdom but scientific authority for its effectiveness. Nevertheless, there is no credible proof of any instance of psychotherapy's effectiveness, let alone demonstrations of its ubiquitous success (Epstein 1995). Prudent skepticism has not been refuted by the annual cataract of literally tens of thousands of published research studies. As a result, the outcomes of psychotherapy, and consequently the tenets of social efficiency, are at best indeterminate. Yet even a cautious reanalysis of the literature suggests that psychotherapy is routinely ineffective and possibly even harmful. As the superficial and convenient arrangements of contemporary social welfare policy are exposed as inadequate, attention is drawn back, logically and politically despite the reluctance of American taxpayers to act as good neighbors, to a more generous structural strategy for social problems.

In 1980, Smith, Glass, and Miller published their citation classic, *The Benefits of Psychotherapy* (BOP), in refutation of a small number of critics, notably Rachman (1971), Eysenck (1952), and the earliest publication of the Bergin and Lambert enterprise (Bergin 1971; Bergin and Lambert 1978; Lambert, Christensen, and DeJulio 1986; Lambert and Bergin 1994), who had contested the claims of psychotherapy's effectiveness.[6] In a weak and methodologically porous comparison, Eysenck (1952) claimed that patients may have actually been harmed by treatment. However, the studies he relied on for this conclusion, updated in 1965 (Eysenck and Rachman), were very faulty, leading one critic to comment that "within the framework of Eysenck's nonexperimental data base, there are limits to one's certainty about any conclusions" (Office of Technology Assessment 1980, 41). However, Rachman raised an unrefuted issue with the methods of the outcome research, namely, the routine absence of adequate controls and the possibility that "spontaneous remission" (perhaps due to the seasonality of the condition or the maturation of patients), and not treatment itself, was responsible for positive outcomes. The suspicion that many emotionally functional although unhappy people seek treatment (perhaps Gross's [1978] YAVIS syndrome of those in psychotherapy for largely recreational purposes) gave force to Rachman's argument for randomized nontreatment controls and even placebo controls.

Whereas Bergin (1971) suggested that psychotherapy provides "moderate positive benefits," his review tended to support Eysenck and Rachman's notion that any enthusiasm for effectiveness needs to be tempered by natural cure and patient deterioration. In later editions, he recants even this faint doubt with the discovery that placebo effects contribute importantly to therapeutic outcomes. "Psychotherapy is laden with nonspecific or placebo factors . . . but these influences, when specified, may prove to be the essence of what provides therapeutic benefit. Instead of 'controlling' for them in research designs by adopting a spurious parallel with medical placebos, we may be dismissing the active ingredients we are looking for" (Bergin and Lambert 1978, 817). But the confirmation of placebo effects—simple belief in the curative process—would knock the whole professional core out of practice, reducing behavioral change to a form of positive thinking not requiring the deep insights and advanced graduate training of therapists. As a tenet of research logic, placebo effects are typically discounted from positive outcomes to estimate the true contribution of therapy, the value-added by going to a trained psychotherapist. Moreover, the Bergin and Lambert enterprise relied on a questionable base of studies and intuitive summaries of their conclusions.

BOP was remarkable on two counts. First, it concluded that psychotherapy was broadly and deeply effective. Second, it claimed that this conclusion was scientifically sustained by a large base of credible outcome research and by an unimpeachable method, meta-analysis, to "colligate" the findings of those studies.[7] Previous summaries of the literature had relied on either naive "box scores" of outcomes (Luborsky, Singer, and Luborsky 1975) or intuitive commentaries that, although occasionally elegant, were customarily incomplete or easily reinterpreted (e.g., the Bergin and Lambert enterprise). Yet neither conclusion can be sustained; BOP's meta-analytic procedures were flawed, and the base of the research is universally porous, laughably so in many cases. In essence, BOP summarized, and poorly in the event, the universal biases of American preferences for cheap answers to its deep problems, giving a quantitative dimension and hoary respectability to a form of alternative medicine but failing to fulfill its own ambitions to achieve scientifically credible standards of proof.

BOP concluded that psychotherapy was very effective:

[T]he average person who would score at the 50th percentile of the untreated control population, could expect to rise to the 80th percentile with respect to that population after receiving psychotherapy. . . . Little evidence was found for the alleged existence of negative effects of psychotherapy. . . . Only 9 percent of the effect sizes were negative. . . . Nor was there convincing evidence in the dispersion on the treated groups that some members became better and some worse as a result of psychotherapy. (Smith, Glass, and Miller 1980, 88)

It is worth noting that this thirty-percentage-point improvement covers fully 80 percent of the total range of possible improvement. Cognitive therapy, based on the happy conviction that people can think their way out of emotional problems, was even more successful, with 99 percent of treated patients better off than controls.

A multitude of problems impedes all of BOP's conclusions. For placebo-controlled studies, BOP's results were far more modest, with only 10 percent of treated patients better off than controls.[8] In a reanalysis of findings, Prioleau, Murdock, and Brody (1983) reduced this small finding even further, to 7 percent. However, BOP devalued placebo controls, arguing that wait-list controls, which fared poorly against treated groups (and therefore boosted estimates of effectiveness), were sufficient. Nevertheless, even the remaining small estimate of the success of psychotherapy is questionable, since BOP's own correlational analysis concluded that measurement reactivity—the degree to which measures of outcomes are reactive to the test situation instead of the patient's condition—accounted for 3 percent of the outcome variance.

Furthermore, and contrary to its stated commitment to consider only rigorous research, BOP relied on a host of questionable studies (analog research, uncontrolled investigations, and findings that did not reach statistical significance) whose methodological pitfalls routinely exposed their findings to the biases of researchers and clinicians. Indeed, BOP piously derided rigorous standards of research as a "device" for ignoring important studies by mindless conformity with "'textbook' standards; these methodological rules, learned as dicta in graduate school and regarded as the touchstone of publishable articles in prestigious journals, were applied arbitrarily; for example, note again Rachman's high-handed dismissal on methodological grounds of study after study of psychotherapy outcome" (Rachman 1971, 38).

Nevertheless, BOP still accepted the burden of proving effectiveness, rejecting the notion that the skeptic bears the responsibility of disproof. However, a reanalysis of BOP actually reprises concern with the safety of treatment. First, the study presents effect sizes as though they are populations of outcomes instead of samples of underlying populations. BOP's effect sizes were computed from standard error types of statistics instead of standard deviations, implying an enormous underlying variability in patient outcomes. Thus, the outcomes of psychotherapy appear to be wildly unpredictable, not tightly clustered as BOP suggests (Epstein 1984a, 1984b). Moreover, many of BOP's source studies are played on unreliable instruments to measure outcomes, naively asserting the accuracy of patient self-reports. Additionally, the research was customarily conducted in optimal settings where highly regarded therapists (typically attached to university research centers) practiced under close scrutiny. The routine conditions of community care are far less accountable and far more tolerant of marginal professionals.

Thus, BOP's acclaimed benefit of thirty percentage points is reduced to ten percentage points by placebo comparisons, to seven percentage points by Prioleau, Murdock, and Brody's (1983) reanalysis, down to perhaps four percentage points by measurement reactivity, further by their questionable statistical assumptions, and even further by the likely biases of their porous base of studies. Moreover, Rosenthal and Rubin (1978) have estimated that by themselves "interpersonal expectancy effects"— researcher biases that confirm their hypotheses—in areas such as psychotherapy research falsely account for a greater amount of reported benefits (more than one standard deviation) than BOP's initial claim of psychotherapy's benefits (0.85 standard deviations). In the end, then, the true effects of psychotherapy may well be below the mean of the untreated groups; at best, treatment appears to be ineffective, while it may be routinely harmful.

Yet despite a great number of problems with BOP's analysis and conclusions, many summaries—meta-analyses, as well as intuitive and box score reviews—dutifully supported its endorsement of psychotherapy. Numerous studies corroborated BOP's basic procedures and findings (e.g., Landman and Dawes 1982; Shapiro 1985; Andrews and Harvey 1981; Shapiro and Shapiro 1982; Giblin, Sprenkle, and Sheehan 1985). Weisz et al.'s (1987) meta-analysis reported an effect size of 0.79 (twenty-nine percentage points), and Casey and Berman (1985) reported 0.71 (twenty-six percentage points) favoring treated children over untreated controls. Howard, Kopta, and Krause (1986) discerned huge benefits after only eight sessions of treatment. Patterson (1984) emphasized that the "magnitude of the evidence" in support of the benefits of psychotherapy "is nothing short of amazing" (437). Miller and Berman (1983) and Tillitski (1990) found in the manner of Luborsky, Singer, and Luborsky that all psychotherapies seem to be effective. At the same time, the base of studies was expanding, with additional support for its efficacy in treating headache, depression, insomnia, anorexia nervosa, and many other conditions.

Occasionally some doubt was raised about therapy (Stuart 1973; Kline 1988; Dawes 1994; Dineen 1996), but even the skeptics sheltered a portion of the field from their general indictment, just as Eysenck and Rachman had maintained a faith in behavioral treatment. Nevertheless, these few restraints were inundated by the tsunami of research and social support for psychotherapy. Patients adore it; indeed, some appear to be addicted. Practitioners build careers; insurance companies make profits; and the American taxpayer saves money. Yet the literature of psychotherapy has never produced any scientifically credible evidence that any of its interventions, in any setting, for any condition, has been routinely effective. To the contrary, the field's research is universally compromised by sampling problems, inappropriate or absent controls, measurement biases, and the rest. Its very best research, counting studies such as the National Institutes of Mental (NIMH) Health Treatment of Depression Collaborative Research Project (CRP), were prematurely funded in light of their serious methodological problems.

In spite of impressive national acclaim by the NIMH, a very costly research procedure, widespread participation, and prominent publication, both the conduct and the reporting of CRP belie any conformity with the canons of science (Elkin et al. 1989; Imber et al. 1990; Sotsky et al. 1991). The various authors' finding that psychotherapy was effective against depression is contradicted by their actual research, which reported no significant differences between their placebo-control and their short-term (sixteen-week) psychotherapeutic interventions. Moreover, measures were suspect and dependent on patient self-report; attrition, at almost 40 percent, was an enormous problem. CRP demonstrated little more than the ineffectiveness of superficial care for serious mental problems. In the end, CRP applied alternative science to alternative medicine.

Seligman's (1995) more recent test of psychotherapy's effectiveness should have been dismissed by journal referees as preposterous on methodological grounds without ever emerging in print. Instead, Seligman, a recent president of the American Psychological Association, succeeded in publishing his gloss on the practice of psychotherapy in a prominent journal. Moreover, he dismissed the need for either appropriate sampling or randomized controls while still insisting on the scientific credibility of the research. Indeed, the fact that such atavistic research was even conducted, let alone well published, reinforces the observation that the meaning of psychotherapy, its actual effectiveness, has less to do with its effectiveness than with its ceremonial role and its popularity.

Seligman evaluated the outcomes of psychotherapy by appending a few questions about utilization and satisfaction to the annual reader survey of *Consumer Reports*. He found both widespread use of and high levels of satisfaction with psychotherapy, largely endorsing the earlier findings of Luborsky, Singer, and Luborsky (1975) that all forms of psychotherapy appear to be equally successful. Yet the sample was not representative of patients; the response rate was minuscule, while the respondents were probably not even representative of the sample; the questions (and responses) were uninterpretable in terms of behavioral outcomes; and the actual conditions of therapy (duration, the presenting problem, and so forth) were not credibly explored.

Only 13 percent (22,000) of the 184,000 sampled readers of *Consumer Reports* responded to the survey, and of these, only 4,100 sought help for their mental health problem from a doctor, a mental health professional, or a support group. The respondent group was well educated and wealthy, decidedly not representative of the American public and probably not representative of either those in therapy or those with mental and emotional problems. Moreover, these individuals' decision to subscribe to *Consumer Reports* probably implies greater social and economic success and better adaptive skills and therefore less psychopathology than in the common pool of patients. More problematically, all the responses were obviously self-reports, and no effort was made to check their accuracy. Self-report, particularly on presenting problems, outcomes of therapy, and even satisfaction, is enormously unreliable and sensitive to conditions that probably have little to do with behavioral change. Most unfortunately, the study lacked any controls, thus preventing the attribution of reported changes to the therapy instead of Rachman's spontaneous remission. Seligman's claim that "the data set is thus a rich one, probably uniquely rich" (1995, 967) is absurd unless *rich* is taken to mean "highly amusing" rather than "containing a large amount of choice ingredients" (*American Heritage Dictionary* 1992).

Seligman refused to accept the obvious, invalidating pitfalls of his methodology. Instead, he offered specious internal comparisons and vague unreferenced allusions to the characteristics of patients that endorse their credibility as respondents while depreciating the value of controlled trials. The essay actually consumed more space anticipating potential criticisms of its methodology than presenting its conclusions. Along the way, Seligman created a new criterion for research—human significance—that somehow extends the reach of both clinical and statistical significance: "The [*Consumer Reports*] study leaves little doubt about the human significance of its findings" because respondents rated their own, personal, individual outcomes (970). Yethe failed to prove the human value of his research, especially since the respondent pool may have disproportionately contained Gross's YAVIS types or "therapy junkies" whose self-aggrandized unhappiness fails to inform social policy or the treatment of serious personal and social problems. The possibility that habituation to treatment stimulates overripe evaluations cannot be simply disregarded in a survey with such a tiny response rate, particularly among respondents who were so highly homogeneous and unrepresentative to begin with.

If human significance were really taken to heart, the professional organizations of psychotherapy might make more intensive efforts to scrutinize the behaviors of its practitioners and not simply wait for malpractice suits to cleanse the field. The field probably contains a large number of well-meaning, mature, and responsible practitioners whose only offenses may be ineffectiveness, the time wasted by their patients, and perhaps an expected amount of self-deception. However, along with the search to fill emotional voids with roles in curative heroics and psychological redemption, psychotherapy seems to attract predators—the bunco artists of alternative medicine, as well as the maladapts who perpetrate indignities on their patients. As Seligman himself points out, the issue of accountability exists more in common practice than in the universities and institutes that produce the outcome studies of reputedly highly competent practitioners under laboratory conditions. Others with less need to keep criticism within the psychotherapy clubhouse have taken a darker view of practice (Masson 1988; Dineen 1996).[9]

The long history of defensiveness among practitioners of pseudo-science anticipates the attack on randomized controlled trials by Seligman (1996), *Consumer Reports* (Kotkin, Daviet, and Gurin 1996), and others (e.g., Silbershatz 1999). Still, numerous complaints were registered against Seligman's research.[10] Nevertheless, the conclusion that "invalid is invalid" (Brock et al. 1996, 1083) does not seem to tarnish the celebrity of psychotherapy. The tactical problems in conducting controlled trials, not the least of which is the general lack of will to do so, do not by themselves improve the credibility of flawed, weaker methodologies. If indeed the outcomes of psychotherapy are practical impossibilities of measurement, then the field's effectiveness remains indeterminate at best. Meanwhile, the conversion of this ignorance into cultural wisdom and broad social acceptance signals a political motive rather than a demonstration of rational authority. In the end, to call the research of psychotherapy science is to repeat Mary Baker Eddy's usage, not Newton's rigor.

The Surgeon General's 1999 report on the state of mental health in the United States is the most recent gloss of psychotherapy's potency (U.S. Department of Health and Human Services 1999). Yet it is certainly the most enthusiastic of any recent mental health evaluation, probably because it is oblivious to the problems of proof and to disconfirming evidence. Indeed, its public and prestigious provenance speaks more of government's propaganda on behalf of mental health professionals than of a serious attempt to address the needs of citizens for effective care. The report is a thoroughgoing refusal to entertain the least challenge either to the effectiveness of psychotherapy or to the scientific credibility of its research despite its ponderous assertion of the necessity for experimental methods. Indeed, its extensive bibliography erases the skeptics from consideration. However, its commitments to credible science are discarded in composing the crucial chapters that discuss the outcomes of psychotherapy for children, adults, and the elderly. Ignoring the appalling scientific lapses that are routine in the report's base of research, the central conclusions of the report are portals of faith for testimonials to effectiveness. All treatment approaches are given a respectful presentation; almost all conditions are amenable to treatment; the extant empirical tests of clinical effectiveness are accepted without critical analysis of their pitfalls. Doubt is banished knowingly through an evaluative review prepared by the principal stakeholders of current treatment—therapists, researchers, professional associations, and "citizen" alliances.

Psychotherapy constitutes a community, perhaps a cult, of the credulous, undisturbed by skepticism, largely because the society seems pleased with its ceremonial support of the corrective myth of mental health treatment, the assurance that emotional and mental problems are amenable to relatively inexpensive and compatible cures. Both the field's intransigent rejection of systematic evaluation and its tenacious hold on the society's allegiance are patent in light of a persistent belief in the efficacy of even Freudian psychoanalysis. Certainly, this form of therapy has been long depleted of any respectable scientific proof of effectiveness. Indeed, it has taken a scorching within its own literature, as well as in prominent, exhaustively complete critiques of its theory, its practice, and its culture (Grunbaum 1984; Macmillan 1997; Ferris 1999). Freud himself despaired of his patients getting beyond their cherished neuroses. Yet even after extensive debunking, the persistent attachment to psychoanalysis exemplifies the extraordinary resistance of the broader field, of its patients, and of the culture to address the deficiencies of socially efficient interventions and thereby the enduring deprivations of its less fortunate citizens.

The perverse popularity of ineffective clinical forms that perform important political ceremonies is a door, opened by the reaction to Crews's criticism of Freudian psychoanalysis, into the minds of both the therapeutic community and the society (Crews 1993; *New York Review of Books* 1994a, 1994b). Crews valiantly challenges the effectiveness and theoretical value of psychoanalysis on very standard grounds of rational coherence and credibility. The fractious disagreements stimulated by his inspection of the prophet's works are remnants of the war that was fought and lost over modern psychotherapy; the scientific mood succumbed to the assault of its ever more politically comfortable critics.

The "Exchanges"(*New York Review of Books* 1994a, 1994b), like much of the debate in the field, substitute an ad hominem style for scientific debate. The effectiveness of psychoanalysis, extended into a general consideration of psychotherapy itself, is at issue, not the personal deficits of Freud nor the motives of Crews. While Crews may have erred on small points of history and doctrine—but even these errors are not apparent—his article and his response to his critics in the two *Exchanges* go far to describe the capricious and unscientific origins of Freudian psychoanalysis, a failure of its scholarly enterprise that continues today in all of psychotherapy. Not only is psychoanalysis a pseudoscience, but for the very same reasons—largely a refusal to accept the standard methodological canons of clinical proof—the entire field of contemporary psychotherapy is also scientifically bogus.

The refusal of Crews's critics to accept rigorous tests of outcomes, apparently continuing Freud's idiosyncratic and highly individualistic methods for evaluating his insights, expresses the resistance of the field itself to accountability. As though self-regard were sufficient protection against both a biased selection of research subjects and a roseate estimate of its own effectiveness, Ostrow offers the experience of thirty-seven of his own patients as proof of the field's treatment power, and Peyser offers a single case example (*New York Review of Books* 1994a, 35, 37). Indeed an enchantment with its own cleverness has precipitated the "epistemic fix" of psychotherapy itself: lucrative practice and social popularity, if not actually prestige, without credible proof of clinical strength. The same has been true at one time or another for séances, astrology, herb therapy, aroma therapy, Rolfing, acupuncture, chiropractic, and Scientology.

The conclusion of unremittingly misleading and unreliable research is not made lightly. None of Luborsky's cited "reviews of comparative psychotherapy studies"—notably BOP and his own research—withstand probing scrutiny (*New York Review of Books* 1994a, 37). All of the field's research is grievously marred, with small samples that are also frequently inappropriate for the research, self-serving measurement, inappropriate controls, biased and unreliable measures, biased and compromised evaluators, inadequate follow-up periods, high attrition rates among research subjects, inaccurate analyses, unjustified conclusions, and others (Epstein 1995). As a consequence, the weak base of primary studies does not justify the summary conclusions of the reviews. But even those reviews are flawed on their own terms: improper statistical procedures, an uncritical acceptance of woefully inadequate studies, slanted interpretations, and so forth.

A truly scientific field accepts the burden to prove its effectiveness and goes about developing tests of its outcomes that are methodologically sufficient to refute plausible points of skepticism: that its interventions may be frequently harmful; that it provides only the ceremony of cure and not actual cure; that it addicts patients to treatment; that evidence of positive outcomes are creations of its biased research; that its patients and research subjects do not need treatment in the first place. From the time of Freud and continuing to the present, the psychotherapeutic community has ignored the ennobling activation of self-doubt that is central to the communal practice of true science. Even the few clinical trials that it has conducted of its effectiveness seem to be self-serving, presided over by scholars whose true faith beguiles their skepticism. As a result, the field's positive effects, if they exist at all, can be explained by alternatives that are far less flattering of the field's pretensions to psychic healing and behavioral change. Indeed, as Luborsky claims, psychoanalysis may be no less effective than other psychotherapeutic treatments, but then again, all those treatments are probably no more effective than placebos for psychotherapy or time itself, the customary metaphor for inexplicable remission.

Yet psychotherapy persists in spite of its indeterminate outcomes and its hostility to objective, systematic research. Psychotherapeutic theory undergirds most treatment and rehabilitation programs for addicts, juvenile delinquents, criminals, the mentally ill (except psychotics), welfare recipients, and others. Analytic and therapeutic theory has also been adapted to management, administration, sales, advertising, education, and health care. Yet, again, its obvious popularity is not buttressed by any definitive proof of its treatment effectiveness. The field of psychotherapy is a puzzle of organizational vigor that lacks the nourishment of a true production function.

The outcome literature of psychotherapy is denial, and successful denial at that, of the failure to achieve cure, prevention, and treatment of both personal deviance and subsequent social problems. But denial of this magnitude suggests very powerful social motives that cling to the field's ambiguities and weaknesses. The refusal to let go of psychotherapy, let alone Freudian psychoanalysis, speaks to a neurotic dependency on supportive ideology, the political dividend of ritualizing communal belief through the propagation of corrective myths. Psychotherapy is actually a chapter in the bible of America's civil religion dealing with opportunities to "restoreth the soul" and, miraculously, without disturbing the culture's calm waters or private accounts.

In spite of the obvious fact that false claims of effectiveness do not serve the interests of service recipients, they do provide a convenience for the culture. They also provide the therapist with a respected livelihood. Therapy sets the onus of change on the patient, in denial of both the social roots of deviance and the social responsibility to provide more equality in home life, education, community care and safety, employment, housing, health care, and the other embedded patterns of modern life. Bogus science well serves a socially efficient, postmodern role in creating the symbols of caring but devoid of the material sustenance of greater equality. Indeed, false reports of psychotherapy's effectiveness forestall the socially disruptive, expensive, and immensely unpopular policies that might address serious social problems in serious ways. Not surprisingly but still ironically, the postmodern critique is maturing to fulfill the needs of the targets of its early fury. What began as a plea by the politically marginal in battling an unjust elite has been converted by popular election into the weak research that justifies the subjective truths of its own opposition. The language of psychotherapy has become the language of neglect.

Practice: The Evaluation Champions of the Personal Social Services

The personal social services recapitulate psychotherapy. Despite their scientific pretensions and professional ambitions, they are largely ideological, ritualizations of social values more than profound production functions of cure, rehabilitation, or prevention. This bleak conclusion could be falsified by social welfare interventions that demonstrably meet their goals. Yet the vast literature of the personal social services has failed ever to provide scientifically credible evidence of their effectiveness either in meeting their narrow program objectives or, more important, in addressing the underlying social problems that inspired them in the first place.

The personal social services periodically present general summaries of their effectiveness that are benchmarks of both social and professional progress. These analytic compilations of the best research available are particularly influential in immature disciplines that lack definitive tests of theory or practice but that have amassed an extensive, varied, and increasingly recondite literature. Since the early 1970s and with increasing intensity and frequency since Fischer's (1973b) review, researchers have taken on the task of exploring some portion of the more prominent journals to catalog the application of credible science to social service outcomes. But for a brief and quiet interlude of skepticism and self-doubt, the reviews of the outcome research conclude with near uniformity that rigorous methods are being increasingly applied to the evaluation of personal social services and that the outcomes themselves are improving. Yet only one conclusion is more uniformly consistent than the field's roseate claims: they are universally groundless. There is no scientifically credible research that can sustain the buoyancy of improved methods or outcomes. Each apparent advance in statistical sophistication, sample size, or measurement is overmatched by the resistance of credulous and beholden researchers: incomplete blinding, breached randomization, inappropriate analysis and biased reporting, along with the nearly intractable reliance on subject self-report. When the outcomes as reported in the "Results" section do not adequately sustain the corrective virtues of social service theory, they are aged, scrubbed, dressed in new clothing, and rehabilitated as hopeful leads in the "Discussion."

The dreary task of deflating plangent and excessive claims to rigor and authority is largely ignored or written off as maladaption and heresy. Rather than challenging the skeptic with an empirical fusillade of noisy redundancy, it would be better for each review to simply offer a few champions of its search, say no more than five of the best studies they unearth, that would stand as proxy for the multitude of their other discoveries. Boiling down the stew of research to a rich *gelee* would nurture a more focused discussion.

Putting Families First

Putting Families First (PFF) is among the most methodologically sound evaluations ever conducted of any social service.[11] It is probably social work's champion of champions, its *capo di tutti capi* of empirical research, comparing favorably with the most elaborate outcome research, such as the Seattle/Denver Income Maintenance Experiments, Stein and Test's (1980) experiment with the deinstitutionalization of mental hospital patients, and the Manpower Demonstration Research Corporation's many vocational training studies. Yet in the end, PFF's profound methodological pitfalls, as well as those of the other social experiments, repeat the conclusions of psychotherapy—indeterminacy, plausible ineffectiveness, and possibly even harm. All the other studies of personal social service outcomes identified in the multitude of the field's reviews of its empirical progress fall far short of PFF, pressing for a condemnatory assessment of the research enterprise in the personal social services, the inability to provide rational information for social decision making, and the failure of current social welfare interventions to address social problems.

PFF's evaluation of family preservation services in Illinois employed a controlled prospective research design: the experimental groups received family preservation services; the control groups did not (Schuerman, Rzepnicki, and Littell 1994). A variety of other necessary methodological protections were employed: large samples drawn from a variety of sites; random selection and assignment of subjects; multiple measures and follow-up assessments. Assuring the integrity of the research, experimental subjects apparently received a greater number and intensity of services than did controls; in some sites, experimental subjects reportedly received almost ten hours of care per week, while controls typically received less than one hour per week. The purpose of the expensive and complex procedures that PFF employed was to assure the rational, that is, scientific, credibility of the findings.

Family preservation services are designed to prevent the dissolution of families "at imminent risk of placement" by providing them with intensive short-term services. Successful interventions presumably reduce the need for public child welfare placements (Pecora, Fraser, and Haapala 1992). Frequently modeled after Homebuilders and other similar programs, family preservation services include concrete services such as baby-sitting, respite care, clothing, employment, financial assistance, food, and so forth, as well as a variety of counseling services provided to families, individuals, and groups and for problems of addiction, psychiatric disorders, and behavioral dysfunctions. The services are typically provided for less than six months. As Rossi (1991) points out, the idea of family preservation is broadly appealing. Both conservatives and liberals like to reduce public costs, in this case, by avoiding extended child welfare placements, and enjoy association with efforts to succor the beleaguered modern family.

In the end, PFF announced that family preservation services did not preserve families; there was no difference in placement rates between controls and experimental groups. This conclusion was both practically and theoretically important. On the one hand, it identified a failure of existing services and therefore maintained concern with the problems of dysfunctional families and with the need for continuing public child welfare services. On the other hand, the failure suggested that the theory of service was inaccurate: relatively inexpensive shortcuts to goals were again ineffective. If the finding of ineffectiveness was accurate, then family preservation services were either inadequate or mistargeted—a question of resources or technique. The authors preferred the latter conclusion, but with little authority from their own research.

PFF compromised methodological rigor so often that the experiment sustains no finding and no conclusion. Moreover, the invalidating pitfalls of its design emerged early, calling ethical attention to a research enterprise that lacked any ability to fulfill its promise of credible findings but that knowingly continued to pester staff and service recipients for unanswerable research questions. In the first instance, PFF breached randomization in about one-quarter of its cases, 7 percent because of court orders and the remainder because of worker decisions. Because these cases were excluded from the analysis, the samples of the study become unrepresentative of "families at imminent risk of placement." Second, imminent risk itself was only poorly understood, that is, the basic target group was not adequately defined. Third, the measures of outcomes (except disposition, of course) were unreliable. The researchers acknowledge that "evaluations of family preservation will continue to make use of measures of uncertain reliability, validity, and sensitivity," but they pugnaciously go on to employ them as though they had merit (Schuerman, Rzepnicki, and Littell 1994, 212–13).

Fourth, the disposition of a case—whether a child is maintained in the family or placed into emergency care or foster care—is a very uncertain measure of the child's benefit, especially since placement decisions reflect worker preferences and agency demands that are quite distinct from the best interests of the child. Only the actual condition of the child evaluates the prudence of the placement decision. The assumption that the *type* of placement (adoption, foster care, group home, residential treatment, and so forth) adequately indicates the *quality* of placement verges on intentional cruelty. Moreover, it is a plausible point of skepticism, especially in light of the large number of deaths of children under the supervision of child welfare agencies, to ask whether child welfare workers suppress placements to preserve families by their decisions when they cannot preserve them by their services.

Fifth, methods to gather data varied between control and experimental groups, while the interviewers who took early measures were far less experienced than those who conducted the follow-up interviews. Sixth, neither interviewers, service workers, nor service recipients were blind to the assignment of subjects to control or experimental groups. Seventh, treatment integrity may not have been assured; receipt of services relied on worker reports without corroboration by the researchers. Finally, PFF is haunted by a demonstration effect and possibly even Heckman's randomization bias (Manski and Garfinkel 1992). It is likely that the experiment is unrepresentative of the typical service situation, distorted by unusual worker and agency motivations created by the novelty of family preservation care. Furthermore, the imposition of randomization, especially when participating agencies are not randomly chosen, causes perturbations—some agencies opt out, and some workers subvert randomization (as occurred)—that compromise the representativeness of the samples, probably in unknown ways.

Still PFF, unusual in reaching conclusions of ineffectiveness, was superior in methodological rigor, such as it was, to the porous research that commonly invades the social service literature. Yet even PFF's negative conclusions are suspect as ideological expressions, particularly since the authors seemingly began their study with a then-fashionable preference for restrictive government, that is, a bias against an expanded public role:

> The expansion of the purview of the child welfare system that has occurred in the last few decades should be stopped and reversed. This requires that lines be carefully drawn between our aspirations and what can be reasonably expected. . . . The state cannot accept responsibility for the optimal development of all children. Nor should it even endeavor to assure the "well-being" of all children given the impossibility of achieving that goal, even if well-being could be adequately defined and measured. . . . Emotional harms can, of course, have serious effects on the child, on the development of services to help parents better relate to their children. But these services should be voluntary, outside the abuse and neglect response system. (Schuerman, Rzepnicki, and Littell 1994, 245)

Indeed, this position, preemptively heralded as one of the study's apostolic findings, simply offers an uninformed opinion, in spite of being held by professors at the University of Chicago, that problems of children in the public sector are largely the result of failed professional techniques of intervention rather than grossly underfunded services and social inattention. Schuerman, Rzepnicki, and Littell seem to plead for a greater concentration of funds on those truly in need. Yet the collected acta of the personal social services have little, if any, ability to demonstrate that the most troubled are in any way amenable to this kind of care or to point to any evidence that the dilute tea of PFF's recommendations has ever adequately calmed troubled families. PFF itself lacks any authority of design to state what might work; it only measured, and poorly at that, whether intensive family preservation services in Illinois were in fact successful.

Recall, too, that the research was unable to accurately predict "imminent risk of placement"; indeed, the workers' assessments of risk may simply have been the artifacts of their highly idiosyncratic impressions. The authors' surmises about the appropriate state role are even more tentative than their conclusions concerning PFF effectiveness. Moreover, to the extent that their limited-state suggestions recapitulate intensive case services, behavioral methods, or contracting—the modestly more generous levels of social work's recent epiphanies that may have cost about as much as PFF per service recipient—then they are fated for the same doom as a corrective.

Yet none of the analytic reviews of the personal social services identify studies that routinely mirror even the quality of PFF. Indeed, the reviews most frequently accept a level of evaluation that reveals little more than the adolescent cliquishness of the social services—the unscripted conspiracy among researchers, agencies, and the social will to propagate corrective myths through an implacable opposition to credible evaluation.

The Reviews of the Research

The interlude of criticism in the history of the personal social services traces back to Wootton's (1959) publication of a political and social critique of psychotherapy. However, *Social Science and Social Pathology* was widely ignored in the United States, whose brief question period opened in the early 1970s with Fischer's (1973a, 1973b) critique of social work and Segal's (1972) review of personal social service effectiveness. Normalcy (i.e., self-serving gullibility) was triumphantly restored only eight years later with Fischer's epiphany of a "new spirit" of science in the field that extolled the influence of his 1973 study (Fischer 1981).

Wootton, an English magistrate, argued that the psychopathology research was methodologically "unfortunate" and that services were ideologically misdirected to treat "the infected individual rather than to eliminate the infection from the environment" (1959, 328). She identified income inequality and poverty as the culprit in individual psychopathology. However, in the manner of Fabian socialists and their attachment to the socially efficient Pygmalion myth, she tended to underestimate the costs of eliminating economic poverty and simply ignored cultural poverty, the notion that socially dysfunctional behaviors emerge from deficits in cultural institutions other than the market.

In a similar mood impelled by a commitment to structural interventions, Segal (1972), Fischer (1973a), and Wood (1978) followed with reviews of the social work literature in the United States that identified few credible studies and even fewer that reported effective interventions. Segal could identify "no study of outcome with respect to social work therapeutic interventions with both an adequate control group design

and positive results" (1972, 3). He even suggested that the stronger studies produced more negative outcomes. Of the eleven studies that met Fischer's (1973a) minimal methodological criteria, in about half, "clients
receiving services in the experimental group were shown to demonstrate
improved functioning at a lesser rate than control subjects" (15–16). One
of his studies (Blenkner, Bloom, and Nielsen 1971) even reported serious
deterioration and mortality among experimental subjects. Wood's review
identified twenty-two studies (many also included by Fischer and Segal)
that met her inclusion criteria and covered a broad area of the personal
social services, not just social casework or psychotherapeutic care.
Although only six of her studies reported positive outcomes, Wood tried
to redeem the whole field on these frail pillars.

Critical analyses of then contemporary service effectiveness were also
conducted by Martinson, who famously concluded that in the field of
corrections "nothing works" (Martinson 1974; Ginzburg et al. 1988). A
few additional analyses contradicted the happy conclusions of Smith,
Glass, and Miller. However, the frontier of skepticism closed in 1981, at
least in social work, with the publication of Joel Fischer's impassioned
personal testimony to the triumph of science in social work.

Only eight years after his corrosive reference to social work as Casey-
at-the-Bat (Fischer 1973a), Fischer (1981) felt confident in heralding the
new era of scientific practice on the basis of "material presented at social
work conferences, from the literature and from less concrete sources of
evidence" (199). "In its most salient characteristics, the paradigm shift
appears to involve a movement toward more systematic, rational, empirically oriented development and use of knowledge for practice" (Fischer
1981, 199). Fischer (1978) began warming up for his revolution with the
discovery of a few rays of sunshine; "perhaps the most striking of these is
the research on behavior modification" with humans. Obedient to the
new orthodoxy, one review after another of the outcome literature dutifully unearthed evidence of a scientific blooming that enhanced progress
in achieving service goals. Yet careful scrutiny deflates the claims to scientific rigor of even the best among their base of studies. Not one study
passes a minimal scientific muster—let alone the more rigorous criterion
of full-blown clinical trials that incorporate blinding, multiple reliable
measures, large stable and relevant samples, and applicable follow-up
periods—to adduce credible evidence that any service intervention has
been effective. Still, the reviews consistently report hopeful leads, modest
effectiveness, little steps for little feet, responsible programming, lights in
the dark, and intellectual achievement that provide reason for optimism,
pride, and civic advance. Just as consistently, the reviews flout prudent
skepticism with bogus science: inappropriate controls, the absence of
methodological protections against researcher biases of one sort or
another, and unreliable and invalid measurement instruments. Indeed,

the professional commitments of the researchers (i.e., their expectancy biases) may be better predictors of reported service outcomes than any objective condition of practice. Out of profound respect for the nature of political discourse, social science and social services require interpretation as a variety of ecclesiastical experience.

With their hard eyes focused on maintaining faith in the corrective myth, the summary reviews since Wood (1978) at worst have reached cautious conclusions of growing efficacy and at best have been paeans to professionalization and rationality. Reid and Hanrahan (1982) found "grounds for optimism" in social work services. Rubin (1985) found "more grounds for optimism." Thomlison (1984) reassured the nation that Martinson was wrong and that "something works." Andrews et al. (1990) even identified the essential "something" as differential treatment, one of the oldest trees in witchcraft's primeval pharmacopoeia. From England, Sheldon (1986) reassured the former colonials that they were on the right track.

Yet these reviews, apart from the meta-analyses and their lax inclusion criteria, generally identified only a small number of methodologically acceptable studies, usually on the order of one dozen or so. Most telling, even the best of the enumerated research failed to constitute decisive tests of effectiveness or even to consistently apply the announced standards of the reviews. With no exception, the studies compared very poorly with the best research in the field, imperfect as it is (Epstein 1993a). Frequently the selected studies reported far more negative findings than the reviews acknowledged.

Feldman, Wodarski, and Caplinger (1983; also Feldman and Caplinger 1977) has been cited as evidence of growing rational respectability, notably by Reid and Hanrahan (1982) and Sheldon (1986). Yet The Saint Louis Experiment, which studied the ability of group work to correct delinquent behaviors among adolescents, chose an experimental group with less reported deviancy than a comparable group of middle-class children drawn randomly from a suburban community center, failed to blind evaluators, and failed to adequately control for the interventions (or even to detail them well). In addition, the outcome measures were unreliable (contrary to the authors' claims, .51 is awful); attrition and censoring reached 60 percent by the end of the intervention and 80 percent by the follow-up. Nevertheless, the authors draw the following wildly self-congratulatory conclusion: "The St. Louis Experiment is likely to generate renewed interest in integrative treatment programs for antisocial youths. . . . Transportation excluded the yearly cost for a program such as the St. Louis Experiment would be unlikely to exceed $150 per youth in 1983 dollars" (Feldman, Wadaiski, and Capligu 1983). Despite the inability to attend to deep social problems, cheap solutions have their charms. This research was funded by the NIMH, and the authors have moved on to prestigious academic positions on the strength of this and a torrent of similar publications.

Among Rubin's (1985) twelve methodologically sound studies, only one is rigorous. Yet even Stein and Test's (1980) famous demonstration that community care was possible for long-staying psychotics was problematic. Their study population, drawn from a group of disproportionately family-related individuals in rural Wisconsin, one of the nation's more ethnically homogeneous states, was not representative of impersonalized, competitive, and even antagonistic urban settings in which the mentally ill have been routinely abandoned by their families. Furthermore, the demonstration was conducted by a highly trained and motivated staff that is very rare in the typical service setting. Moreover, the research concluded that deinstitutionalization, if it was to be successful, cost *more* than hospital care. Yet Stein and Test's experiment is routinely cited by public authorities as testimony to the feasibility of deinstitutionalization and *less* expenditure for the mentally ill in community care. Thus a humanitarian experiment to reduce suffering ironically came to justify the widespread neglect of the mental health system.

None of Rubin's other eleven studies were methodologically comparable to that of Stein and Test. Five were very inadequate and trivial. Of the seven papers that he claimed certified positive outcomes, one did not meet his own inclusion criteria, two did not report positive outcomes, another was sunk by high differential attrition, and five had very small samples. Similarly, Sheldon's (1986) base of credible studies withers away under even superficial reading. Many of his studies, such as Rose and Marshall (1974), lacking any controls or protections against bias, could not have passed the muster of the American reviews.

Beginning with Videka-Sherman's (1988) two meta-analyses (reported in a single paper), the quantity of evaluative research and evidence for progress in achieving program goals appeared to quicken. Videka-Sherman (1988) handled more than sixty studies in her two meta-analyses and predictably identified pervasive evidence of effectiveness. Yet her own analyses undercut her conclusions. Her literal conclusion in the first meta-analysis that "the average experimental client had a better outcome than 69 percent of control group clients" (328) ignores the fact they started off at 50 percent. The actual tallied improvement of 19 percent needs to be further discounted by other methodological shortcomings. Only four of the relevant thirty-eight studies, in one portion of her analysis, randomly sampled their subjects from the underlying problem population. Only a small minority of studies employed random assignment between control and experimental groups. Moreover, psychological outcomes were almost invariably measured by patient self-report or practitioner assessments, leading Videka-Sherman to acknowledge that measures "tended to be reactive" (327). Together with their many other methodological pitfalls, few of the studies could achieve "high internal validity," a synonym for scientific credibility. The second meta-analysis was even weaker, routinely relying on quasi-experimental designs, that is, methods without true controls.

Subsequent to Videka-Sherman, two major reviews counted an even greater rate of methodologically rigorous studies. Gorey (1996) continued the optimism of effectiveness, although Rosen, Proctor, and Staudt (1999) sounded a cautious warning. During only a five-year window, opening in 1990, Gorey (1996) identified fully 88 acceptable outcome studies that were published in thirteen "prestigious" social work journals. The number of acceptable evaluative studies that Gorey identified was four times that of Wood and eight times that of Fischer (1973a), who covered a much longer period of time. Reviewing a similar four-and-a-half-year period beginning in 1993, in a somewhat different sample of thirteen social work journals, Rosen, Proctor, and Staudt identified 126 "control-oriented" articles that investigated 147 interventions. Of the 147 interventions, only 65 (appearing in 53 articles) met their criteria of methodological acceptability. Gorey concludes, as did Videka-Sherman, that a large proportion—"more than three quarters"—of those who receive social work services are better off than the average person who does not. However, Rosen, Proctor, and Staudt (1999) were more concerned that such a small proportion of the field's research, less than 10 percent of articles in leading journals, was both methodologically acceptable (at least to them) and devoted to the evaluation of service effectiveness.

Lamentably, both of these recent reviews employed extremely lax inclusion criteria that vitiate all of Gorey's happy conclusions, amplifying Rosen, Proctor, and Staudt's polite concern to frank condemnation. Indeed, the included studies are not at all scientifically credible; at best, they are tentative, unreplicated pilot studies that might stimulate more rigorous and definitive testing in a maturing scientific community. Neither review produced even hobbled champions to contend with the best in the field, imperfect as they are. A startling proportion of the studies were single-subject designs, lacking even rudimentary controls for seasonality and "spontaneous" remission. Many samples were tiny and defy serious attention on these grounds alone. Blinding and other confirmational response protections were customarily absent, a detail that slips past Gorey in spite of his earlier finding that there was a strong institutional bias: "The average effect reported by researchers affiliated with the institutions being evaluated was twice as large as the estimated effect based on external evaluations" (Cryns, Gorey, and Brice 1989, 215). Researchers and practitioners themselves routinely evaluated outcomes and frequently relied on patient self-report. Instruments rarely enjoyed high levels of reliability. Nevertheless, these research reports, anthologized in textbooks, cited for academic promotion, and intoned as eulogies, constitute the rational claims, that is, the scientific authority, of the personal social services.

Yet Gorey accepted any study for his analysis that permitted the computation of an effect size, in other words, any study that computed a standard deviation and a mean and included any comparison group at all. Statistical significance gave way to his concern with clinical significance, a term of art that refers to the practitioner's intuitive sense of the value of the findings for treatment.[12] "Most social workers want more information about the magnitude of the intervention's effects or its effect size, which is more directly related to its clinical or policy significance . . . and more useful for grappling with cost-benefit concerns" (Gorey 1996, 120). Yes, but the information may also be quite illusory, especially in light of the common advocacy bias of social service research whereby devotees of an intervention push positive effects through porous evaluative methodologies, a distortion that is facilitated by small samples.

Gorey also failed to adjust his findings for placebo effects, which probably would have shrunk them by more than two-thirds, following the experience in psychotherapy. Further reductions for other likely biases might have pushed actual outcomes into the willow world of clinical virtue, that is, services may be routinely harmful. While large findings may be clinically interesting, they are not clinically true until they have been run through a gauntlet of randomized trials. To allow the cravings of social workers for social standing to distort the objective outcomes of research sacrifices service recipients to professional ambitions. But this may be the whole point of both the debased scholarship and its continuing political support—the ascendancy of ceremonial, corrective myths over the production functions of cure, prevention, and rehabilitation.

There is additional recognition that the volume of evaluative research in the personal social services is inadequate, having little influence on agencies or practitioners. Nevertheless, the commentary rarely transcends professorial admonitions and reaches for an interpretation of institutionalized obedience to explain the technical inadequacy of the literature. Largely corroborating Tripodi (1984), Fraser et al. (1991) reported that social workers published only fourteen experimental program evaluations in their base of ten research journals from 1985 through 1988. They warned that social work is vulnerable to grave criticism without systematic knowledge. However, in spite of its long-standing absence, they did not handle the fact of the field's robust persistence. Glisson (1995) also identified few methodologically rigorous studies of social work outcomes during a twelve-year period in five prominent journals. It is telling that his concern focused as much on the abandonment of traditional social work practice with the poor, foster care and adoptions, and welfare policy as it did on the poor quality of the research. Samples were customarily unrepresentative, and methods were inadequate for the purposes of the studies.

Rosen, Proctor, and Staudt's (1999) fifty-three studies, presumably the most credible research published between 1993 and 1997 in social work and possibly in the personal social services, are tatters of science. Only seven of the fifty-three passed Santangelo's (unpublished) minimal screen: fifty research participants, randomized groups, and nontrivial interventions. Yet of these seven champions of the Rosen, Proctor, and Staudt tournament of valued research, only one study, by Bowen and Neenan (1993), cannot be quickly dismissed on methodological grounds, and this study concluded that assured day care failed to reduce reliance on welfare. Riccio and Hasenfeld (1996) suffer from the problems that bedevil any conclusion drawn from California's Greater Avenues for Independenceexperiment to provide jobs for welfare recipients (Epstein 1997). Icard, Schilling, and El-Bassel (1995) utilize outcome measures that are not directly related to the high-risk AIDS behaviors that justified their experiment in the first place. Three of the seven employed study groups of only about twenty: Magen and Rose (1994) come up with largely negative findings in spite of torturing their data for hope, while Rife and Belcher (1994) fail to identify the degree to which professional supports may have contributed to the success of the job club; Reid et al. (1994) exhibit small changes that may simply result from surveillance and not the elegance of intervention they claim, while one of their central measures, grade change, may be reactive to teacher participation. In an apparent replication of Reid et al. (1994) but with slightly larger samples, Reid and Bailey-Dempsey (1995) are also impaired by a lack of blinding in critical measurements but also an uncertain randomization procedure. Moreover, many of the seven studies simply ignore the demand characteristics of their experiments, the possibility that subtle encouragements by researchers and practitioners elicit compatible self-reports (i.e., confirmational responses) from participants rather than true changes in target behaviors.

These seven highly imperfect studies sit atop more than fifty years of research in social work. The remaining forty-six Rosen, Proctor, and Staudt studies are simply pitiful, including single subject designs and even case studies as valuable forms of program evaluation. Thus, the best research in the social services is so methodologically impaired and routinely trivial as to suggest the pointlessness of funding social service professionals either to develop study agendas in the first place or to evaluate their own enterprise.

It is ironic and even hypocritical that many of the scolds are themselves the purveyors of the very problems they decry, producing volumes of undistinguished research. The standards for acceptable research even in these critical commentaries remain lax and susceptible to a variety of serious threats to internal validity. Claims to effectiveness in the personal social services based on quasi experiments, pretest/posttest and single subject methods, and surveys remain problematic. Beyond the charm of comedy, it is worth wondering whether the lack of influence of the research is a commentary on the practitioner's true belief in her own efficacy or her rebuff to the improbable research itself or simply a case of thoroughgoing and willful ignorance.

The periods of doubt and the more common eras of credulity may both be accommodations to contemporary taste. During the quaint rebellions of the 1960s and 1970s, social work produced the mock heroics of public confessions. Then, recognizing the perils of acknowledged fecklessness, the literature quickly banished self-doubt, contriving evidence of effectiveness. But the body of the research, universally crippled by debilitating methodological pitfalls, fails to support any rational conclusion except indeterminacy and the wry supposition that the intellectual life of the social services does little more than endorse popular political preferences: skepticism in an age of doubt and belief in an age of faith.

Bulletins of Social Progress

The scientism of the personal social services is evident in the variety of bulletins of rational progress and watchtowers of the civic religion constructed regularly by even prominent presses. *Social Programs That Work* (Crane 1998) and *Violence in Families* (Chalk and King 1998) are as profoundly vacuous as the other innumerable attempts to retrieve personal social services from their morass of indeterminacy.[13] *Social Programs That Work* offers little credible testimony to the effectiveness of programs to compensate for educational deficiencies, improve nourishment, treat juvenile delinquents, provide employment for welfare recipients, and prevent drug abuse. To the contrary, the book's porous base of studies encourages skepticism toward the scholarly enterprise in social welfare, underlining its desperate search both for intellectual coherence and for effectiveness in the thin array of contemporary provisions for people in need.

The enumerated successes of *Social Programs That Work* (Crane 1998) are predicated largely on the heroic and charismatic efforts of a few supremely talented individuals who not coincidentally may be creaming a large underserved group to select a small number of likely candidates for success. Moreover, the programs are demonstrations that have not been routinized; invariably they recruit enthusiastic, special faculty to participate in experimental programs and cannot discount the unusual efforts and motivations of their staffs from their findings. All the presented successes are largely unreplicated and uninstitutionalized experiments that rarely acknowledge their idiosyncratic characteristics, preferring to abstract global conclusions of technical prowess from a tiny base of experience. As Crane points out, "[O]nly a small percentage of social programs offer convincing evidence that they generate both substantial effects and benefits that exceed costs"; thus this low success rate implies that "the very best programs [need] to be replicated on a large scale." Yet Crane is unwilling to consider that the successful programs (conceding the point for the moment), especially because of their rarity, are accidents of sampling or distortions of measurement.

Of the nine programs presented, five are educational interventions intended to improve basic academic skills. The four others were designed to improve nutrition, prevent substance abuse (two programs), and treat serious juvenile offenders. The nine programs are deemed successful because their gains are statistically significant, large, cost effective, and persistent, and most notably because the quality of the evaluation confers scientific credibility on the findings. Yet, in fact, the evaluations of the programs were in every case problematic. As Crane acknowledges: "Unfortunately, it is impossible to be sure that the distinctions between the treatment and comparison groups are produced by the program and not by initial differences in the makeup of the group. . . . [U]nobservable differences could be generating variable outcomes. Thus nonexperimental evaluations carry less weight" (1998, 16). Few of the evaluations were experimental, and the experimental designs were vitiated in each case by problems of representativeness and measurement. Crane concedes that in most cases "unique qualities" of the programs probably explain their gains, and that in any event these benefits often rapidly faded in the manner of Headstart. Moreover, because of the unusual circumstances of the experiments, the questionable evaluative procedures, and the difficulty in interpreting the meaning of the findings, Crane feels compelled to repeat again and again that the results are preliminary, conflicting with his insistent claim (and the purpose of the National Center for Research on Social Programs that subsidized the search for effective programs) to have discovered the North Stars of social welfare policy.

Yet it is simply laughable to assert that drug use has been prevented among adolescents by life skills training or that serious juvenile offenders have been treated when the evidence is at the level provided by the research of Botvin and of Chamberlain and Moore. The studies on life skills training and treatment foster care and most of the other research that Crane praises are stunning departures from customary rigor, not testimony to science.[14] Moreover, Crane's appreciation for mandatory work requirements, a defining element of the 1996 welfare reform legislation, needs greater appreciation for Mead's patent biases and the thoroughgoing problems, particularly the wildly inflated claims, of the manpower training literature itself.[15]

The nine programs and Mead's endorsement of mandatory work training presented in *Programs That Work* are corrective myths, endorsing the standard logic of professional intervention that socially efficient solutions to difficult cultural problems are possible within the context of existing social institutions, notably the school. Yet many of their very preliminary, questionable, and evanescent benefits are amenable to much different interpretation. Particularly the gains enjoyed by the Abecedarian program that began its interventions at the age of six weeks and by The Women, Infants, and Children Program hint powerfully at the need for intensive, long-term institutional equality more than the isolated value of bedraggled, partial, itinerant social welfare programs. That is, rather than a bit of an educational prop here and there, the deep issues of American deprivation need to be addressed by very costly surrogates for failed families, communities, schools, and employment. *Social Programs That Work* do not really work except to continue the fiction of social efficiency and to accentuate the political process through which social services are imagined, tested, and gussied up for social dialectics.

The experience of these programs belies any sort of coherent social decision-making process that addresses need, goal selection, comparison of alternatives, and then selection and implementation. Instead, and with the full-gospel choral support of prestigious institutions such as the Ford Foundation, these programs pass cultural muster as missionary dramas of abiding faith in the value of the individual, American progress, and the good works, volition, and grace of the program's apostle. The successful mission underscores the tenets of the civil church through programmatic attention to personal deviance while ignoring the structural deficiencies of American society. These Aesopian fables reinforce an extreme individualism (and social isolationism) through the euhemeristic myths of personal effort and earnestness in the character of the programs' developers. Without a single reference to cactus, sagebrush, a hanging tree, or a gunfight, the process assumes that social reform is a chapter in the book of the American frontier—the conflict between good and evil—that recalls John Wayne, Paul Bunyan, and Johnny Appleseed in the guise of each programmatic missionary. Diogenes the social worker is still on the road.

In 1995 the *New York Times* printed a front-page summary of an apparently successful experience, the Quantum Program, to motivate the average inner-city high school student toward graduation and college (Dugger 1995, 1). The program evaluations, by a Brandeis professor, *credibly* sustain its success: nineteen of twenty-five youths in the experiment graduated from high school, and eighteen went on to college, compared with only twelve high school graduates and seven who went on to college among the controls (Hahn 1994). The Quantum experiment employed randomized procedures, and its outcome measures were very hard, referencing easily corroborated objective conditions—graduation and college enrollment—rather than the uncertain self-reports of subjects or the judgments of service providers. Both the control group that received only what the school generally offered its students and the experimental group were composed of twenty-five randomly selected, entering high school students. The experimental interventions included a variety of tutoring and educational supplementation. However, at its heart the program depended on the skills of a counselor, "Reuben Mills, a brash, 22-year old youth worker fresh out of college," to motivate twenty-five new high school students for at least three years. Mills, an extraordinarily charismatic person with the sustaining motivation to improve life in the ghetto community in which he was raised, put in a week of endless hours and effort. He was also able to develop critical relationships with each of his charges: "What poor children from crumbled families and neighborhoods need most is an adult who cares about them and sticks with them for years" (Dugger 1995, 1).

Yet the evaluation of the program was in no way controlled for the unusual, if not unique, contributions of Reuben Mills and the unusual demonstration conditions under which he was recruited. There is no real success in a demonstration unless it can be replicated, and the Quantum experiment, like those cited in *Social Programs That Work*, reports its parables without consideration of the ideographic conditions that may account for their success. It is worth remembering that high school counseling departments and a variety of other therapeutic and community programs are set up precisely to mentor students in the manner of Mills. They routinely fail. Mills succeeded for four years, but his victory cannot be routinely replicated, and it is doubtful that he will put off a social and personal life in permanent sacrifice to cohort after cohort of incoming high school students.

Each one million problematic high school students would require forty thousand Reuben Millses willing to put in hundred-hour weeks for modest pay. The United States cannot provide a sufficient number of foster parents of even marginal quality, let alone a deluge of immensely talented mentors for troubled youth. The epoxy-resin attachment of the American people to the recurrent romance of *The Blackboard Jungle* has meaning as a dialectical form of social denial: difficult children succeed because of the skill and dedication of their teachers, and therefore greater and very expensive investments in family, community, and education are not needed. However, the preferences of the American people for small public budgets does not make much programmatic sense, relying as it does on prayer and the rare miracles of saints in substitution for institutionalized equality. The heroic efforts of Mills are heartwarming reiterations of American folklore that romanticize the unique value of the American character: the pioneer as social worker on the frontier of social need, the triumph of American ingenuity, the successful mission of personal faith in civic service, and, always, the superiority of the naive, intuitive, voluntary, innocent, tough-but-fair, amateur over the

bureaucratic professional, and always as an instance of a personal calling to service.

But the Quantum experiment and the parables and legends of *Social
Programs That Work* are not helpful social science but a diversion from the
reality and intractability of social problems in America. In just this way
and through the distortion of the social sciences, the Russell Sage Foundation and the intellectual life of the nation generally ennoble individualism in denial of social responsibility and possible remedy.

Similarly, *Violence in Families* (Chalk and King 1998) is a typical extrav-
aganza of the National Academy of Sciences (NAS) that customarily follows the institutionalized preferences of the nation more than the dictates
of science.[16] However, none of the base of research cited in the volume
provides any scientific authority for its conclusions and recommendations, which are to be understood as consequences of established social
values, not serious approximations of social reality. Speaking with the
NAS's typical evasiveness and chopped logic when facing tough questions, its Committee on the Assessment of Family Violence Interventions
scrupulously detailed the appalling condition of the field's research but
then blithely made recommendations that ignored its own criticisms.
Ironically, the committee even isolates the family preservation research as
providing "a rigorous set of studies [that] offers important guidance to
policy makers and service providers" (Chalk and King 1988, 294). But the
report ignores the most appropriate guidance of PFF and refuses to
acknowledge the futility of these heepish ploys. Rather, it recommends
that "intensive family preservation services represent an important part
of the continuum of family support services" (303). The startling contrast
between Rossi's (1991) condemnation of both family preservation
research and services and the NAS's report suggests very different
notions of science and therefore very different motivations in approaching social policy.

The committee's own commentary on the field's research into violence
in families undercuts its conclusions:

> It is premature to offer policy recommendations for most family violence
> interventions in the absence of a research base that consists of well-
> designed evaluations. However, the committee has identified two areas
> (home visitation and family preservation services) in which a *rigorous set of
> studies offers important guidance to policy makers and service providers.* In four
> other areas . . . the committee has drawn on its judgment and deliberations
> to encourage policy makers and service providers to take actions that are
> consistent with the state of the current research base. (Chalk and King 1998,
> 294, emphasis added)

The committee obviously ignored PFF and Rossi and just as obviously
set uniquely convenient standards of credibility for social research.[17] But

the committee would be left with no opportunity for its portentous wisdom about violence treatment and prevention—except that the outcomes of the programs are indeterminate and probably fictive—if it applied credible scientific standards to screen the base of studies. However, the literature's debased quality did not inhibit the committee from cold fusion pronouncements, accepted blithely by the nation's intellectual community without any of the recriminations that Fleischmann and Pons (Broaal 1991, 130) suffered. The purity of physics rebukes and derides the compromises of social welfare.

Indeed, to get past the weak research and come up with credible recommendations, the committee would need to invoke a broader social philosophy and connect it to a number of observations about programs designed to treat family violence. Those programs are short-term and superficial; they are almost universally focused on correcting embedded human dysfunctions through an individual, characterological, or subcultural approach. If family violence is to be either prevented or treated, then more attention may need to be paid to the social context of violence in America. That is, a structural strategy attending to the imperfections and inequalities of American society, rather than a treatment strategy focused on the individual, begs for consideration. However, the provision of greater social equality is much more expensive than social therapy or psychotherapy for perpetrators and their victims. Following its custom and assigned social role, the NAS initiates its presumably impartial, expert, and scientific investigation of a social problem with an ideological commitment to social efficiency that actually compromises any vaunted commitment to objective reality (and science). In just such a way, institutions of American life and the organizations they engender propagate embedded preferences in support of social policy.

Similar analyses come to similar conclusions about social services intended for foster children, the elderly, addicts, juvenile delinquents, criminals, the unskilled, the long-term unemployed, troubled children, adolescents, and adults, and so on. Indeed, foster children are uniquely deserving citizens, and the continuing, institutionalized failure to provide them culturally generous levels of care or to accurately describe their situations gets past any pretense of American charity to the nation's embedded cruelty.

Bulk-Cargo Empiricism and Hoo-Ha Science

Presumably, social progress entails shedding ineffective institutions and adopting those that work. The refusal to credibly evaluate the effectiveness of the social services generally, indeed, the distortion of objective and coherent research in order to promulgate corrective myths, denies society the ability to consider the value of its social arrangements. The research rarely conducts prospective experiments, and its few instances are marred by breeches of randomization, inappropriate measurement, reliance on recall, and confirmation biases. The more common study lacks controls or applies inappropriate controls, employs patently unreliable measurement instruments, ignores its own evidence in considering results, suffers from small, unrepresentative samples, and frequently relies on the practitioner's own evaluation of her work. The typical summations of the research smooth out its rough edges as Aesopian fables of social virtue and program effectiveness. As a consequence, the justifications of social services—the theoretical basis for expecting particular interventions to achieve defined social goals—have not been tested.

Nevertheless, the frog of research has been kissed into splendor by the princess of belief. The body of bogus research apparently constitutes an adequate political justification—sermons for the converted—for adopting corrective myths and applying the rule of social efficiency to social policy choices. Yet despite broad social satisfaction with the homilies of scientific prowess, all that has been produced is another twentieth-century update of a pernicious nineteenth-century Romanticism. Rather than a scientifically maturing body of methods for investigating social outcomes, the contemporary conditions of practice research and of the social sciences generally are little more than an advanced stage—a postmodern genetic sport—of Feynmann's bulk-cargo empiricism. Through the connivance of the researcher's own ambitions, the practitioner's self-regard, and society's convenience, hoo-ha science subverts rationality with the supreme subjectivity and smug self-assurance of exaggerated individualism in service to the frequent, mindless orthodoxies of culture. As a reasonable, thoughtful justification of contemporary social welfare policy, the corrective myth and its supportive literature are about as tasteless and unconvincing as a hairover.

Modern culture is easily susceptible to myth, and in this regard technology's modern communicants remain mystically in touch with their primordial germ cells. A clever artist is probably at this moment sculpting obsolete appliances into objects of high household culture—personal totems that restoreth with quiet piety both the soul and civil obedience. In spite of centuries of scientific realism, the need to believe, rarely impelled beyond itself as the curiosity to know, continues as the most profound human craving. The terror of uncertainty and chaos, tribalism and the vilification of rivals, greed, and above all an embedded cruelty expressed throughout American social welfare policy are constant and often dominant motives; the inescapable technological progress of contemporary culture is profoundly cheapened by the paleolithic emotions of its citizens. A candid, broad acceptance of ignorance (the most plausible summation of the research of the personal social services and its only true contribution to the policy debate) might be the best corrective for social conflict and its cruel consequences in social policy. It might also provide the core recognition for a binding humane consensus.[18] Despite oracular loyalty to the eighteenth-century patriarchs of democracy and the American way of life, the society operates off of profoundly Romantic assumptions—the clairvoyance of social saviors—about the nature of man and society, promulgated in the nation's civil religions.

Notes

1. Heritability is the "magnitude of genetic influence." It is estimated in twin studies as twice the difference between behavioral correlations of identical and of fraternal twins reared together (Plomin 1990, 48).

2. Here again, the lack of the FES's reliability, by decreasing the reported correlations between environment and behavioral outcomes and increasing their variance, conveniently increases the power of genetic explanations in support of MST's basic thesis. Bouchard and McGue (1990) should have more directly confronted the problems of the FES. In an apparent confusion of range and variance, they conclude, "The increased variance of the FES here relative to the normative sample demonstrates that restriction of range in the self-reported rearing environments of this adoptee sample cannot be the explanation of any failure to find significant relationships in the present study" (272) between the FES and personality. The same cannot be said about the increased variance caused by measurement error, which depresses any ability to estimate the true relationship. In addition, the groups of identical and fraternal twins apparently differ in key environmental variables: time together prior to separation (5.1 vs. 12.7 months, respectively) and total contact time (26.5 vs. 13.1 years, respectively; Bouchard and McGue 1990, table 1, 268).

3. The research procedures and climate may themselves create confirmation response bias. Did interviewers convey their expectations for the twins to report similarly? Did the biases work out differentially for different groups of twins? Are the twins recruited to endorse the heritability theses of behavioral genetics through the clubby atmosphere created in many twin, adoption, and sibling studies by Fourth of July get-togethers and celebrations at critical research junctures? In the manner of the Orphan Train Society or the dwarf cohorts studied at Johns Hopkins, is an esprit de corps created among the siblings as they sympathize with each other and search for comforting explanations of their behaviors? Do the researchers supply those comforts?

4. Unlike Murray, who is a committed political conservative with a long history of having a free way with data, Bouchard conducts his investigations without the baggage of racism, condescension, and social superiority. Rather than Bouchard's characterization of Murray as an intellectual gadfly, it is Bouchard who seems to fulfill this role by staying clear of extrapolations from MST to social policy, although the field of behavioral genetics does not seem to share this inhibition (Bouchard 1995).

5. Numerous studies, notably Fanshel and Shinn 1978, have employed IQ as dependent variables.

6. Early critical studies included Gottshalk Fox, and Bates 1973; Frank and Frank 1991; Park and Covi 1965; Errera et al. 1967; Strupp and Hadley 1979; Rieff 1966; Truax and Carkhuff 1967; and perhaps a few others.

7. Meta-analysis is a technique to compare the conclusions of disparate studies on the basis of effect sizes. An effect size quantifies the degree of similarity between experimental group outcomes and control group outcomes: the difference of means between experimental and control groups divided by the standard deviation of the control.

8. Lambert, Weber, and Sykes 1993 tended to confirm this observation estimating that placebo effects routinely accounted for 0.43 standard deviations (seventeen out of a possible fifty percentage points) of improvement. They even suggested that uncontrolled studies could be conducted by simply deducting this amount from reported outcomes. Unfortunately, the creation of a standard for placebo effects would only challenge the field to cross this hurdle in its poorly conducted research, with each generation of researcher facing an Olympic competition after each succeeding estimate of generational expectancy biases. See discussion of Rosenthal and Rubin, below.

9. Decoy research in the manner of Rosenhans' classic study (1973) has a great attractiveness to assess ethical behaviors in practice and even perhaps as a professional sting operation. If the FBI can hold congressmen accountable, then surely the American Psychological Association or some patients' rights group might decide to do the same with therapists. Psychotherapists would be visited by decoys with rehearsed complaints and presentations in order to evaluate (1) the consistency of diagnosis and treatment and (2) the proprieties of practice. Through a second method, effectiveness might be tested by randomly selecting community practitioners whose patients, past and present, would be surveyed relating to issues of ethics, as well as to satisfaction with practice and outcomes. Indeed, this sort of common accountability should be a condition of practice and licensing. Yet it is doubtful that 10 percent of practitioners would agree to such conditions.

10. See the commentaries by Hunt; Brock et al.; and Mintz, Drake, and Crits-Cristoph in the October 1996 issue of *American Psychologist*.

11. Brief portions of the description of PFF and the summaries of social work's outcomes in the next section are adapted from Epstein 1997.

12. More reasonably and traditionally, clinical significance is a more rigorous criterion than statistical significance for accepting findings. It presupposes that differences between control and experimental groups are not due to sampling error (chance) and that clinical value implies a certain minimum benefit. In this way, small but statistically significant results may not have a clinical value. Yet in light of the many small-sample studies, clinical significance has curiously come to imply large results that may not be statistically significant.

13. *Violence in Families* is one in a series of seven volumes. The yearly publication announcements from the herd of presses that attend to the social services—

the University of Chicago Press, Oxford University Press, and Columbia University Press, on the more literate, erudite hand, and Allyn and Bacon, DeGruyter, Sage, Wadsworth, and Brooks/Cole, on the other—list literally hundreds of similar volumes in numerous specialized areas. In the end, though, they all rely on the same sorry base of research. The two books chosen for analysis are among the best put together and best published, the champions of the field.

14. See detailed criticisms of Botvin's drug prevention research in Epstein 1995, 72–74, and of treatment foster care in Epstein 1999, 119–20.

15. See in particular Epstein 1997, chap. 5.

16. For a sample of the NAS's sacrifice of science to professional fashion, contemporary tastes, and bureaucratic imperatives, see Gerstein and Harwood 1990; Jaynes and Williams 1989.

17. The debilitating lapses of family preservation programs and research, along with other treatments for the violence that attends family dissolution, are discussed throughout Epstein 1999.

18. Then again, Ernest Becker would probably disagree, arguing that the denial of *The Denial of Death* is an impossible expectation for human existence.

Chapter 3

The American Ethos 1:
Two Civil Religions

The search for the determinants of social decision making in the United States (as well as elsewhere) has been frustrated by both methodological pitfalls and political considerations. The apparent organizational elements of American politics (interest groups, public opinion, elites, legislative coalitions, presidential influence, and so on) are probably the least fruitful areas in which to search. They are the temporary and coincidental elaborations of more fundamental processes by which society reaches consensus. In spite of their common association with live decision making, they are probably as inconsequential to policy outcomes as serving trays are to the quality of a meal. The formal organizations of social decision making can be described with some precision. However, they engage in processes that remain vague and poorly specified, converting the objective realities of economic conditions, social environment, and tradition into the sublime subjectivities of political choice.[1]

The apparent and formal entities of political decision making seem to mediate more fundamental social preferences that are institutionalized in the culture as a series of enduring behavioral patterns—family, peer group, community, education, entertainment, work, and so forth. These persistent organizations constitute the structures of society, its institutions, while the underlying preferences off of which they are elaborated constitute a civil religion. In its ecclesiastical role, a civil religion conducts the ceremonies and festivals that reinforce orthodox social values and consequently socialization and political cohesion. More important, however, a civil religion is the incarnation of the underlying preferences of the culture that legitimates claims on social resources. In this sense, the American civil religion coincides with American politics while, again, both are probably impelled by deeper social processes and preferences. While the American civil religion itself begs for explanation, it still appears to infuse culture with its binding authorities.

There must be something prior to the exercise of power, some telling point of legitimacy that can be separated from the processes that mediate decisions. In this sense, coalitions, interest groups, and the rest derive their influence from a source; they do not create themselves. A civil religion is the avatar of this source.[2] Yet, in turn, the source must be explained. However, with each regression from immediate effects, the methodological task becomes progressively unmanageable. Prospective data obviously cannot be retrieved from historical action, and the present always imposes its assumptions on the past.[3]

The consistency of American decision making over the years belies the contention that the society endorses a multiplicity of competing social visions even while it is seems hospitable to an immense diversity of peoples. The consistency of certain central choices throughout modern American history, especially relative to its socioeconomic stratification, contradicts the notion of great ideological diversity. To the contrary, a relatively conservative preference for subcultural and characterological explanations of social outcomes, with only brief interludes of national emergency that impelled situational remedies, has typified most social groups: the rich and the poor, men and women, blacks and whites, union and nonunion households, and so on.

The civil religion defines social problems, those conditions of society that are accepted as problematic and consequently those conditions that the society will try to change. Thus poverty has rarely been defined in the United States as a common problem of the culture but rather has been customarily understood to indicate individual failure, and usually grave moral imperfection. Consequently, programs to change the individual instead of the society have been central to American antipoverty strategies. While undercutting pressure on public purses, these policies have typically accepted the cruel inattention of a largely unregulated marketplace to the needs of poor and dependent people. The myth of self-reliance and personal responsibility is clasped to the American bosom even in the face of the overwhelming personal incapacity to modify events and the relatively few opportunities that the culture affords for even modest success. The quiet and meek acceptance by working people of their declining fortunes since the early 1970s is a true conundrum of political motivation, only unraveled by a pervasive civic puritanism that is hostile to the nation's republican pretensions (Luttwak 1999). Indeed, the socioeconomic stratification of American society is the central topic of political discourse, and its legitimacy is coincidental with the nation's civil religion.

Welfare policy, narrowly conceived as the few programs for the destitute, is particularly central to political discourse because it provides a widely attended platform to discuss the legitimacy of the socioeconomic stratification of American society, the most fundamental expression of its outcomes. Customarily, not even tax policy, annually affecting trillions of dollars, raises as much heat as the periodic debates over Food Stamps and Aid to Families with Dependent Children (AFDC), although the most recent welfare reform was occasion for more consensus than dispute between liberals and conservatives. Indeed, the country has reached broad agreement on what both the poor and the wealthy deserve largely because of a deep, abiding agreement on fundamental social and economic values that has rarely been disrupted.

Civil Religion

Rousseau and Tocqueville, and seemingly the entire literature of civil religion, discuss civil religion as an actual fully embodied institution of ritual, ceremony, dogma, clergy, and even church. Rarely is civil religion seen simply as a profound albeit amorphous institution of pervasive belief relying on transcendent authority, customarily divine but not necessarily so, to legitimate society's choice. The contemporary analysis of America's civil religion has continued with the same assumption, notably through the discussion stimulated by Bellah's (1967) seminal essay and continued more generally in the search for the determinants of America's political choices.

Yet religion as more than the sociology and history of particular organizations and social structures is the incarnation of particular values that actually determine social choice. While the idealized statements inspired by civil religions are frequently revealing of aspirations, and particularly the hopes that rebound from unacceptable reality, they more frequently obscure the effective beliefs of a culture, the operant motives that determine its social policies. Formal religion, ceremonial religion, public religion, and public theology are ritualistic in simply reiterating the established canon of power, its justifications for particular social and political choices. The invocation of equality, freedom, democracy, plurality, and tolerance as touchstones of the American ideology and the clichés of every patriotic gush has very little to say about the continuing inequalities and unfreedoms of American life. The civil religion of a society, to the extent that it exists, most importantly includes the society's actual values and the forms in which those values are justified, this latter including rituals, ceremonies, historical allusions, and even specific sectarian religious texts. Civil religion, while certainly including the elaborated sanctions for social choice, also recognizes the less dogmatic and doctrinaire, the more mystical processes that actually create tradition or at least mirror the changing plate tectonics of social experience. Thus, in order to separate the proactive from the reactive, and the creative from the expressive functions of civil religion, it is crucial to distinguish what is mere ritual from the pervasive attitudes that precede or coincide with social choice.

Civil religion is a metaphor of religion, more than the actualization of a broad Judeo-Christian tradition institutionalized as a secular or nondenominational church (although this is also frequently the case). The American civil religion is composed of deeply held, nearly ubiquitous beliefs that may predetermine but at least justify social policy choices and indeed sectarian religious practice as well. These beliefs largely conform to the tenets of philosophic liberalism at the heart of modern conservatism: faith in the market instead of government, with the consequent preference to rely on the mystical ability of the invisible hand rather than the Holy Ghost of central planning (or social engineering) in pursuit of democratic and republican goals; subcultural and characterological rather than structural (i.e., situational) explanations for social outcomes; and, therefore, a fierce determination to hold individuals responsible for their own social and economic standing.

The heart of these beliefs seems to conform loosely to Puritan and Calvinist Protestant theology. Bellah, Linder, and Davis, among many others, have followed Weber in assuming that religious morality— the theological commitments of particular churches—strongly influences numerous secular outcomes, notably capitalism. However, recalling Tawney's criticism of Weber, it is worth considering that no line of causation has been proven. Against Weber's theme, capitalism may have created Protestantism, or both may be the complementary products of more fundamental factors. Yet whatever their origins, a series of beliefs that are invoked in justification of social choices appear to be embedded in American society. Thus, it is not the empty formalism of the American tradition of freedom and equality that creates power, but rather the broad and pervasive attachment to actual values (which are frequently quite ignoble, parochial, predatory, self-centered, injudicious, bigoted, narrow, and cruel) that legitimates social choice as the will of the people, signs of God's favor, and evidence of American exceptionalism.

The democratically held preferences of American society, their ubiquity and depth, rather than any idealized, transcendent source of divine right, actually create authority, although appeals to the spiritual and divine usually embellish broadly popular choices as the common cant of social decision making. The statement that these values are the tenets of America's civil religion recognizes, on the one hand, their endurance and their elevation to the level of gnomic, self-discovered truth and, on the other hand, the series of goals and objectives that are naturally promoted by the state as it fulfills its democratic mandate. The banal fact that democracy frequently leads to injustice seems still to be true.

Not surprisingly, a cohesive society creates a cohesive series of beliefs, whereas a fractured society hosts many fiercely competitive social visions. But all social factions, in pursuing legitimacy and authority (power), invoke their beliefs not simply as empirical propositions but as religiously sanctioned, inveterate truths that transcend the mundane but also impose concrete conditions on society. American social welfare policy has been very consistent through the years, largely because American society, despite its violence, has also held to a consistent set of conservative social values. The fact of social parsimony and its frequent cruelty does not fly in the face of the society's civil religion but rather serves to mark a line between its vaporous and ceremonial claims to decency (or at least continuity with its creation myth) and the tenets of its operative consensus. This consistency between the nation's institutionalized values and its social policy choices has been justified within a civil religion, fiercely defended as articles of secular faith, but faith nonetheless.

The frequent heartlessness of the operant American civil religion may isolate the affections of the spiritual Christian, but it does not change the popularity of its tenets nor the degree to which the American people are passively content with its effects. Rationality has played little role in American social welfare decision making, which has worked itself out through the self-evident splendor of the nation's history and destiny. Religion, notably civil religion, is not just an idealization of faith but an adjunct to political necessity. Accordingly, social welfare policy in the United States has been a conscious choice and for historically coherent reasons—the self-perceived convenience of powerful groups. While its form has occasionally changed, its meaning has remained largely consistent for the poor and lower-status groups that consistently lose out.

Dying in 1778 and spared the excesses of the French Revolution, Rousseau, who coined the phrase "civil religion," was able to preserve an Enlightenment fervor for "rational" social interventions that included a state-sponsored civil religion to create "a system that was a single whole, that is to say a good one" (Rousseau 1954, 209) Rousseau's civil religion functioned for social cohesion and republican values:

> [E]ach citizen must have a religion requiring him to cherish his duties. . . . Outside of these areas . . . each citizen can hold any opinions he pleases. . . . It follows from the above . . . that the sovereign is entitled to fix the tenets of a purely civil creed, or profession of faith. These would not be, strictly speaking, dogmas of a religious character, but rather sentiments deemed indispensable for participation in society—i.e., sentiments without which no man can be either a good citizen or a loyal subject. (Rousseau 1954, 219–20)

Rousseau invoked through the state the sublime role of standard religion—"an ultimate sanction capable of putting the law above men" (Sherover 1980, 117, quoting Grimsley)—by combining secular and theological authority in a civil religion:

Rousseau's principle in the purely civil profession of faith is that of the need for a commitment to the import of the possibilities of freedom. It is a recognition that free institutions require a kind of devotion akin to that traditionally associated with religious commitment. It is a recognition that an organized community must be able to presuppose the loyalty and good faith of its members. (Sherover 1980, 121)

The recognition that a pervasive ethos creates harmony among social institutions has inspired political radicals and visionaries, including the literary list of the Enlightenment, as well as Marx, Lenin, and Mao, to create artificially what society failed to provide naturally. Less ambitious and less prescriptive, classic American reformers, the founding patriarchs, and other moderates as well also subscribed to the obvious usefulness of common beliefs in creating a nation. However, none have proven the ability of their planned interventions to do so: the French Revolution descended into blood and dictatorship; the communist revolutions, notably in China and Russia, seem to have killed as many as they converted and without achieving republican ideals; the reformist tradition of American society may have perversely facilitated the depravities of the market at the price of societal decency. In this light, America's very modest personal social services and welfare programs, designed to realize socially efficient reforms, have compromised every role except as ideological ceremonies of the operative civil religion. Rousseau argued against an *exclusive* national religion and in favor of religious tolerance. Still, he never let go of the notion that the state should promote republican ideals forcefully as religious tenets, so strongly did he believe that a nation "cannot possibly survive with a population of bastards," that is, with citizens unbaptized into the civil sacraments of a nation.

America's early republicans, notably Adams and Madison, had less grandiose expectations for central control and opted, in conformity with philosophic liberalism, most notably the strain professed by the Scottish Enlightenment, to allow civil society to determine its own principles without imposing a "civil profession of faith" (Kelly 1984, 241). Tocqueville applauded their restraint, finding in the Protestant religious diversity of the early republic the source of its civic virtue. Tocqueville, the enthusiast of the American experiment, even felt that a mature civil religion drawn from Puritan roots was realized in the United States. Kessler 1994 applauds Tocqueville for "capturing, as no one else did, the essence of mainline Christianity in the 1830s, that is the various ways it accommodated to equality in order to insure its survival" (169–70) and thus sustain the civil religion.

In fact, however, in his discussion of equality Tocqueville was actually capturing the essence of individualism that America derived from Puritanism's assumption of the equality of souls rather than any equality of social circumstance. Equality of the soul underpins the Puritan doctrine of free agency—the ability, indeed the obligation, of each individual for moral choice. Thus, American individualism, predicated upon the belief that each person has *in fact* the freedom to determine his or her moral worth, is secularized at the core of America's civil religion as the belief that each person also has the freedom of opportunity to determine his or her own social circumstances. In this way, as an extreme form of personal responsibility adapted for America's operative civil ethos, Protestant moral equality, the object of Tocqueville's comments on religion in the United States, comes to justify social inequality. Tocqueville, in spite of his frequent imitation of Dr. Pangloss, could not have been blind to the reality of American society in the 1830s—almost a century before the enfranchisement of women, at the height of American slavery, and with a deep antagonism toward native Americans and many immigrant groups. Throughout *Democracy in America,* Tocqueville subtly employs the theoretical and moral sense of equality to gloss over, indeed to tacitly justify, much of the apparent social and economic inequality he surely witnessed.

Documenting the frequent victory of ascriptive civic ideals in American social policy, Smith criticizes Tocqueville and Hartz as apologists for the early American republic. Indeed, the rhetoric of reaction and ascribed assumptions of group inferiority are baneful companions of every American impulse for change and participate forcefully in America's social dialectics (Hirschman 1991). While today predatory ascriptive isolation is not legal, its companion attitudes are common enough to explain the meanness of traditional American social welfare policy and by extension a large portion of its social and economic stratification. It is telling that the United States is more segregated racially almost four decades after the civil rights legislation of the 1960s than it was during the Jim Crow era (Massey and Denton 1993).[4] A large portion of the American experience substantiates Rousseau's comment about civil and theological intolerance: "[W]herever you find either of the two you find the other" (Rousseau 1954, 221).

The Ceremonial Civil Religion

Bellah's (1967) seminal essay clarified the lineage of the American civil religion, although he preferred to view civil religion as the ritualization of the society's "highest aspirations." Along with many of his contemporaries, Bellah largely ignored the conflict between the nation's operative civil religion that provides political justification for social choices and what he and many others thought it should be. Indeed, Bellah's statement of the American covenant—a myth of origin, a chosen people, salvation, worldly success, tolerance (cultural pluralism), and hostility to alternative forms (notably socialism)—has a universalist quality. There is pathos and perhaps even blindness in the insistence that the nation conform with its lofty ideals as though these ritualistic aspirations were actually intended as more than the subterfuge of historical continuity and political authority. America is like other cultures in proselytizing its civil mythology of exceptionalism through public rituals of divine favor, supracultural truth, and its unique historical, if not actually evolutionary, importance for all mankind.

However, it seems pointedly naive to take a nation's legends as archaeological evidence of cultural reality and insist that folklore is the operant core of civic preferences. The religion of daily life has a more trenchant relation to individual choices that as group preferences perhaps explain what a society collectively decides. While the wellsprings of common action may be veiled from consciousness, the actual choices themselves are frank and obvious, especially as they are enacted into public policy, which at least in the United States is usually an afterthought of the society's private realities and agreements. Put another way, whatever a society chooses to do—cruel or humane—it justifies in socially coherent, although by no means rational, forms. Its actual civil religion is displayed in the persistence and consistency of specific policy choices that conform with its preferences. In this sense, a civil religion is necessarily a "more generic form of religion," but largely because the society provides a common and binding social experience and a demotic understanding of that experience.

Religion itself, as either church or belief, probably reflects social experience more than it forms it. Civil religion obviously serves as "a doctrine of solidarity" (Kelly 1984, 233). However, the solidarity is incidentally a product of its beliefs; more important, social cohesion reflects common experience that acts through tenets of a civil religion as guides to common action, that is, private behavior and collective, policy choice. Rational inquiry and reasoned discourse are incapable of discerning the elements of a civil religion, let alone imposing it on a nation. Notwithstanding the adventures of sociology, society works itself out in mysterious ways and with only the rarest departures from profoundly subjective, that is, political processes.

Following Bellah (1967), civil religion in the Unites States is constructed from "certain common elements of religious orientation that the great majority of Americans share" (4). It is expressed through a set of both theological and secular beliefs (e.g., salvation and individualism), symbols (e.g., icons, crosses, and the American flag), and rituals. In serving civic ends, God is in her Ten Commandments mood, "unitarian" as well as "on the austere side, much more related to order, law, and right than to salvation and love"(7). God displays her special concern for America as the promised land communicated through the rhetoric of the civil religion that embellishes close parallels with the ancient Israelites (if not always modern Jews) and their flight from bondage in Egypt (the Old World): "God has led [her] people to establish a new sort of social order that shall be a light unto all the nations" (8). The rhetoric of patriotism is the devotional focus of public ceremonies—Thanksgiving, Memorial Day, the Fourth of July, and so forth—that constantly reinforce the sacred conformities of American obedience. While the civil religion is quite specific in form, mandating the touchstones of public discussion, it retains a flexibility, characteristic of the social institution of the church, at least to accommodate to the style of contemporary discourse and preferences. Past the empty formalism of beliefs in an amorphous catechism of liberty, justice, and equality, the public rituals of the civil religion lack substance, simply providing a civil communion, a renewal of membership in the body of the republic.

Bellah and most others who explore American civil religion are particularly concerned to trace the lineage of the public ceremonies and rituals, most frequently noting the continuing influence of Puritan and Calvinist theology, historical traumas such as the Revolutionary War and the Civil War, and the revelations, epiphanies, and commitments of America's philosophes, notably Adams, Jefferson, Hamilton, Madison, and Franklin. In place of the dogmatic assurances of the prophets and the original patriarchs of the Old Testament, "the words and acts of the [American] founding fathers . . . shaped the form and tone of the civil religion as it has been maintained ever since" (Bellah 1967, 7). Bellah, for one, was initially sanguine about America's civil religion, which "at its best is a genuine apprehension of universal and transcendent *religious reality*" (refusing to consider even briefly the possibility of this oxymoron in his construction). In his early essay, Bellah occasionally acknowledged antidemocratic uses of the civil religion: "American-Legion type of ideology . . . to attack nonconformist and liberal ideas and groups of all kinds . . . manifest destiny . . . the shameful treatment of the Indians." Yet in the next breath he retrieves its idealistic value, since "it has been difficult to use the words of Jefferson and Lincoln to support special interests and undermine personal freedom" (14). Yet, quite obviously, Bellah restricts the civil religion to euphuistic state speeches and not to the nation's consistent preferences for denial and parsimony that still persist.

Bellah gave greater definition to the nation's civil religion in later works that also expressed his distress and perhaps a sourness, notably occasioned by the Vietnam War and continuing poverty, that its universal ideals were ignored in the social reality of policy choice (Bellah 1975; Bellah and Hammond 1980). Yet he consistently derives the moral tenets and forms of the civil religion from textual analyses and not from the direct scrutiny of American opinion, intentions, and choices. At least in this regard, Bellah's analysis and similar ones, caught in the ethical formalism of theological exegesis and its dogmatic limitations, largely fail to appreciate the subtleties of societal processes and the determining regularities of culture.[5]

As Mead 1977 argues, the Old World religions were modified for the needs of the new republic. His simple thesis turns on its head Bellah's ubiquitous assumption that "the common moral assumptions" of a society "rest upon a common set of religious understandings" (16). Indeed, it seems as reasonable to assert that morality, as a preference for particular behaviors, mediates social experience and thus determines formal religion and civil religion as well. Yet Mead's preference to explain American belief as an extension of the Enlightenment Christianity of the founders is as romantic a notion as Bellah's, drawing a line between the intuitions of the historian and the obligatory rigors of social science, if not always of the social scientist.

"The darker side of history tends to be phased out" in handling civil religion, notably during the founding period of the republic (O'Brien 1999, 83). Mead might have profitably contrasted Jefferson's political imagination—Enlightened, humane, democratic, and republican—with Jefferson the successful politician.

> The spotlight has been on the benign things that Jefferson said, from time to time, about—for example—Indians and slaves and not on what he actually did, and refrained from doing. He said many benign things about American Indians on familiar "noble redman" lines. But his instructions to American officials dealing with Indians were free from such sentimentality. Finding that such officials were trying to check the access of Indians to firewater, in order to save their lives, he instructed such officials to desist from such interference with the natural course of things. The sooner the Indians died out, or at least declined into helplessness, the better it would be. The custodians of the civic [sic] religion tended to dwell on the nice things he said and to ignore the lethal harshness of his actual policy. (O'Brien 2000, 83) The "great Virginian" was also no champion of blacks and hoped to repatriate them to Africa, having concluded in his *Autobiography* that "native habit, opinion has drawn indelible lines of distinction between" the races (O'Brien 2000, 83). Which lesson of the founders was learned: the theological and civic posturing, or the pragmatic and facile concession to the cruelty of popular social policy, or both? Civil religion as effective hypocrisy, that is, political melodrama, is not adequately appreciated.

Yet Marty (1959) and then Herberg (1960) raise tolerance to the level of "ultimacy" in America's civil religion, recognizing its political and social value but critical of its reflective emptiness. Marty describes the emergence of a post-Protestant "religion-in-general," a fourth American communion that serves as its civil religion. He laments its reduction of the Bible's magnificent God to "a harmless little divinity," understandable and manageable, comforting, "an American jolly good fellow" who serves the secular ambitions of believers. At its core, Marty's civil religion is based on "faith in faith" that draws its content from the demands of secular society for cohesion rather than from any supracultural ethical doctrine. Yet Marty sees great value in America's civil religion, its "over-arching nationalization of that religion-in-general which is the product of the erosion of particularity and which makes religions' distinctions irrelevant" (178). Consequently, tolerance as cultural pluralism, the heart of American democracy, becomes very salient.

Influenced by Marty, Herberg identifies the civil religion of America as the common ground, the melting pot, between Protestantism, Catholicism, and Judaism. Yet religion of democracy, the "authentic character of Jewish-Christian faith," is falsified, and the faith itself reduced to the status of an American culture-religion" (Herberg 1960, 262). With only the vague content that Marty defined, the established religions promote the value of faith itself ("the positive attitude of believing") to worldly success, cultural enrichment, personal contentment, peace of mind, and spiritual euphoria: "So thoroughly secularist has American religion become that the familiar distinction between religion and secularism appears to be losing much of its meaning" (Herberg 1960, 270). As a consequence, American religion has become "so empty and contentless, so conformist, so utilitarian, so sentimental, so individualistic, so self-righteous" (270). This bothers Herberg considerably, since he argues that the role of a proper value-based religion is "prophetic transcendence" in judgment of both social and personal behavior. In contrast, civil religion "has always meant the sanctification of the society and culture of which it is a reflection," and in particular the "religious validation of the social patterns and cultural values associated with the American Way of Life, notably laissez-faire capitalism" (263). Rather than acting as a brake on the civil religion, the church religions have been overwhelmed by social imperatives, with both becoming apologists for the culture as it is practiced.

Williams (1952) not only applauds the notion of American civil religion as the religion of democracy but also argues that "the state must be brought into the picture; governmental agencies must teach the democratic ideal as religion" (371):

> I see no escape from the conclusion that, in the present world situation, America runs a grave danger from lack of attention to the spiritual core which is the heart of her national existence. If we are to avoid this danger, democracy must become an object of religious dedication. Americans must come to look on the democratic ideal . . . as the Will of God or, if they please, the Law of Nature. They must strive for a common understanding of this ideal and for a devotion which taps the deepest motivations. The times demand a dedication which is comparable to Christian and Jewish dedication at their best. (368)

Williams's enthusiastic faith in democracy, implying political plurality and tolerance, was understandable as a contemporary reaction to fascism and communism. Yet it remains ethnocentrically naive in explicit advocacy of the "metaphysical sanctions" and "ceremonial reinforcements" of a civil religion established by government. Indeed, while retreating to the rhetoric of public corruption and moral crisis, Williams is curiously oblivious of the traditional reluctance of American philosophic liberalism to cede great discretion to central government and of the nation's historical suspicion of all power, including church power.

Compulsion, as Mead insists, was a common device to protect the faith of fourteen centuries of orthodox Christianity. The attitude of intolerance, while not actually commemorated by any of the civil religion's rituals, has certainly been a characteristic part of the American ethos through four centuries of social policy: witness the pervasive and long-standing interpersonal violence of the society itself; its reaction to labor organizing, unpopular political factions, and civil rights protests; its bare-knuckle rites of passage into at least male adulthood; and its contemporary bloodlust for the death penalty. While "Enlightenment" Christianity seems to have slowly replaced its "orthodox" precursor, the substitution has occurred more in the ceremonies of the republic than perhaps in its decisive beliefs. Indeed, the civil religion of the United States reconciles both forms through a series of common rituals and a bland ahistorical civil catechism whose function is less to reflect underlying values than to provide a sense of continuity with the Genesis myths of the republic and its manifest righteousness.

Yet tolerance, or perhaps the appearance of tolerance, was not a triumph of the spirit that suffused the United States either in its infancy or as a mature postindustrial nation. Rather, it emerged from the political failure of fiercely self-confident religious factions to secure a ruling consensus and impose their own particular religious styles. The United States may have been saved from a theocracy of Christian mullahs more by the irascible ethnocentricity and intense bigotry of its immigrants than by any democratic, republican mood that they brought along with them or learned here. Ironically, a nation brimming with protections for minorities and the faith of the founders in equality and democracy has frequently abided, perhaps complacently, the abrogation of basic rights and civic tolerance. The political desire to suppress those protections has persisted through centuries in the breasts of America's Sunday republicans.

The Operative Civil Religion of America

Among many others, Smith's (1997) compendium of America's historical improprieties documents the failure of religious tolerance as a social ethic. Mead traced this divide to the early religious pitfalls of America: "[T]he separation of 'Salvation' from social and political responsibility; the appearance of offering a choice between being a faithful church member and being an informed and loyal citizen of the Republic" (Mead 1977, 132). America's civil religion repairs the pitfall by confounding moral impulse, enshrined for popular tastes as evidence of exceptional divine favor, with decisive social preferences. Civil religion develops sacred rituals of secular ideals to provide mystical (gnomic, following Bloom 1992) justification for more profane choices: peace pursued through war, intolerance in the service of an accepting society, and above all a self-certifying, self-revealed assurance of truth. A sheepishness—perhaps ontic depression in the guise of morality—sublimated into both myth and idealized public ceremony prevents the frank adulation of cruelty. While cruelty and a mean parochialism often dictate social policy, the republican values of generosity and greater equality may be dangerous to denigrate. Rather, the subterfuge of myth played out through the idealized rituals of the civil religion encourages the tranquil dominance of popular preferences—the operative values of the civil religion—and a tentativeness toward their wisdom and propriety.

Indeed, the civil religion of the United States may be the primary ideological pitfall into which the nation has stumbled, encouraging a civic profession of faith through amateurish and disingenuous voluntary associations at the expense of effective action through government. Mead traces the civic impulse to Lyman Beecher's theology, a form of social gospel. While the moral incentive originated in the churches, such voluntary associations were independent of the churches and were not the churches in action; they did provide "an influence . . . distinct from that of the government, independent of popular suffrage, superior in potency to individual efforts, and competent to enlist and preserve the public opinion" (Mead 1977, 130, on Beecher).

This lofty mission was degraded in the reality of pathetic social programs such as the Y's and the settlement houses, as well as the charity organization societies of the Progressive years that continue today among the multiplicity of voluntary and charitable organizations that, among other more directly political roles as policy advocates, provide personal social services while fulfilling other roles by advocating particular social welfare policies. Individually and collectively, these agencies and their services are better understood as the programmatic failures but political successes of social efficiency than as serious confrontations with social need. The programs themselves are the social welfare rituals (the corrective myths) of the civil religion.

It is difficult to find in the gravitas and religiosity of Lyman Beecher or his children, Harriet and Henry Ward, or their well-educated, well-meaning, and financially unchallenged friends, the least hint of hypocritical intent or insincerity. Yet they could not protect the presentation of their motives, and their noble impulses were unkindly appropriated to construct an elegant justification for the small-government, incessantly private preferences of America's civil religion. Indeed, the good intentions of the Beechers have been diverted through numerous modern epigones to authorize the cruel ceremonies—the personal social services and contemporary public assistance—of the operant civil religion, the antagonisms of the American public toward dependency and the poor.[6] Perhaps the Western religious mind, Enlightenment Christianity, the post-Protestant national religion-in-general, the religion of pluralism, and theological analysis itself will attend to the immaterial epiphanies of the spirit in neglect of concrete political conflict. However, it is more likely that political consensus will shape its justification through the gaseous moralizing of public sanctimony, its "nationalistic religiosity" (Marx 1974, 225).

It is curious how infrequently the public rituals of the civil religion are questioned as windows into the nation's soul: in reference to the 1960 opening of Camelot—the Inaugural Speech—"Bellah would have us believe that President Kennedy and his supporters really were committed, above all else, to a global struggle against tyranny, poverty, disease, and war" (Marx 1974, 224). There is a stolid refusal to interpret religion in its operative sense; its rituals are taken on their face while, Herberg and others insist, that the American civil religion is both noble and "the operative religion of the American people supplying American society with its overarching sense of unity amidst conflict" (Richey and Jones 1974, 8). Herberg is no booster of Main Street, but he still fails to probe the religion of Americanism past its smugness.

Civil and religious ritual is frequently a form of denial that, in extolling the virtuous and ideal, provides a tacit excuse for the vulgar motives that actually explain social choice. In this way, the American civil religion that issues the text for Memorial Day—"celebrative of democracy, the constitution, and national unity, of free enterprise economics, of social egalitarianism and, most interesting, of religion" (Richey and Jones 1974, 8)—camouflages as patriotism the embedded intolerance of the operative American civil religion, its quiet sanctimony and ingenerosity toward the unchurched, unorganized, and unrepresented. The ritualistic religion of American republicanism needs to keep posted before itself the reality of the nation's rejection of republican forms, notably the extraordinarily low turnout of voters, with fewer than 50 percent of eligible voters participating in even presidential elections.

Customarily, religious rituals are substantively vague emotional lozenges that commemorate patriots, heroes, saints, and prophets. Through communion in the sacred, they endorse the righteousness of believers. Participatory ceremonies encourage self-certification and revelation of superiority and chosenness. In this way, the public rituals of the American civil religion can be reinterpreted as essentially ethnocentric, nationalistic, nativist, and even idolatrous, providing tacit permission to restrict the franchise of the United States to a group of chosen citizens, in other words, permission for intolerance and suspicion, and a warrant to ostracize the outsider, the renegade, and the heretic. Therefore, the true test of a religion is witnessed in the quality of its believers—what they do. In this sense, the true meaning of the American civil religion is found in the social policies it inspires. The struggle of intellectuals and saviors over social ideals is very different from engagement in the choices of society; their eviscerated studies flatten out as evocative decorations for patriotic events: balloons, party hats, and noisemakers. At worst, they are simply generating propaganda and a justification for its dissemination through government.

Yet in calling for a renewal of the American civil religion, populist fantasy—"a language born of the common American life"—perversely assumes that the depravities of American society have been the wreckage of voracious elites, that somehow broad democratic participation is a curative for a stony heart, that Rousseau's general will and the will of the people are synonymous (Shanks 1995). Shanks has given this romance its greatest elegance as civil religion. Unlike the functionalism of Bellah, Herberg, and others "concerned about the sacralization of good social order," his civil theology is intended to inspire a republican epiphany among citizens that avoids any role as handmaiden for the state or for tradition (5). Rather, in Shanks's hands, "the affirmation of the proper independence, from the state, of civil society" (7) is a sophisticated reprise of a social gospel as much committed to freedom of the civic spirit as Lyman Beecher's children were abolitionists of chattel slavery. Europe's Christian Democrats and America's "biblical Christians" could take heart from a view of civil religion as the Golden Calf: "Indeed its seems . . . that in a certain sense, today, the practice of prayer has acquired a whole new purpose. Namely: to operate as a medicine against propaganda" (11). Very much in the Williams school of democracy as civil religion, Shanks proposes a "good civil religion: where one deliberately drops one's defenses against the critical voice of the outsider. In the uncivil world such voices are shut out by propaganda on the one hand, and by official secrecy on the other" (13). Yet again, in pursuit of the ideal, there is little attention to operative religious beliefs or to the reasons for them. Fierce commitments to populist democracy, even buttressed by generous public education, and to the curative power of free debate have the ring of historical denial, the aesthete's blindness to life as it is lived.

Social Ethics

Similarly attending more to civic salvation than to the perversities of social choice, the attention paid to social ethics also produces otherworldly moans from the sanctuaries of monastery and academia. After two thousand years of Christianity, the world has still failed to achieve Shanks's "anti-politics" of goodness, perhaps suggesting that the natural experiment of religion will not resurrect Eden. Indeed, Christianity has far more often acted as the idolater of the state rather than its recusant or critic: the behavior of the Vatican during the Second World War, the Inquisition, witch trials, scapegoating, torture, forced conversions, expulsions, the bloodletting of state churches. Yet even recognition of these misfortunes has little power to slake the fervor of conservative American Christianity for its righteous centrality in guiding the nation's morality: "[A]lthough civil religion may resemble Christianity at many points, it is far different from the biblical faith and should be exposed as an ersatz faith, a substitute religion which has no legitimate claim to the allegiance of Jesus' disciples" (Linder and Pierard 1978, 136).

Betsworth is enchanted with the self-validating postmodern truth that "narrative is the form of rationality especially appropriate for ethics, a conviction that one story is more adequate than another in enabling one to recognize truth and to conform one's character to that truth" (1990, 181). This revolution in human consciousness is pressed, of course, in spite of the fact that it does not seem to work out that way except as a narrow reflection of largely uninformed and ingenerous self-interest.

Weighing in against authoritarianism and the tyranny of the market, Hearn (1997) is also oblivious of political history in recommending yet another revival of localism, "the sociological option, and it may become more prominent as more people recognize the futility of finding security in the market economy and the welfare state" (174). Recalling a previous generation's "backyard revolutions," Hearn scratches up evidence for this epiphany of societal transformation from a few case examples of neighborhood self-help in which the poor but industrious citizenry realize the hopes of Jeffersonian democracy through after-school tutoring and art classes, nightly street patrols, and voluntary home health services of questionable duration, reliability, and quality.[7] He forgets the failures of a century of community organization and development, of socialist and populist politics, of contemporary labor union organization, and of the debacle of the citizen organization impulses of the 1960s, its War on Poverty. These failures are long associated with the absence of concrete goals; electoral fraud; cronyism and nepotism; the minuscule turnout of residents, members, and citizens to participate in committees and meetings after the kickoff barbeque; co-optation of leadership; the creation of authoritarian elites; and, the worst affront to the crusading reformer, recognition that the noble citizenry were largely content with things as they were. Yet judging from the nation's operative civil religion, it is most likely that the sociological option will continue to be less often chosen as people find little pleasure in neighborhood politics that exhaust them through hours of unpaid effort made in futile substitution for professional services and that realize in the end only the emptiness of the intellectual's tin plated republicanism. Indeed, lessons in participatory democracy have not dispelled the fatalism and torpor of working-class life, less often teaching the joys of neighborliness than the plebian wisdom that it is better to be rich than poor.

America's broadly democratic choices—the free market over tight regulation and high taxation; parsimonious public assistance over generosity; social isolation over social integration—are frequently cruel but justified through a civil religion of daunting historical consistency. The American romance with its polished goals cheapens national discourse by its refusal to come to grips with the predatory in American life, acknowledging the powerful evidence of embedded civic preferences for inadequate and even mean social policies. America's civil religion as public catharsis through festival, ritual, and oratory exaggerates its ethical and moral idealism, concerning itself with the formalism of civic piety at the expense of the perfervid social attitudes that actually affirm social choice. While religion itself may frequently take on the serious aesthetic and spiritual burden of the sacred in social life, civil religion as a necessarily political consensus cannot; it is profoundly mundane and profane.

The ceremonial civil religion essentially restates Enlightenment ideals, transmitting the chosenness of the American people. It is bland and inoffensive, providing the binding ceremonies of historical continuity. However, the operative preferences of the United States, applied with the intensity of revealed truth and personal salvation, have consistently endorsed conservative values. Enacted in social policies that sustain the high-risk, high-penalty lottery of personal success and wealth, America's operative civil religion specifies its preferences for extreme individualism and for market freedoms over the role of government in addressing social injustice and economic inequality.

Rousseau's Bastards

The theological critique of public faith frets over the loyalty of its rituals to republican and ethical ideals. Well and good as far as this stale tour through the American museum goes. Bellah and the others who created a scholarship of the American civil religion pick through the ruins of national cathedrals, Gettysburg Addresses, and Macy Thanksgiving parades as though they were unearthing the essential commitments of an Enlightenment civilization, too self-conscious and modest to utter its own noble reality. Yet America's ceremonies of commemoration and its rituals of solidarity subtly convert the sacred vapors of national tragedy, sacrifice, and suffering into the fog of national denial. The process springs spontaneously from willing citizens demanding a mythology to sweeten their operant ethos—their cruelty and selfishness—as morally imperative and historically true.

A more pointed sociology of the American civil religion begins with the inveterate and pervasive opinions of the American people that are associated so hermetically with their policy choices that they are to be understood as either reasons for choosing, or justifications for having chosen, or both. In this light, civil religion, whatever its actual ethos, binds a nation together, providing a common reason and justification for its policy choices. Its idealized rituals and symbols—"scepters and crowns, fried oysters and velvet gowns" (Marquis 1930, 24)—especially as paradoxes of its operant values, are forms of denial, myths that reconcile aspiration to the reality of its preferences, which are most frequently not simply accommodations to the ineluctability of nature but an expression of a very judgmental, if not actually free, collective will. Theologically, the nation's departure from its ideals seeks a remedy in an epiphany of the good. Sociologically, the nation uses the ceremonies of its civil faith as instances of national convenience in propagating its embedded values. America's national cohesion is secured by broad and historical agreement over common beliefs and shared forms of denial. This well-integrated and well-defended national personality, its operant civil religion, seems closed to any glib strategy (couch, gun, or appeal to decency) to challenge its cultural choices.

Contrary to Rousseau, a nation does thrive with citizens who reject the sacraments of decency. America has contrived a harmony between its civil religion and its social policy notwithstanding the piteous wails of its aesthetic Christians and its feckless liberals. The discussion of an American civil religion has customarily been "a pastime for intellectual elites," which would not necessarily be a problem if it concerned only water polo or croquet. However, these moralizing intellectual elites are usually also social, economic, and near-hereditary elites disengaged from the common experience of citizenship and carrying a unique stake in its future (Kelly 1984, 223). Not surprisingly, in many of these hands the civil religion has been shaped as a vehicle for preaching and edification, for proselytizing a patriotism of idealized values—religion-in-general, culture-religion—that nourishes their own conception of republican obligations and virtues.

Yet the notion of a civil religion in contrast simply to a civil ethos is quite valuable in amplifying the emotional environment in which Americans have chosen a consistent series of social welfare policies. Indeed, religion distinguishes a complex of values held by faith that emphasizes the profoundly subjective, even mystical, rather than the coherent and reasonable, let alone rational, manner by which citizens come to believe in the correctness of their values. The devotional commitments of America's civil religion, its actual preferences, are to be found in the pervasive and intense beliefs of the American people that consistently accompany and justify their policy choices, as well as in the provisions of the policies themselves. The actual civil religion is very different, far crueler, than the ritualistic prose of its ceremonial form.

The two perspectives from which public belief is analyzed—sociological and theological—are in conflict with each other, largely because the preference for text, monument, and public profession of faith interprets the civil religion on its face as an idealization of experience. The weakness for accepting ritual as institutional truth is understandable in the community of religious scholars whose goal is to define the apostolic standard for moral and ethical behavior. The theological community, producing the nation's manpower for the ceremonies of life's transitions, is content with the disparity between ideals and behavior that not parenthetically marks the mission for many of their churches. On the other hand, the sociology of any cultural institution seeks objective and perhaps even rational explanation for a variety of outcomes, in this case social welfare policy. Objective analysis avoids at least the pitfall of regressing to the fantastic in order to approach the ideal.

The actual choices of the American people speak volumes about their basic values. Public opinion surveys open windows into the beliefs of America and Beelah for one picks through presidential speeches as though they were a special disclosing fluid. However, as long as the argument can be sustained that American social policy is a democratic expression of the nation's desires, notwithstanding an elite imposition here and a purchased legislature there, the programs of the welfare state themselves are the most accurate estimate of the operative American civil religion.

Notes

1. Indeed, these political processes may even be ineffable and perhaps a bit mystical, since awareness itself of change and of the preferences of political players has unpredictable effects on the direction of both social tastes and, consequently, political choices. At best, empirical research describes the elements of politics, identifying coincidental relations. Rarely if ever does opportunity present itself for more trenchant causal analyses.

2. Yet civil religion is not as diffuse a notion as the earlier idea of national character. The search for national character, notably by Sorokin, Znanieki and Wilson, and others, stumbled into numerous pitfalls of chauvinism, methodological absurdity, and an abiding authoritarian rigidity that sought to fit rococo reality into the convenient, tight categories of cultural pride. By itself, the constancy of ascriptive ideals in American politics should be sufficient to mellow ethnocentric vainglory into pensive indecision.

3. The most debilitating assumption is the symmetry of cause—that historical and contemporary actors are moved by similar motives and that similar material elements had similar social, political, and psychological meaning. This proposition of historical symmetry is itself untestable in both fact and theory. If one could take a time machine back to survey prior attitudes, the first effect would certainly be a disruption of the past by the visitors and their survey instruments.

4. Recent declines in segregation patterns since Massey and Denton's 1993 analysis have been relatively small (Taylor 2000).

5. Apart from those listed below, Richey and Jones (1974) expanded Bellah's sense of civil religion but still maintained a central theme favoring it as a statement of the avowed and the ideal but never as operative preferences, that is, a justification of the actual ethos.

6. The resurgence of "faith based social welfare" and "compassionate Republicanism" is a more explicit statement of this antagonism. It is not that George W. Bush has adopted from Olasky a remarkably quaint anachronism of service dating back to the Gilded Age and its slavish attention to the social whims of the robber barons. Rather, he has correctly identified patrician charity, along with its implicit and harsh denigration of recipients, as the will of contemporary voters. This idea of highly discretionary charity suffuses the 1996 welfare reforms, a widely popular piece of legislation.

7. See, for example, *The Backyard Revolution* and the other operettas of localism, including Alinsky's fulminating sentimentality (1969).

Chapter 1

The American Ethos 2:
America Speaks—The Polls
and Policy Choice

The ideological logic of centering an analysis of policy making on public opinion is structural, substituting embedded belief for the more common demographics of economics, housing, social status, family patterns, race and ethnicity, and the rest. It is an open question as to what controls the operative and enduring ethos of the United States—whether the conscious, moral sense of the American people, or simply the received values by which they continue to abide, or both. However, the fact of a culturally coherent series of preferences is less ambiguous. This civil religion, while certainly associated with the accomplishments of America's extraordinary high culture, also seems to carry along, perhaps even as the price of its success, an unfortunate malice of unconcern.

American citizens' beliefs in civic obligation and social welfare are described in hundreds of opinion polls conducted since the mid-1930s by numerous independent organizations. However, these types of surveys are circumscribed severely by a number of technical and interpretive faults and ambiguities.[1] Nevertheless, the polls provide a more democratic and direct test of the existence of an American religion than the exegeses of historical speculation, especially those with little empirical foundation that simply screen text and ceremony through the author's own worldview. Still, the direct interpretation of actual social policies, so long as the criterion of democratic choice is met, is perhaps the best indication of America's preferences.

More than six decades of polls describe a surprising consistency of American public opinion both across time and among groups. While there is apparent evidence to support the notion of social progress in the United States, advances have consistently been accompanied by an intolerant disregard for the needs of many groups. However, the evidence of progress becomes less compelling as the "philosophic" opinions of the American people—their support for a ceremonial civil religion, the touchstones of patriotic identity and historical continuity—are separated from their attitudes toward specific public policies.

Customarily, a great consensus supports public social welfare policies. At least superficially, there appears to be little evidence of a contentious rift between elite and popular attitudes or between public policy and public opinion. In light of the harmony of opinion across most sub-groups, the question of whether the population has become mesmerized by elite propaganda or whether leadership actually represents the will of the people becomes operationally unanswerable. Yet the fluidity of the American decision-making process rebukes those who insist on specific conspiracies of elite interests and therefore on the inherent innocence and goodness of "the people" that would be released through more authentic democratic participation.

While culture itself is the grandest of all conspirators, American politics are open, elites are often deeply in conflict with each other; information is ambiguous and frequently inaccurate although famously available; judgment is impaired; coordinated manipulation of national opinion is too costly and complicated to hide; and, most tellingly, the winners in the American game, notably businesspeople, are broadly admired and envied. The profound freedoms of ultimate choice are so frightening and chaotic, bringing psychological nihilism to the front of consciousness, that propaganda—the convincing sophistry of partisan doctrines—is probably accepted gratefully as comforting delusion. If the American people are led, it is certainly neither blindly nor unwillingly; they put on their own harnesses.

American public opinion toward social welfare, rarely generous or accepting, has become increasingly conservative, with declining evidence that Americans put much faith in structural, that is, situational, explanations for social outcomes. To the contrary, what appears to be the American public's reflexive and empty endorsement of freedom and tolerance is translated into a broad and deep sense that individuals are largely responsible for their own outcomes, that the economy and society play a small role in determining winners and losers, saints and sinners. Perhaps for the first time since the 1920s, the national discussion of welfare that led up to the public assistance legislation of 1996 quickly reached a broad consensus on the need for changes that enacted stringently charactero-logical assumptions about personal deviance.

The optimistic reading of American social welfare policy and attitudes (e.g., McClosky and Zaller 1984; Cook and Barrett 1992) is easily amenable to a far gloomier interpretation. Similarly, the long tradition of mining rationality from the opinion polls, continued eloquently by Page and Shapiro (1992), tends to confound the ritualistic, congregational responses of the American public, perhaps the result of too many public school repetitions of the Pledge of Allegiance and "God Bless America," with the underlying policy consensus. The Enlightenment notion of progress through rationality is too quickly applied to American society without attention to the ambiguities of surveys, notably response falsification, or to the actual meaning of the public policies that have been enacted and repeatedly sustained by many different groups of Americans. Americans report belief in the generalized republican virtues of democracy at the same time that they report more specific attitudes and preferences that endorse a cruelty and meanness of purse toward those in need.

Still, the surveys seem to indicate that tolerance has been increasing over the years, and some traditionally deprived groups, notably African Americans, Native Americans, Hispanic Americans, homosexuals, and particularly women, appear to be making socioeconomic headway, at least over the long haul.[2] At the same time, American attitudes seem to broadly accept the quickening pace of economic inequality while endorsing public policies that rigidify those differences; working people and the poor in the United States have been harmed economically and socially throughout the recent decades of globalization, technological change, and economic growth. Yet Americans, including stunning proportions of the groups that have been harmed, are clearly advocates of the negative freedoms of the marketplace while consistently and characteristically opposed to the positive freedoms that only government seems capable of providing. As an extension of the preference for the marketplace, the advances in American public life have been more procedural than substantive, more formal than real: a growing enfranchisement across the expanse of American history but a declining use of that franchise along with growing economic and social inequality.

It is facile and perhaps too solicitous of political vanity to reach the judgment of recent American history that the nation has made notable social gains even while conceding that it still has a ways to go, implying as it does a moral growth that parallels the size of its gross domestic product. The United States may have made progress, but it is still a relatively unforgiving place, offering its prayers of obeisance to a number of sinister influences. Indeed, its cruelty, hallowed in its operative civil religion and tediously masked by the emphatic patriotism of its public rituals, has a tradition that is as long and profound in American history as the nation's westward expansion and economic imperialism. America reaches for the narcotic of ascriptive inferiority as quickly as it pours veneration into the cups of its successful businesspeople.

In a masterful compilation of extensive polling data, McClosky and Zaller (1984) demonstrate an ambiguous American ethos: "[T]he welfare state, like laissez-faire capitalism, remains deeply controversial" (282) among the general public as well as among elites. Americans appear to recognize "the enduring appeal of the traditional values of independence

and self-reliance" (270) that lie at the center of subcultural and characterological explanations for social outcomes. During the Second World
War and eight years after the passage of the first Social Security Act, 44
percent of Americans considered that a "cradle to grave" program of
minimum security was "impossible and undesirable"; in 1958, 53 percent
of Americans thought that "the government should just let each person
get ahead on his own" (another 23 percent were neutral); in two separate
polls conducted between 1975 and 1979, about 50 percent of Americans
thought that "the poor should help themselves," while only about one-
quarter thought they should "receive special government help" (another
25 percent were neutral; McClosky and Zaller 1984, table 9–1, 271).

At the same time the American people overwhelmingly—sometimes
in excess of 80 percent—appear to endorse government assistance when
citizens "cannot find jobs, have no visible means of subsistence, or seriously need help" (272), attitudes at the core of structural ideology. Yet the
American people quietly endure high rates of homelessness and unemployment with little complaint against government. McClosky and
Zallers's liberal optimism that "only about a third of the American public
now accepts the notion that the poor are poor because 'they are lazy and
lack self-disciple,' and even fewer (24%) believe that poverty is caused by
the failure of the poor 'to try hard enough to get ahead,'" is bracketed by
nonresponse rates within the questions of over 50 percent (268). That is,
more than 50 percent of respondents "decline[d] to choose" (125)
between the structural and the subcultural options, a sleight of intellect
by McClosky and Zaller that raises questions about the extent of masked
bias in the rest of their analysis.

McClosky and Zaller endorse the common perception of social
progress in the United States while acknowledging a tension between the
ideologies of "democracy" and "capitalism," a duality that largely repeats
the contrast of liberalism with conservatism and of structuralism with the
subcultural and characterological point of view. Yet they rely on a historical reading of social policy to interpret the contradictory data. They conclude from the growing "regulation of business . . . in almost every sphere
of economic enterprise" that "the democratic tradition is more securely
rooted in the nation's political culture than is the capitalist tradition" (293).
The triumph of liberal democracy—the republicanism of more classical
analyses—grows out of their general findings that ideology matters and,
curiously, that the public tends to support those social welfare programs
that conform best with capitalistic individualism. Nonetheless, their gloss
of regulation neglects the long-standing criticism that the regulatory agencies have been co-opted by the regulated industries. Their analysis also
obscures the reality of the social welfare programs themselves, assuming
an effectiveness in addressing need that few actually realize. Their conformity with "capitalistic individualism" translates into an uncritical rati-

fication of market judgments that impede the ability of the American welfare state to address poverty or even to secure a comfortable retirement for most workers. Indeed, the United States remains the least effective among the modern industrialized nations in reducing poverty through taxes and public transfer programs (Gilens 1999, 205).

More problematically, the reported preferences of the American public can in great part be understood by the choice of words and the context of the survey questions themselves (see note 1). "Cradle to grave" seems to be a daunting, even authoritarian, expression of public responsibility that discourages agreement. "Letting each person get ahead on his own" is more benign than the cold distance of "the government in Washington"; an expression such as "our national government" would carry a far warmer, more inviting connotation. Sentences that begin with "in order to improve their condition" predispose a respondent toward a response of self-reliance by suggesting that the condition of people is their own responsibility. Indeed, methodological pitfalls reconcile the reported contradictions of McClosky and Zaller's data better than their quick interpretation of American history. As a result, the possibility of entrenched individuality and a permanently ascendant "capitalistic" culture seems at least as likely as their rejuvenated democracy.

In a frequently cited work, Cook and Barrett (1992) reduce the ambiguities of McClosky and Zaller, seeing in the reported ethos of the American people a desire for sharing and tolerance that flatly contradicts the popularity of Reagan's retrenchment of the liberal welfare state. In spite of the electorate's clear preference for the Reagan presidency in both 1980 and 1984, Cook and Barrett insist that the American people strongly desired an expansion of the welfare state in 1986. They found only the merest desire to decrease any of the seven largest social welfare programs among the public or Congress. Only 8 percent of congressional respondents and 16 percent of the public wanted to decrease Aid to Families with Dependent Children (AFDC), and only a quarter of each group wanted to decrease Food Stamps, the least popular program. In contrast, a majority of the public wished to increase Social Security, Supplemental Security Income, and Medicare, while a substantial proportion of the public favored increases in Medicaid (47 percent), Unemployment Insurance (32 percent), AFDC (33 percent), and even Food Stamps (25 percent). Moreover, taken together with the large percentages of popular and elite opinion that wished to maintain current levels, the support for the welfare state, and an expanded one, seems overwhelming (Cook and Barrett 1992, tables 3.1 and 3.4)Yet even on their own terms, the data are easily amenable to reinterpretation as the great support of the American people for a very minimal and inadequate welfare state, which is its reality, and even for the appearance of charitability and generosity but not its substance.

In addition, Cook and Barrett's data show that members of Congress—the elites—as well as the public hold a high priority for the provision of food and cash assistance to disabled and poor elderly, while the congressional respondents ranked the needs of poor children as the highest priority. Still, Cook and Barrett are loathe to actually question the sincerity of these opinions by considering the actual, long-standing inadequacy of these types of programs or the inaction in legislatures (national and state) to mount improved interventions, notably for children in public care. Indeed, the contrast between the reality and the report of the needs of impoverished elderly, let alone those of poor children, begins to suggest the limits of opinion polling in probing the public's true intentions. The most recent congressional revision of the child welfare laws (the Adoption and Safe Families Act of 1997) is perhaps even rebarbative, hardly in keeping with a notion of elites working for their own priorities, fulfilling their reported preferences, or pursuing noble goals.

Yet Cook and Barrett's survey is also deeply flawed methodologically, not only by wording and the positioning of its questions but also by an unfortunate sampling procedure.[3] Their analysis consistently interprets the superficial conformities of respondents with the ceremonial clichés of good citizenship and the standard pulpit morality as though they were the public's live preferences. Cook and Barrett defensively reach back to a 1944 study in order to conclude that the anonymity of their survey in collecting responses is adequate to overcome the respondents' defenses and obtain their non–socially desirable attitudes. Furthermore, they argue that in 1986, at the height of President Reagan's popularity, a socially desirable response could fall on either side of their questions. Yet a phone survey is not quite as anonymous as they insist; there is, after all, a warm human interaction between the respondent and the interviewer that probably elicits agreement with the standard virtues, notably charitability, of the nation's ceremonial civil religion. Respondents were essentially repeating public rhetoric. President Reagan, as the most prominent example, always defined the poor as the beneficiaries of his policies—securing for them a noble independence and improving their moral worth—even while those policies diminished their welfare by cutting their cash subsidies, failing to provide jobs, and putting many out on the streets.

The preponderant reports of more than sixty years of polling provide data that depict a great consistency between elites, popular opinion, and the actual choices of American social policy (Gilens 1999; Teles 1998; Public Agenda 1995; Shapiro et al. 1995; Mayer 1992; Shapiro et al. 1987a, 1987b). These data starkly refute the fillip of popularity that Cook and Barret, or even McClosky and Zaller, give to welfare state liberals. At the same time, these analyses provide little evidence to sustain Page and Shapiro's (1992) belief in the growing rationality of the American public.

To the contrary, they begin to suggest a characteristic indifference, even spitefulness, toward fellow citizens and a consistent deceptiveness, perhaps hypocrisy, in reporting beliefs.

Public Agenda's (1995) survey, conducted shortly before the welfare reforms of 1996, enumerates pervasive American attitudes: an overwhelming proportion of Americans want to help the poor and even think that government has an important role in doing so. However, the specificities of helping hardly evoke the gentle Cub Scout's supervision of a geriatric crossing or the hospital vigil of a concerned community or the biblical nobility of anonymous charity or a grandmother hovering over the hungry and the sick. The "philosophic," or ritualistic, attitude of compassion masks a far crueler series of preferences that largely explain the severity of American public assistance. Although 59 percent of the general public feel that "the system costs taxpayers too much" (Public Agenda 1985, 40), they apparently report less concern with the cost of welfare (even though perceptions of its true costs are wildly inflated) than with its insidious effects: "By more than four to one (65 to 14 percent), Americans say the most upsetting thing about welfare is that 'it encourages people to adopt the wrong lifestyle and values . . .'" (9).

In line with this sentiment, huge proportions of Americans, and very similar proportions of both blacks and whites, believe that "people abuse the [welfare] system by staying on too long and not trying hard enough to get off" (73 percent); "welfare is passed on from generation to generation" (68 percent); "people cheat and commit fraud to get welfare benefits" (64%); "welfare encourages teenagers to have kids out of wedlock" (60 percent); and so forth. Only 13 percent of all repondants feel that "welfare benefits are too low." Nineteen percent feel that "the system makes getting benefits a humiliating experience," although it is not clear whether respondents approve of this or not (Public Agenda 1995, 40).

American's perceptions of welfare recipients are deeply condemnatory, and it is quite likely that the antagonism toward the welfare system itself is a displacement of these attitudes. However, blacks and whites occasionally differ in their attitudes toward recipients, but then usually only slightly. "Compared to other Americans," 49 percent of blacks and 67 percent of whites feel that welfare recipients are "more likely to think that society owes them something"; "are lazier" (45 percent vs. 53 percent); and "have fewer job opportunities" (48 percent vs. 45 percent; Public Agenda 1995, 47). Quite notably, these small differences imply an interracial consensus on conservative, characterological themes.

With such great belief in both the harm that the welfare system causes and the characterological problems of the recipients, the public reports great enthusiasm for stringent, if not actually harsh, changes in existing programs: "surprise visits to the homes of welfare recipients to make sure they deserve their benefits" (64 percent); "requiring enrollment in job training and education programs" (77 percent); "not increasing benefits when mothers on welfare have more children," that is, "family caps" (60 percent); "putting a strict time limit on how long people receive welfare benefits" (57 percent); "requiring welfare recipients to do community service, like cleaning parks, in exchange for their benefits" (57 percent); and so forth. These demands are even more constrained than the frequently discretionary provisions of the 1996 welfare reform act itself. Still, only 19 percent of respondents wished to reduce benefits, while 68 percent supported day care, and 55 percent would continue Medicaid for welfare recipients when they went to work. Many other surveys (e.g., Weaver, Shapiro, and Jacoba 1995), agree that Americans believe passionately that welfare recipients should work—no free rides—while they are reluctant to acknowledge hardly any condition under which the seemingly healthy are excused from work or conformity with common values. Indeed, the belief in a large number of able-bodied poor, today's "sturdy vagrants," is a catechistic pillar of the operative civil religion more than any sort of objective fact. It is an expression of true faith, revealing more about the believer's political commitments than about salvation.

The American public is also traditionally very reluctant to develop the supports necessary to provide work. While most Americans say they want health and child care benefits to follow welfare recipients into work, they have provided little live support for legislation (e.g., universal child care and public jobs) that moves in this direction. Furthermore, almost all the assumptions behind the public's prevalent attitudes toward both welfare and welfare recipients are incorrect: a more expansive definition of welfare (largely coextensive with programs for low-income people, not just the poor) consumes only about 10 percent of the federal budget, whereas a definition restricted to the poor themselves includes welfare programs that cost no more than about 3 percent of the federal budget;[4] many adults on welfare cannot work, suffering injuries and illnesses that are debilitating but not severe enough to qualify them for Supplemental Security Income; jobs are frequently unavailable; welfare payments are terribly inadequate, providing through AFDC (now Temporary Assistance for Needy Families [TANF]) and Food Stamps typically less than 60 percent of America's very stingy poverty line; housing assistance outside of public housing is rare; the public seems pointedly oblivious of the fact that two-thirds of welfare recipients are children; the vaunted programs of the 1996 welfare reform are either unfunded (training and education), underfunded (child day care and Medicaid), proven failures (family caps and case management), speculative (time limits), or obnoxious intrusions that have caused more resentment than virtue (surprise home visits, bureaucratic discretion, counseling).

Public Agenda sums up the "values that we live by" as helpful, frustrated, perhaps occasionally misguided, but well-meaning. Gilens (1999), however, may be closer to the operative truth and still consistent with the reported data. He places the onus for inadequate welfare policy on the "negative stereotypes" and free-market beliefs held by the American people, although he dances delicately away from a confrontation with frank racism and meanness. After all, inadvertent misperceptions are fairly easy to correct by better media coverage, but racism would seem to be socially implacable, especially after so many decades of civil rights activism.

> One reason that America has not devoted more resources to fighting poverty is the public's concern with the undeserving poor. Americans' cynicism toward welfare recipients, sustained by misperceptions of the racial composition of the poverty population and negative stereotypes of blacks, limits the easiest and by many accounts most effective anti-poverty measure: giving money to those who lack it. The distinction between the deserving and the undeserving poor is an old one, as is the stereotype of blacks as lazy. . . . The already existing belief that blacks were lazy contributed to the negative media coverage of the black poor over the ensuing decades, and this coverage has in turn helped to perpetuate the stereotype of blacks as lazy and the black poor as undeserving. (Gilens 1999, 205)

Gans (1995) has argued that the long-standing negative stereotypes of the poor are being ascribed to a growing concept of an American underclass, perhaps supplanting despised ethnic groups and races as the demons of public discourse. The American underclass may contain a disproportionate number of blacks and other minorities, but, more important, it provides an interdenominational, equal-opportunity, color-blind stage for the nation to play out its social melodramas of civic virtue and a righteous depository for its cathartic wrath.

Stability of Attitudes over Time

Despite a plangent republican and democratic voice in the polls, a more telling series of social attitudes have been largely consistent and antagonistic toward the provision of welfare for as long as systematic opinion surveys have been conducted. These values constitute the operative core of the American civil religion that inspires the self-deceptive rituals of public life. The strong subcultural and characterological strains of individualism in American thought, often masking a darker tendency toward ascriptive denigration, express and summarize the way that the American experience has been taken to heart by Americans. These are constant forces that accompany social progress as a strong minority opinion, but they are often the determinative motives that explain public policy, political success, and American civil society. American ways of doing things become institutionalized in American culture not necessarily because they realize American goals but frequently because they simply symbolize and enact American preferences.

Teles (1998) argues forcefully that in one important regard American attitudes toward welfare have changed. Between 1961 and 1993, he reports, there was a reversal of opinion in the proportions of Americans who felt that "too little" or "too much" was being spent on welfare: fewer than 10 percent in 1961 but 55 percent in 1993 felt that too much was being spent on welfare, whereas 60 percent in 1961 but 20 percent in 1993 felt that too little was being spent. At the same time, Americans consistently endorsed preferences for work over cash assistance. These preferences, he argues, were not reflected by "elites," which for Teles contains only intellectuals, not wealthy interests or even elected representatives. "In American democracy, the public needs elites [intellectuals] to give form and structure to their preferences, if those preferences are to have social and political impact" (Teles 1998, 165). Thus Teles concludes that the 1996 welfare reforms were widely popular but successful legislation was frustrated for decades by divisions among intellectuals that blocked the design of appropriate programs to realize the public's desires. Teles supports the 1996 welfare changes as moves in the right direction in spite of the opposition of many thoughtful analysts.[5]

However, as Schiltz (1970) documents, by the early 1960s, Americans' antagonism to cash relief had simply returned to the customary levels of the 1930s and 1940s. But for one outlier in 1948 and another in 1961, consistently small proportions of Americans have supported increases in public assistance (Schiltz 1970, 152). Indeed, Teles (1998, 48) seems to make far too much of a single 1961 poll.[6] Yet he is quite in line with the body of polls that report Americans' transcendent belief in work. Even in the depths of the Great Depression, with unemployment over 30 percent, fully 55 percent of Americans agreed that "there are many persons in your community on WPA [work relief] who could get jobs if they tried" (Schiltz 1970, 156). The extraordinary stamina of this denial even in the face of pervasive economic collapse contradicts any sense of the public as rational or even as compelled by objective social and economic reality. Indeed, the national antagonism to public assistance gives impetus to thedenigration of those in need—lazy, improvident, and immoral—as the ostensible grounds for cheapening their claims. In the end, Teles probably exaggerates the political conflict over welfare between intellectuals and the public. Moreover, rather than any dramatic change, popular attitudes toward public assistance over the decades have been very stable and actually hostile to those in need, notwithstanding the refulgent, global goodwill. Thus, while affirming steadfast American attitudes, Mayer (1997) takes liberalism to task for its own losses and not the nation for any imagined conservative shift.

The major problem with contemporary American liberalism is not that public opinion has grown more conservative, but that liberalism itself has
moved *too far* to the left. Over the last thirty years, the basic set of policy
positions espoused by American liberal[s] . . . has undergone a profound
transformation that has set them at odds with large segments of the American public. (Mayer 1997, 318, emphasis in original)

Cleavage among Groups

The cleavages of American public opinion are both rare and customarily
small (Shapiro et al. 1986; Schiltz 1970). Consistent opinions exist even
across the natural divisions of class, race, and gender. On classic questions of group interest, race appears to be one of the few exceptions, but
even this is diminishing (see Shapiro et al. 1986; Public Agenda 1995,
tables 6 and 7).

Page and Shapiro (1992) provide one of the rare comparisons of social
attitudes across income groups. Based on data from the General Social
Survey between 1972 and 1990, they conclude that "Americans of high
and low income . . . disagree somewhat about" social welfare. Yet the
largest differences, those between "upper income" and "lowest income"
groups, rarely exceed twenty-five percentage points, while changes from
year to year are largely parallel among all groups.[7] However, once differences between the very wealthiest and poorest groups, the upper and
lower 10 percent, are removed, attitude differences among the remaining
80 percent of income groups are insubstantial, with approximately 50
percent of all groups customarily reporting through the years that too
much is spent on welfare. Differences between the top and bottom
income deciles in the percentage reporting that too much is spent on welfare were less than 30 percent in about half of the years between 1973 and
1998; in the remainder, they were about 40 percent. The absence of substantial differences by income is all that much more surprising because
family incomes among the bottom 10 percent fell well *below* the poverty
line in virtually every year. While the top and bottom income groups of
African Americans differed by similar amounts, fewer African Americans
than whites felt that government was spending too much on welfare. The
difference between African Americans and whites of about 25 percent in
1972 decreased over the years; by 1998 there was hardly any difference by
race.[8] Moreover, attitudes toward welfare are also largely similar among
ethnic groups and between men and women.

The pattern of immaterial differences across time and income groups
as well as a consistent "substantial parallelism" in changes from year to
year characterize reports of happiness, life purpose, community participation, and attitudes toward politics, organized labor, government, help
for the poor, and so forth. The consensus appears hostile toward a large-

government, redistributive agenda and satisfied with life in general. Yet whatever the ambiguities of interpreting specific polls and responses, the more telling point is the degree of agreement. Even many of the very poor seem to agree that they should be that way.[9]

Quite naturally, the great attitudinal consistency of Americans across time, income, ethnicity, and gender groups has stabilized the roles of social welfare programs—the insurances, as well as public assistance and the personal social services. The most significant changes have included the addition of Medicare and Medicaid in the 1960s; increased real Old Age Insurance payments and consequently increased replacement rates; the creation of the Supplemental Security Income program that federalized indigent relief for the elderly, the blind, and the totally and permanently disabled; and the welfare reforms of 1996 that eliminated the AFDC program and its provision as an entitlement for the poor. But in spite of these changes, the American social welfare system reflects a deep political consensus to provide only parsimonious and inadequate care.

Social Insurance

Many early criticisms of the basic Social Security pension program—OASI, now OASDI and Medicare—are still pertinent today, perhaps more so. "In many respects the [early] law was an astonishingly inept and conservative piece of legislation" (Schiltz 1970, 41, quoting Leuchtenberg). While the base of coverage was restricted in 1939 to about 55 percent of the civilian workforce, by 1996 its coverage was nearly universal, about 96 percent (except as noted, all data from Ways and Means Committee 1998). However, benefits are still inadequate, especially for low-income workers, who typically retire without additional income or savings. In 1996, the average monthly benefit was barely above poverty levels, providing only $759 for retired workers and $1,186 for retired workers and their spouses. The maximum family benefit for an average wage worker was $1,666 per month but represented a payment threshold that only a minority of retirees crossed. Social Security retirement replaced less than 60 percent of the preretirement income of low wage earners in 2000, with estimates declining to less than 50 percent by 2030. Typically and logically, complementary retirement income declines with wages; thus, low wage earners typically have no income when they retire other than their Social Security checks. Social Security payments constitute more than 80 percent of the entire incomes of the poorest 40 percent of retirees; 18 percent of beneficiaries, typically the poorest, rely entirely on Social Security (Social Security Administration 1998). While Social Security keeps an enormous proportion of the elderly above the poverty line, almost 50 percent of all aged households lived on incomes below $15,000 per year in

1996; about 30 percent lived on less than $10,000 (Social Security Administration 1998).

While retirement test exempt amounts appear to be generous, especially after 1996, only about one-third of the 9.5 million eligible recipients under the age of seventy elected to work, and the overwhelming number earned less than $10,000 per year in 1994, while 42 percent earned less than $5,000 per year. The recent decision to eliminate the retirement test altogether will affect only a small number of retirees, usually the wealthier ones. At the same time, the tax strategy for the program is at best proportionate and, in consideration of an upper limit on the earnings base, regressive (notwithstanding the small minimum benefit).

The rustic expectations of the 1930s do not carry over well to the new urban millennium. The framers of the Old Age Insurance program assumed that the income needs of workers would decline as their children became self-sufficient and their homes were paid for, the two largest expenses of the middle years. Therefore, replacement rates of only about 50 percent would be sufficient, especially when augmented with savings. Unfortunately, few if any workers with modest incomes are able to save substantial amounts for their retirement or work part-time; they typically are not part of other retirement plans; medical expenses, notably for coinsurance and drugs, consume a large amount of retirement income; low-income workers more often rent than own their housing. In short, the expenses of the golden years do not obediently decline along with income. As a result, Social Security provides little security for most workers with modest incomes, obliging many to reluctantly continue employment, and providing little retirement comfort, let alone forgiveness for decades of toil. In defiance of ancient Chinese wisdom—"winners and losers, in the end the same thing"—the retirement provisions of the social insurances are better understood as rigid and parsimonious extensions of America's income stratification than as a generous recognition of the democracy of old age or a lifetime of citizenship.

Lubove's conclusions are still pertinent today:

> Eligibility and benefits in the contributory old-age and insurance titles were closely work-related, government contributions were omitted, and fiscal conservatism prevailed in the emphasis upon reserves and the equity principles of private insurance.... [T]he American welfare state remains underdeveloped by income-maintenance criteria. Our economic security system was designed in the 1930's, and can ... be interpreted as an effort to provide some measure of economic security without significantly affecting income distribution. In dollar volume the social insurances overwhelm the tax-supported public assistance programs, implying a determination to keep economic security as contributory and closely work-related as possible. (Lubove 1968, 175, 179)

Yet the social insurances have always been broadly popular, perhaps because of their stringency, recalling Gilens's observation that the American people insist that their social welfare programs conform with their privatistic values. Unfortunately, these demands subvert the ability of the programs to achieve their goals. With little difference by income, education, region, or occupation, large majorities of all groups supported expansion of the Old Age Insurance program between 1938 and 1948 (Shiltz 1970). Yet those receiving "relief" customarily provided a very weak supportive voice, a curiosity perhaps to be seen in conflict with any notion of class interest or self-interest and more as a window into the psychology of deservingness, denial, and self-hatred, emotions that put people on the couch rather than on the grandstand of rationality. Perhaps to absolve themselves of hurtful labels, those most in need are sometimes most perversely loyal to the principles that created their need in the first place.

The tepid early program and its inadequate present form reflect popular attachment to the principle of self-sufficiency. Roosevelt's comments of 1935 capture this continuing mood:

> The lessons of history, confirmed by the evidence immediately before me, show conclusively that continued dependence upon relief induces a spiritual and moral disintegration fundamentally destructive to the national fiber. To dole out relief in this way is to administer a narcotic, a subtle destroyer of the human spirit. It is inimical to the dictates of sound policy. It is in violation of the traditions of America. (Schiltz 1970, 30, quoting Roosevelt)

In spite of the fact that Social Security is financed through intergenerational transfers that do *not* constitute any sort of judicable claim, the American public, poignantly including those on relief, needed to be cozened with the ritual of self-support (their taxed contributions) and the myth of self-sufficiency and worthiness. Indeed, while popular opinion appeared to support more generous alternatives to Old Age Insurance, notably the Townsend plan that was to be funded through a progressive income tax, the modest benefits of the current Old Age Insurance program seemed to fulfill those ambitions.[10]

Public opinion consistently expresses a paradox about the social insurances (and often other programs as well): on the one hand, a strong desire for greater spending on Social Security and, on the other, a strong antagonism to increased taxes, even considering the regressive Social Security tax to be more fair than the progressive federal income tax. Baggette, Shapiro, and Jacobs (1995) report consistent majorities since the 1970s and across different polls that desire an expanded, more generous Social Security system, refusing to accept cuts in benefits or cost-of-living adjustments for other purposes such as to reduce either the federal budget deficit or defense spending. At the same time, majorities also report that Social Security taxes are "somewhat" or "excessively" high. Yet the public overwhelmingly prefers to reduce federal income taxes rather than Social Security taxes. Nevertheless, support for Social Security increases may not be literal, perhaps reflecting an uneasiness that the system is in trouble and that retirement benefits are insecure. Quite naturally, recipients want painless security and free benefits, while taxpayers want lighter burdens. The program itself, rather than the contradictory public opinions, represents the politically acceptable trade-off. It seems clear that the American public, in the early years of the Social Security Act and more recently, has refused to seriously handle the financial inadequacies of the elderly through public provisions—either through Old Age Assistance or through the far stingier, means-tested Supplemental Security Income Program.

Public Assistance

The other programs of the American welfare state, especially those without effective political representation, even more clearly embody the basic preferences of the American public. Payments in 1997 for children in foster care, for the permanently and totally disabled outside of total care facilities, and for poor families with children left most in poverty. Indeed, the 1996 welfare changes "reformed" Food Stamps to put up only enough for five days of food per week (Ways and Means Committee 1998). These miserly programs reflect more than sixty years of embedded, even majority, preferences for characterological and conservative assumptions about the counterproductive influence of welfare (except where indicated, subsequent data are drawn from the tabulations contained in Weaver, Shapiro, and Jacobs 1995; and Shapiro et al. 1987a, 1987b).

Large majorities of the American public believe that public assistance programs work poorly because they discourage virtue, that is, work, while encouraging vice such as divorce and out-of-wedlock birth. While more than 80 percent of Americans report great sympathy for the poor, only about 40 percent feel the same about people on welfare. The nation has consistently split about evenly over responsibility for poverty and consequently the government's role in relieving need. However, more recent polls are tilting in favor of characterological explanations ("people not doing enough") and therefore reduced government assistance, redistribution, taxes, and spending. But a structural sense of responsibility for individual failure has rarely expressed itself as a dominant preference. In sharp distinction to Cook and Barrett (1992), decades of opinion surveys consistently report a minority of support for increases in welfare programs, but a larger minority consistently want them cut. Indeed, consistent majorities report that people on welfare are getting "more than they need." But whatever the ambiguities over general propositions, an enormous majority, sometimes more than 75 percent, have endorsed the limitations of public assistance, wishing to maintain existing welfare programs or to cut their benefits. Not surprisingly, Weaver, Shapiro, and Jacobs (1995) report substantial and sometimes huge support (even greater than Public Agenda 1995) for many of the harsh remedies and goals enacted in 1996: workfare (87 to 89 percent), self-sufficiency (90 to 93 percent), time limits (89 percent), and family caps, that is, a refusal to increase "benefits when people on welfare have additional children" (46 to 68 percent). It is again both strange and telling that so many of those on welfare are antagonistic to government programs and so unsympathetic to others receiving assistance.

The contradictions between global good feelings and their realization in specific programs are profound. Erskine (1975) reports great support for the government to handle poverty and the problems of unemployment but small support for the unemployment program. Throughout the polls, notably in the summaries (Weaver, Shapiro, and Jacobs 1995; Shapiro et al. 1987a, 1987b), large proportions of Americans want government to do something about social problems, but far smaller proportions endorse specific government interventions. The conflicts become even more apparent when support is discounted by aversion to taxes. Yet, as Gilens (1999) observes, there is "substantial concurrence between public attitudes . . . and public policy" (174). Indeed, the actual program provisions are the strongest evidence of the public's actual preferences—its trade-offs between competitive inclinations.

Rationization without Rationality or Compassion

The strong and consistent opinions of the American public tend to obscure the fact that people's opinions are often inaccurate estimates of social reality, hardly rational approximations of anything but the respondents' inner states, if even this. The pollsters and political science generally have developed an excessive stake both in their survey data and in the sincerity, let alone the knowledge, of respondents. Rather than expert estimates or informed judgments, the reported opinions are more often the projections, displacements, sublimations, and rationalizations of citizens that collectively constitute the ideological support for particular social policies. The resentment of a black woman in Birmingham, Alabama, is understandable: "I had a cousin on welfare, and it was nothing for her to buy her son [expensive] tennis shoes. I have to buy my shoes on sale" (Public Agenda 1995, 31). What is not so palatable is that the statement is actually making claims about welfare reality that are false but that as moral judgments go far to explain America's operative civil religion. The respondent is stating her own version of the myth of the welfare Cadillac, that the characteristic recipient is a corrupt, lazy, immoral hustler who should be put her place an inferior social and economic position relative to the respondent, who of course is both a prudent shopper and a virtuous citizen. Welfare programs in the United States have typically done just that—fix recipients in the hierarchy of American life—more than relieve want, provide jobs and training, educate, or care for poor children without families. Well below poverty levels, payments for the most deserving and the most in need (foster children and the disabled) put the lie to American compassion. Yet despite a consistency of conservative opposition, there has never been any rigorous demonstration that greater generosity in social welfare programs is economically counterproductive or socially unwise. The greatest impediment, and perhaps the only one, to the adequacy of America's social welfare provisions remains the unwillingness of the American public, not simply their leaders, to more equitably share the nation's bounty.

The apparent contradiction between the "philosophic" good intentions of the American public and its begrudging social welfare choices is reconciled by a process of denial, which is probably the essence of myth. The reconciliation of the two civil religions occurs in the actual provisions of welfare programs, with the ceremonial religion providing the psychological, patriotic, ethical excuses for the paltry social welfare programs elaborated in expression of the American people's operative civil ethos. The ceremonial civil religion of democratic and republican values—participation, equality, generosity, compassion, and justice—masks the deeper, less apparent but operative civil religion, which is far more "capitalistic," privatistic, ascriptive, and ungenerous. Indeed, the rituals of the ceremonial civil religion—frequently the emotional gilded calves of its personal social services—encourage a binding catharsis of self-congratulation that justifies the real preferences of the American people. The contradiction between the ceremonial and the actual may pose a rational inconsistency. However, social decision making is not rational; to the contrary, it finds an easy ability to obscure, soften, and misrepresent harsh policy choices as a wise sternness or a deserved punishment on the basis of altruism hallowed by the ceremonial religion.

Self-deception may be the worst kind precisely because of its effectiveness. The sacred belief in the basic goodness of the American people is itself a tyranny that perpetuates the spasms of vituperation and scapegoating that accompany failed policy. Someone or something is blamed, but rarely the American people themselves, who conveniently displace guilt on the media that misled them or on politicians who defiled the public trust or, in their most evil moods, blacks, Native Americans, Jews, foreigners, immigrants, homosexuals, Catholics, Communists, and the feeble-minded who subvert Americanism. Curiously, even the harshest criticisms of American society and social policy (notably by Anelauskas 1999, and by the many, gloriously unwrinkled neo-Marxists) reserve a special dispensation for the American people themselves as hapless victims of imperialism, capitalism, and propaganda. Mencken and Twain made a living from the rarest artistic perspectives: the foolishness, if not actually the evil, of the American people. Without upholding any special virtue for the market, the notion of a powerful American consensus transforming the classic victim into victimizer is a troubling threat to many ideologues of class.

Yet the most routine truth of American social policy may be that it exists because of its popularity with the American people. Even while a diversity of interests is represented in the ecology of political rivals (the vaunted pluralism of American life) that diversity can be expressed within the same individual as conflicting roles: the upstanding ceremonial front for an operative self-centeredness. The citizen chooses roles to maximize—taxpayer or government beneficiary, parent or child, leader or follower, dissident or conformist, donor or recipient, speculator or conservator, and so forth—and the choices are organized within political factions. Failure of policy and democracy is conveniently displaced with projective velocity onto vulnerable shoulders. What the process lacks in nobility it makes up for with brute political success.

Simply the fact that there may be palpable reasons for public opinion is no proof that it is rational. To the contrary, reasons for the occurrence of any phenomenon are customarily assumed in the metaphysics of contemporary thought. If "rational" was understood to be a near equivalent of "good," as only a word of commendation with little, if any, specific content, then describing public opinion as rational would provoke little debate. Yet rational choice, rational policy, rational public opinion, and rational belief imply a series of justifications that transcend mere agreement. Page and Shapiro's (1992) preference to equate rational with politically coherent creates a serious problem of meaning that allows cultural vanity to slip past objective proof.

Page and Shapiro (1992) argue that "the collective policy preferences of the American public are predominantly rational, in the sense that they are real, . . . stable, . . . mutually consistent, and . . . sensible" (xi). When preferences change, "they almost always do so in understandable and, indeed, predictable ways, reacting in consistent fashion to international events and social and economic changes as reported by the mass media" (xi). For the authors, "real" apparently means amenable to empirical substantiation through opinion polls, while "sensible" translates as culturally acceptable. The ability to predict change in public preferences, in this case, *because of* the independent influence of the mass media, establishes a very clear line of cause. Yet these are the characteristics of *reasonable* political accommodation with social experience but definitely not the hallmarks of rational choice. Social decision making is not rational in the modern sense unless public preferences are informed by rational information. The implication of sensible adjustment to perceived opportunities and threats is that choice is largely irrational, that is, without good information but perhaps with a decent regard for human needs and sensibilities.

At a minimum, rational implies wise goals and effective and efficient means or, with the qualification of economics, at least the best possible choice in light of imperfect and incomplete information. To call a choice rational is to imply scientific rationality, or the objective and logical demonstration of optimality. While a policy may work out well over time and enjoy the support of an enormous number of people, it is not rational unless its value can be objectively demonstrated beyond the fact of its popularity.

The ultimate goal for man—the highest good, the rational end—has defied the most intense efforts of philosophy. Metaphysics has not been replaced by physics, and rationality is limited from the outset. In some form, a society picks goals without the benefit of rational processes or proofs. However, the possibility of rational means (rational policies) remains. Page and Shapiro, along with the tradition whose argument for democracy hinges on the decency and wisdom of the governed, start their analysis with heavy ideological baggage but lightened by a convenient definition of their task. Yet even if the public were minutely informed about every available detail of every issue—and this is preposterous—their choices could not be rational, since the information itself is deeply flawed and biased. The task for rationality in social decision making is to demonstrate the precedent of concern (that decisions were made prior to emotional, irrational commitment relying on objective, logically relevant information), that the choice was optimal, and finally that self-interest followed objective need. These conditions are rarely, if ever, met.

Nevertheless, American decision making is culturally coherent: it conforms with the self-defined interests of powerful groups; it is justified in terms of their generalized goals and preferences; the processes and the preferences underlying the system are widely endorsed; and, not coincidentally, its mythology of justification, its ceremonial civil religion, reinforces the emotional stability of national identity and chosenness that facilitates consensus. The stability of the American system is more a tribute to its stable ethos, its enduring civil religions, than to any ability of the American people to transcend their "passions" in a larger commitment to Enlightenment rationality.

In contrast with Page and Shapiro, the public's "philosophic" attitudes to social welfare are customarily in conflict with the individual program provisions of the American welfare state. Liberal, progressive attitudes are reported at the same time that vicious program elements are supported. Indeed, the deep contradictions of American public opinion justify the duality of public ceremony and tacit belief, the deeply emotional, irrational détente of social decision making.

Yet the program choices themselves are not rational at all in achieving either ultimate goals or avowed social preferences. The welfare programs of the United States meet their goals poorly: Old Age Insurance provides little security and even less reward for a lifetime of work; foster care harms children and puts up a pittance for their care; Food Stamps and AFDC (now TANF) do not address poverty; other low-income programs cover only a tiny fraction of need; and the personal social services customarily lack any true production function. The effects of the welfare state's programs are indeterminate at best and often droll parodies of their promise. But they endure with great political support. While fulfilling occasional and modest production functions, the programs are always civil-religious rituals of profound social and economic preferences that often coincide with predatory but widely popular social values.

Furthermore, the role of the media is very ambiguous, although they probably have little influence as an independent political force. Rather, they compete for audience share by purveying popular belief. Then again, an underlying process of immense complexity may determine both media interpretations and public preferences. It is difficult to maintain that the mass media, staffed and owned by sedulously adaptive social actors, are ever able to stand outside of their own culture. The media may actually be incidental to the deep desires of the public whose inventive pejoratives are constantly being created, in service to the operative civil religion, in support of existing inequalities. The American public's attitudes have been consistently hostile toward people in need and consistently in support of programs that deny them resources, that even humiliate them for their needs. Work for the underclass requires toil, mortification, and penance. Workfare, rather than a public jobs program, elaborates a coercive mood of forced obeisance but not a compassionate or generous view of those in need, not the nobility of work or work as social contribution. To confuse the dressed-up and polite report of survey respondents with the consistency of popular support for actual and harsh social welfare programs is to commit a bald ideological crime.

The media as entertainment frequently reflect the desires of the American public more than they fulfill any noble role in education for democracy. Even Gilens acknowledges the public's disinterest in readily available data that refute racial stereotypes of welfare recipients. He falls back on an injunction for editors to provide more instructive information. Yet there is little, if any, ability to isolate the true source of the public ethos—elite manipulation, or popular experience, or both. Consequently, the public's conscious choice of an uncaring ideology remains a salient explanation for social policy and perhaps more so than elite propaganda that has the virtue of preserving some tenuous sense of American innocence. A stronger indictment of propaganda can be made of the pollsters themselves, who consistently ignore the grievous rational imperfections of their surveys and analyses to arrive at fiercely partisan conclusions that inevitably invoke the authority of the revealed preferences of the popular will.

The polling data provide no consistent evidence of a split between elites and popular opinion, only a reported difference between liberals and conservatives relative to philosophic positions that favor conservative values as the questions get closer to actual programs. There is even some evidence that elites may be more compassionate than the public (see Cook and Barrett's comparison of congressional opinion with public opinion). Indeed, attitudes are strikingly consistent across most groups, even those that would appear to harbor substantially different interests, suggesting that national identity—cultural homogeneity—has triumphed over class, gender, region, and even race. Thus, contemporary American social welfare policy itself, unconfused by imperfectly reported opinion and hidden motive, stands as the most profound, direct, and accurate estimate of the popular will: democratic in defiance of generosity, rationality, and even perhaps wisdom.

Conservatism has largely triumphed over liberalism. The operant civil religion of the United States sustains this victory. Calvinist and Puritan intolerance and an atomistic individualism better explain America's social welfare policy than the opposing impulse to increase social and economic equality through public interventions. Similarly, subcultural and characterological explanations for social outcomes, notably poverty and wealth, have customarily been far more popular than structural explanations of the human condition. The muted strains of genetic superiority, perhaps excused as the way that divine favor expresses itself, often recur to sanction social policy.

The antiseptic cruelty of America's commitment to social efficiency is distant and disdainful, pious and widely popular, without beatings, chains, prisons, or mutilation even while it denies adequate training and education, income, housing, employment, or compassion. The American civil religion perpetuates a fiction of nobility, a subterfuge for the actual meanness of the nation's social welfare for lower-status and poor groups. The universal rituals of caring—the little lies of nationalistic pomp—hide the nation's actual neglect of social need, the failure to provide a substantial remedy for poverty or for social isolation through both public policy and private philanthropy. Indeed, America's true civil religion, that is, its long-standing operative values, has been constantly opposed to any sort of generosity for socially marginal or lower-income groups, and notably those without much political cachet.

Notes

1. Even the best opinion polls stumble. To begin with, samples are frequently unrepresentative because response rates are low, and the researchers have neither the time nor the money to assure greater participation. The refusal to respond of those who are actually reached is often greater than 50 percent. However, an even larger number of potential respondents, identified and pursued, are never reached. It is unlikely that those who are often not at home are like those who are frequently at home. Second, response falsification increases the inaccuracy of polls. In regards to highly charged topics and intimate, cherished behaviors, respondents may be reluctant to report attitudes or behaviors (intolerance, crime, sexual predation) that cut against public standards and to open themselves to even slight disapproval even from an anonymous, distant phone interviewer. But these are precisely the attitudes and behaviors that are frequently of greatest interest. Responses also appear to be very sensitive to the wording of questions and the order in which they appear; words of general commendation elicit more positive responses than words of disapproval (Smith 1987); the response to one question tends to carry over to the next. For example, Cook and Barrett(1992) make much of their counterintuitive findings that Americans support an expanded welfare state; however, many of the positive responses toward welfare reflect the least offensive, charitable wording of their questions about public assistance and the fact that they follow questions about OASDIand Medicare, an extremely popular program. Most respondents are also poorly informed about issues, reporting attitudes more sensitive to the question and possibly also to America's generalized, ceremonial civil religion than to its substance. As many researchers, for example, McClosky and Zaller (1984), have noted, there is wide disparity between these more "philosophic" attitudes and those that actually stimulate social choice or reflect a true preference.

Aside from these technical issues, the survey itself creates an artificial opinion environment: people are questioned individually about their attitudes and intentions when in fact they actually behave in the context of live reference groups. A poll implicitly assumes that policy is a democratically produced consensus of equal respondents when in fact people may reflect the attitudes of their reference groups. Respondents may be less sensitive to reference groups during survey interviews than they are, say, before an election. It would be intriguing to compare the results of two surveys, the typical poll that seeks a spontaneous reply and a mailed questionnaire that encourages respondents to take their time and seek whatever advice they need before responding.

There is also the curious problem that the reports of the polls themselves act to reinforce their own findings by presenting the appearance of consensus to the American people. In light of the likely biases of all surveys, reported data may create a belief in the nation's values or strengthen an existing one where none may actually exist or where the consensus is far weaker. This marketing effect takes place through credulous analysts dependent on the authority of their tools and more insidiously through political candidates and decision makers who regard reported opinions as marching orders from "the people" that preempt the tedious process of public debate.

2. Yet the issue of progress relative to social and economic growth may be another story, since blacks and Hispanics are disproportionately represented among the poorest, while income differentials between blacks and whites and even women and men have not been shrinking dramatically in recent years.

3. A very large nonresponse rate in spite of their preferred tabulations.

4. The contention in Public Agenda (1995) that "the public has a good sense of the programs that fall under the welfare heading" (49 note 1) is probably quite inaccurate. Most studies, let alone the public, have trouble defining the package of federal programs constituting welfare, customarily leaving out Supplemental Security Income, foster care, and the other protective programs, small low-income programs such as heating assistance, as well as the range of educational programs and personal social services. Whatever the definition, the burden of "public assistance" is quite small.

5. Teles also ignores the roles of intellectuals in creating the 1996 welfare changes. The reforms were largely drafted by Baines and Ellwood, reflecting Ellwood's *Poor Support* (1988) as well as Mead's (1992) enthusiasm for mandatory workfare and Murray's (1984) desire for a smaller, decentralized public role in welfare. Indeed, a good case can be made for the customary connivance of intellectual thought with the popular will.

6. And the good Senator Moynihan might have been a bit hasty in sending Teles's "book all over Washington" (from the back jacket of Teles 1998). Teles relied on only one polling source whose pivotal question ("Are we spending too much, too little, or about the right amount on welfare?") probably creates a negative response. Substituting "the poor," "the needy poor," or "the deserving poor" for "welfare" would probably create entirely different biases. This issue of wording led Schiltz to question the meaning and comparability to other responses of the 1948 and 1961 outliers.

7. Page and Shapiro's (1992) four groups—upper, middle, lower middle, and lowest—could not be quartiles, since the General Social Survey does not permit reaggregations of individual responses. At best they are approximations, but the authors do not quantify their categories.

8. These comparisons are based on my tabulations of the GSS through 1998. Unless otherwise indicated, all subsequent conclusions about cleavage are also based on my tabulations of GSS data. All income groups are approximations, generally within a few percentage points of indicated margin except for African Americans in the early and mid-1970s. Strangely, in many years (e.g. 1973–76, 1980–83), the estimated bottom quintile reported a *larger* pro-welfare response than the estimated bottom decile. This recalls the counterintuitive finding during

the Great Depression and shortly after of the very large percentages of those on relief who opposed extension of the Social Security Act (Schiltz 1970). Indeed, the greatest cleavage is among the very bottom, perhaps the lowest 5 percent, and the very top few percentage points. But again this is too small a constituency for a viable political base. Here the differences are on the order of forty to fifty percentage points.

9. Indeed, with few exceptions concentrated at the very lowest incomes, only a small percentage of any income group feels that more should be spent on welfare or that government's role should grow for any aspect of personal social services or poverty reduction. The exceptions are almost invariably located at the very lowest incomes.

10. One of the few very large reported differences of opinion by income occurs over the question of increasing the size of old age benefits in 1939: only 28 percent of the "prosperous" but fully 63 percent of the "poor" supported large benefits (Schiltz 1970, 46, reporting Roper). Yet by 1945, only 41 percent of a national sample felt that benefits had "not gone far enough," 38 percent were content with the current program, and 6 percent wanted to roll back benefits. Still, specific amounts were not queried, only a vague issue of satisfaction with the current program or general questions about spending on the elderly. Schiltz provides a pointed caution about the quality of the survey questions and the general understanding of the public itself relative to the subject of pensions, relief, and social insurance. Reported opinions may clearly have been simply a product of wording and ignorance (Schiltz 1970, 31–41).

Chapter 5

The American Ethos 3: Social Welfare Services as Rituals of the Civil Religion

Any prevalent social value activates the purposive behaviors of social institutions as well as their ceremonies. Most organizations fulfill both production and ceremonial functions. The most market-driven industrial firm also provides approval for the system in which it succeeds. Yet many organizations are largely ceremonial, masking their ideological functions behind specific organizational goals that are not in fact pursued. Thus, some social welfare programs, notably the social insurances and public assistance, offer concrete benefits (e.g., cash, food, medical care) that at least appear to play an intended role in poverty prevention or reduction. Many others, such as the personal social services, offer little substance. However, all social welfare programs also proselytize the values that they enact, even the tacit ones. Thus social welfare provisions, whether or not they provide substantial relief, most emphatically pursue other social ends, notably those that reinforce the broader social system of the United States. The propagation of these values has harmed many Americans despite the nation's vaunted ceremonies of justice, fairness, and compassion. To the contrary, cruelty has been a frequent choice of American social welfare policy.

Cash Transfer Programs as Rituals

Both the social insurances and public assistance programs provide an obvious role in increasing income by transferring cash through government to a variety of eligible groups. Yet the conditions of the transfers constitute distinctive ceremonies that reaffirm public values. The United States is certainly wealthy enough to fill its economic poverty gap, even a larger one measured against a higher threshold than the current poverty line. The nation could also easily afford to increase the pay of lower-wage workers and to provide them more comfortable retirements.[1] It could also afford more realistic subsidies for survivors and the disabled. Yet it chooses not to, largely on grounds that those in need do not deserve greater generosity and that relief itself creates a moral hazard. The classic rhetoric of reaction against assistance for the poor castigates any policy that softens work requirements for encouraging the very behaviors, notably laziness and improvidence, that cause poverty in the first place. Thus a stern necessity—the sentimentalist's tough love—is a necessary condition of ambition and labor force discipline.

The moral hazards argument, posed forcefully by Murray (1984), also justifies social efficiency, recasting selfishness as philanthropy and neglect as deservingness. Yet there is little empirical evidence for the existence of moral hazards. Danziger, Sandefur, and Weinberg (1994), among others, provide a convincing refutation even while they fail to construct a rational, structural explanation for social problems. In lieu of more compelling proof, Murray fell back on thought experiments: the influence of financial incentives on family composition (marriage, divorce, children, and so forth) and work. Curiously, Danziger, Sandefur, and Weinberg also rely on a thought experiment although it is tacit: middle-class outcomes (deferred childbearing, high educational attainment, steady employment, job productivity, and so forth) would occur more frequently if more people had middle-class experiences. Again, however, like the Pygmalion myth, contemporary liberalism assumes that those experiences are relatively inexpensive to provide; indeed, but for Haveman's final chapter, Danziger, Sandefur, and Weinberg largely assert the principle of social efficiency although at more generous levels than Murray.

Few analysts seem willing to face the nearly incorrigible resilience of deviant behavior or the huge costs required to even test greater equality as a preventative intervention. Yet, as others have noted, Murray has a loose way with data, reporting convenient, incomplete information as it serves his purposes. As two examples, he fails to address the fact that illegitimacy rates rose while welfare payments fell, a direct refutation of his predictions. He also misrepresents the cause of the increasing proportion of illegitimacy among African American births. The increased proportion of black children born out of wedlock did not result from an increase in the proportion of unmarried black women who had children; this has stayed constant over the years. It was due to a declining number of total births, presumably as a result of more black families deciding to have fewer children in protection of their newly found middle-class security. More to the point, wealthy populations do not subscribe to the moral hazards principle in raising their own children or indulging themselves. Still, the revelations of social discourse are ideological, not rational, and people tend to stand most emphatically where they sit most comfortably.

Nevertheless, the sincerity of deservingness as the overriding principle of American public welfare and charity is beggared by the treatment of conspicuously worthy members of the society, namely, foster children and the permanently and totally disabled who are poor. The society abides its unpoliticized hypocrisies congenially through the cash transfer programs themselves that express the normative choices of the American people and promulgate its operant civil religion. These choices endorse the nation's social and economic differences. Ceremonially, these programs claim to reward frugality, work, discipline, and dedication; they encourage prudent saving and healthy living; they express the nation's charitability and tolerance; and they promote modesty, chastity, love of home, and personal responsibility. Actually, these virtues are ritualized justifications for the enactment through its social welfare programs of the basic, large, and growing differences of the society itself. Yet there is scant demonstration that any of the society's social and economic differences are either necessary or wise for economic growth and social cohesion, or have much to do with civic contribution and personal nobility. In the absence of rational choice, all that remains is political coherence, the reciprocation of self-interest and power.

Presumably, great wage differentials are necessary to maintain workforce discipline, competition, and effort. Repeated with little forgiveness as the great differentials of public retirement benefits, they are justified as promoting thrift and savings. Work-based differences are sanctioned as rewards for the provident and as punishments for pleasure seekers. Those who do not work are due less than those who do; those who earn more are entitled to greater pensions. The principle of less eligibility is carried through endlessly in American social welfare, with the sins and virtues of parents reflected in higher payments for the surviving children of workers and for those disabled while employed than for poor children without parents or for children of poor parents who are not attached to the workforce. Quite obviously, the distinctions have little merit relative to the needs of the children.

As the appeal of the social insurances grows through their own rituals of support, the distinctions that they make among beneficiaries also become more rigid. Their very popularity can be seen in mirror image as popularity for their long-standing inadequacies—notably the tightfisted benefits for huge numbers of recipients—and for their enacted distinctions among insurance beneficiaries, as well as between insurance beneficiaries and recipients of public assistance. OAI recipients receive far greater benefits than those who have not worked and proportionate to the size of their contributions (to the system). The amount of their contributions is obviously related closely to their earnings and not coincidentally to the status of their employment. Thus, the social insurances relative to public assistance and relative to workers themselves repeat programmatically the core values of the culture, notably market position, that created them. In this sense, cash transfer programs celebrate their own assumptions and promulgate their enacted preferences.

Public assistance programs are designed to promote work by allowing for only a threadbare existence while receiving relief. The reforms of 1996 go so far as to set time limits on relief—twenty-four months or less for each episode and no more than sixty months over a lifetime. The reforms also pursue their characterological assumptions that the poor are immoral and lazy by mandating workfare and "training," by promoting family caps that force case management on unwed mothers, and by increasing administrative discretion, particularly allowing states to deny benefits to those they consider to be uncooperative. In addition, the reforms lower benefits, notably Food Stamps, and restrict program eligibility by dropping addicts, noncitizens, and even many poor children with serious behavioral problems. The few billions of dollars of savings are insignificant in a federal budget approaching $2 trillion, but they cause considerable discomfort for millions of recipients. They also ceremonially endorse particular ideological preferences, and this, after all, may be their principal purpose.

Yet none of the assumptions of character nor of social and economic necessity implicit in the reforms have been rationally demonstrated. An instrument for the measurement of morality continues to frustrate invention, and the poor remain on the same footing as the wealthy with whatever god may exist. Welfare recipients are not clearly able-bodied; many, if not most, have medical, psychiatric, and emotional problems that prevent work but are not serious enough to qualify them for Supplemental Security Income (SSI) as totally and permanently disabled; the overwhelming proportion of welfare recipients, about 70 percent, are children; many recipients lack job skills and are the first ones dropped from employment in a recession; some made poor marriage choices; some became mothers in situations far removed from suburban opportunity, loving families, and nurturing peer groups. Some welfare recipients have incorrigible social deformities but are still acceptable parents. It is important to remember that the United States provides hardly any relief apart from Food Stamps for people who do not have children and who are not gravely impaired by physical and mental problems. As a result, many Americans live outside the common experience of the nation, working rarely, eating poorly, and living in the nation's tin-shack subcultures.

Still, there is no demonstration that increased taxes to care for these people at levels of an appropriate American minimum will have deleterious economic effects by lowering the incentive for work or by hampering investment. On the one hand, the trade-off between the income effect and the substitution effect is not theoretically predictable; indeed, people may work more to compensate for a higher tax bite (Epstein 1997). On the other hand, greater strain on profits may improve the prudence and attentiveness of the nation's moguls to the productivity of their wealth. There is also no demonstration that smaller economic differences will assault the dignity of success. Moreover, the possibility exists that the highest level of economic growth may not be coextensive with the most satisfying culture. Notwithstanding an impressive desert of economic, moral, and social ignorance, the nation has erected an undeniably concrete monument to its actual preferences.

Public assistance programs enshrine the irony of relieving people of poverty at levels substantially below the poverty line. Even poor states under AFDC could have afforded much higher welfare benefits, and more so now under TANF,[2] especially in light of large block grant surpluses due to near-record levels of employment after 1996. As a case in point, Mississippi, perennially the nation's poorest state, was obliged to contribute only about 20 percent of its AFDC payments; it was obliged to spend only about twenty dollars to attract eighty dollars of free federal money to the state. Moreover, the state's portion was largely recouped through sales and property taxes, especially since the benefits turned over more than once in the state's economy.[3] In essence its payments cost little or nothing. Nevertheless, Mississippi chose to fix AFDC benefits at $120 per month for a single mother and two children. Obviously neither compassion for the poor nor economic rationality (let alone greed) had any influence over the state's decision. Instead, the negative attitudes of the state toward poor people—both black and white—and its nearly feudal passion to maintain social differences played a large part in its antagonism to any influence that threatened traditional caste and class relations.

More subtly but just as profoundly, other states and the federal government itself—in other words, the American people—transmit through public assistance programs attitudes toward their recipients that justify the characteristics of the programs themselves. In this way, Food Stamps vouchers, necessitating repeated acts of public humiliation, are justified in the sacred name of honest accountability but underscore the criminal inclinations of every recipient. It is not accidental that the vouchers, pace the Scarlet Letter, are probably more popular than the relief itself. On the one hand, the payments of public assistance stand in testimony to the charitability and compassion of the American people, while on the other hand, the very meagerness of the payments underscores the unworthiness, the lowness, the social marginality of recipients. Thus, the charitability and enduring tolerance of the ceremonial civil religion paper over the cruel cheapness of the operative civil religion.

American public assistance resolves the classic tension between the goals of reducing poverty and reducing dependency in favor of the latter even at a time of unimaginable national wealth and declining need. Indeed, work could be made more attractive relative to welfare through higher Earned Income Tax Credit benefits and other targeted subsidies that relieve the pressure on prices. Yet the 1996 reforms were clearly designed to increase work incentives by devaluing welfare even at the expense of harming recipients, notably children, who cannot work under any circumstances. Again, this very popular choice was made without good information about the side effects of welfare on work performance or family stability. Quite obviously, the nation is actively hostile to social equality as a remedy for economic inequality.

The combination of Food Stamps and TANF, even with some housing assistance, is inadequate to keep body and soul together, let alone a family with children. Welfare recipients obviously, consistently, substantially, and illegally augment their income with money from family, friends, lovers, fathers of their children, and both legal and illegal work.[4] The AFDC law required that welfare benefits be reduced dollar for dollar (exempting the first thirty dollars per month) for all additional income, including gifts, subsidies, and so forth. Yet the illegal income of welfare recipients, notwithstanding official data, has long been recognized and largely accepted. Indeed, this official winking can easily be interpreted as the fee paid to recipients of public welfare in return for acting out their characterological imperfections.[5] In just this way, street people as kinetic public sculpture are a constant reminder of the sins of improvidence. They are perfect cautionary tales, more effective perhaps than Nancy Reagan's campaign to "Just Say No to Drugs" or the stagy pieties of groups such as the Ad Council.

The public's disapproval of public assistance is carried through to the organizational arrangements (office, staff, reporting requirements, etc.) designed for care and surveillance. Welfare offices are regularly dirty, poorly maintained, crowded, uncomfortable, noisy, inadequately ventilated, and dilapidated. Waits for interviews are interminable; case workers are haughty and rude. Eligibility workers are often capricious, making harmful errors for fractious applicants and rewarding the more compliant. Workers often gratuitously convey the very attitudes of disrespect and superiority that undergird the laws they administer. The ritual of welfare with all its formal and informal sting endorses the society's assumptions about recipients, the poor, and status in American society. It provides, at one and the same time, an expression of contempt that bolsters the superiority of those who do not need to rely on welfare and a justification for that contempt. The changing demands for civility that deny the propriety of frank ethnic and racial derogation still provide opportunity for ascriptive isolation, even involving tacit racism.

Personal Social Services as Rituals

Cash transfer programs perform an obviously concrete role—the provision of money—that obscures their ceremonial influence. This is not the case for the personal social services, especially in light of an extensive literature that fails to establish any credible grounds for their effectiveness. By and large personal social services, especially those that attempt to change behavior through one form of psychotherapy or another, are pure rituals of the ceremonial civil religion that also dramatize the subterranean values of the operative ethos. Especially personal social services with therapeutic pretensions proselytize the tenets of social efficiency through intimate personal processes of mentorship and exchange that fix responsibility largely on the individual. Not coincidentally, these ritualized entertainments of blame repudiate greater social equality, the notion that personal services should provide surrogates, and frequently material ones, for missing social institutions—the family, the community, education and socialization, peer groups, work, income, and so forth.

The social welfare agency bridges between services and society, enacting the social will through the persona of a legal entity that defines programs, hires staff, and solicits recipients. Most important, however, the agency justifies the services to the broader culture on grounds of the recipients' needs. The definition of need itself reflects established preferences more than an objective consideration of the actual situation of service recipients. Thus, the agency acts politically, drawing its sanction from the society and campaigning actively within the localized community for particular social values.

Agency services constitute a script of social drama: the board and staff are its heroes; the recipients are its villains. But following the logic of the agency's cultural auspices, the theater of the personal social services is customarily directed not to the service recipient but to the broad political audience of Americans. Despite the profound inability to modify deviant behaviors, the personal social services are still cherished as social rituals that reinforce American values. They set boundaries on behavior that mark out existing social and economic divisions by ascribing derogatory characteristics to those outside of social favor and by embroidering the presumed virtues of the socially orthodox. The export of collective blame has been one of the most enduring elements of civilization, usually effective for all its primitive injustice. In this way, the poor are not simply without money but have earned poverty, hardship, and stigma by improvidence, immorality, impulsiveness, and violence; lower-paid working people are unintelligent sheep who would succeed if they showed some initiative; the homeless are vagabonds; the emotionally ill are malingerers; juvenile delinquents are incorrigible bad seeds, thus relieving the good public of an obligation to redeem them from their own self-defeating behaviors.

While the rules of contemporary public discourse discourage frank racist expression, belief in group incapacity boils below the surface, undercutting the impulse to invest more in family, community, and education: the black-white test score gap proves black intellectual inferiority;

Italians are Mafiosi; Irish are drunks; Jews are devious misers; Latinosare violent peasants; and, with growing frequency, the ethnically and racially mixed exhibit clear signs of hybrid weakness. The intolerance of America is building a color-blind, multiethnic underclass. This exquisite concession to republican discourse invites each American subgroup to divide along lines of worthiness by demeaning its less fortunate members in celebration of American virtue. Pinker, Dawkins, Murray, Harris, Plomin, and even Bouchard provide the integrated, equal-opportunity underclass with theoretical sophistication, rejuvenating a ferocious biological determinism through the neo-Darwinian intellectualisms of behavioral genetics. In short, the long-standing ascriptive tendencies of American society are expressed through personal social services that deny substantive care to those in need and with unfortunate directness translate into the harshness of contemporary social welfare programs. Psychotherapy, case management for unwed teen mothers, and child welfare services, notably foster care, are typical rituals of the American ethos.

Psychotherapy

Drawing inspiration and sanction from an extreme form of American individualism, psychotherapy (including counseling and clinical social work) is a powerful American ritual of blame and deservingness. Winners seek affirmation of their success; losers seek the discipline to take responsibility for themselves. Psychotherapy offers the communion of American society through the expiation of sins and social redemption. It secularizes the binding rituals of a generalized Christianity, incorporating both Catholic and reformed elements. Its mystified priests (psychotherapists) offer an individual relationship with the divine (one's inner spirituality) by channeling conscience and consciousness along pathways to social grace and salvation. The central messages of psychotherapy—individual responsibility and the sacredness of the American ethos—pay homage to the chosenness of American society by decreeing that adaptation is a personal choice. The choice is amenable to rational induction: recognition of a problem, commitment to change, learning the techniques of change, and then reinforcement of conforming behavior. Throughout, the psychotherapist acts as guide, mentor, and surrogate for social approval, affirming conformity with social orthodoxy, that is, restoring the soul of the deviant.

Psychotherapy is often little more than laying on hands or branding immorality, particularly when courts mandate treatment for child molesters, rapists, addicts, drunks, and wife beaters. Similarly when public figures blatantly transgress social sensibilities through drug addiction, racial intolerance, spouse abuse, and so on, they publicly display their remorse as well as their obedience to the social ethos by publicly acknowledging the corrective of psychotherapy. Yet change is improbable for sex offenses, violence, and drug addiction, as well as for other habits that have long resisted any modification. Moreover, public humiliation is more likely to create sullen resentment than to turn on the light of reason. Yet the stigmatizing spectacle of being sent off for resocialization reaffirms social norms. Psychotherapy is a public scolding by professional finger pointers and tongue waggers, aggrandized by the authority of status and science. These rituals educate the culture, defining the individual as the source of his or her own problems. However, by convincing many troubled people that they warrant treatment for their diagnostic labels, psychotherapy produces civil penitents, on the one hand, and a solidarity of the righteous, on the other, that discourages political attention to the imperfections of the society itself. In reality, psychotherapy and the psychological society generally are vehicles of socialization through personal adaptation in preference to institutional reform.

Frank and Frank (1991) draw a valuable parallel between the shaman and the therapist but in an unconvincing attempt to promote the self-healing placebo effect as the core of professional psychotherapy. They miss the force of the process as an application of social judgment through both the therapist and the shaman, who act as partisans not of the patient and the bewitched but of the needs of the society for conformity. The deviant and the possessed both require readjustment to social norms that are implicitly upheld by attending to the individual, in the one case resolving guilt (often with adjuvant medication) and in the other casting out demons.[6] The process is necessarily mystical, tapping into the superstition, vulnerability, and fears of the individual who through mania or misadventure stands outside of the protective skirts of social acceptance.

Without scientifically credible proof of effectiveness, psychotherapy becomes a solely spiritual process with no definable content and no demonstrable production function, dependent for its sanction entirely on the subjective assessment, the satisfaction, of both the patient and the society. With a geographic passion for precise social boundaries, the culture is probably indifferent as to whether the patient changes so long as treatment or punishment does not require large costs or seriously threaten social tranquillity. In the event of individual change, the society pats itself on the back for tolerance, reeducation, and the wisdom of its elders, enjoying a sanctimonious rush as though an errant child returned home to enter the clergy of the reformed. In the face of continued deviance, a socially desirable group of undesirables is created for comparison, threat, social disapproval, and even blood sport (vis-à-vis capital punishment, prefrontal lobotomies, chemical castrations, solitary confinement, and perhaps even child foster care). In each case, psychotherapy flourishes, either as a ritual of the normative or as the justification to punish deviance.

The recent popularity of "spiritual psychotherapy" is a candid admission that the field defies accountability as a modern profession with viable treatments. In actuality, all of psychotherapy is a "spiritual" ritual of social ratification; its interventions have little, if any, material relation to behavioral change. The spiritual therapist is "a virtuous man who has little to repent of or apologize for at the end of his life. . . . How does one arrive at this exalted state of virtue? . . . Such an individual tries to do nothing; he just is" (Karasu 1999, 144). Thus, spiritual therapy is transcendence through the help of the transcended, who "conducts his practice according to these six tenets of transcendence: Love of Others, Love of Work, and Love of Belonging; Belief in the Sacred, Belief in Unity, and Belief in Transformation" (144). The demons of spiritual psychotherapy, its targets of work, are "nonluminous hollows," "posttherapeutic dysphoria," and neglected souls; its goal is "a soulful and spiritual existence" (145). The language of the charlatan and quack is no less incorporeal than the faux science of mainline psychotherapy. Its encyclopedia of cognitive, emotional, and behavioral treatments mock operationalized definition, while the field refuses to credibly test its outcomes, even through black box methods. Indeed, psychotherapy need not comply with the canons of science, since it provides society with a very different service than rational treatment.

The rituals of psychotherapy realize Bloom's (1992) sense of the American religion itself—mystical, ineffable processes that glorify the individual—applying the awful, coercive weight of social disapproval to behavioral apostasy, that is, sin. Since psychotherapy claims to offer live opportunities for personal change, failure reflects the individual's moral intransigence in a society that is obviously tolerant and even generous. Thus, continued deviance justifies harsher remedies that, viewed as a lapse of character exposed through psychotherapy, relieve the society of any obligation for substantial, material responses to need. In this way psychotherapy, with all its stuffy moralizing, undermines greater social and economic equality and the sustaining doctrine that people are largely the products of their environment. Yet by its conformity with social orthodoxy, psychotherapy often reaffirms the shriveled human spirit that it professes to treat.

Case Management for Teen Mothers without Husbands

The 1996 welfare reform included mandatory case management of teen mothers as a preventative for further illegitimate births. On its face, the enthusiasm for case management is puzzling, since all the pilot experiments with intensive supervision and ancillary services (the basic form of case management) have apparently failed (Polit, Kahn, and Stevens 1985; Polit, Quint, and Riccio 1988; Maynard, Nicholson, and Rangarajan 1993;

Long et al. 1996; Quint, Bos, and Polit 1997). Most of the studies incorpo-
rated experimental designs in which the case management group
received general equivalency diploma (GED) preparation, assistance in
finding work (job clubs and job searches), some vocational training, parent training, and some counseling in addition to requisite supervision.
There is even a consistently perverse tendency across the experiments for
the groups that receive case management to exhibit slightly *elevated* inci-
dences of repregnancy, perhaps a result of reinforcing the role of motherhood. Yet case management is better understood as a ritual reinforcing
social preferences than as a serious disruption of the decision by single
women to have children.

Case management appears to provide choices for its clients along with
encouragement to select wisely. In the conservative logic of characterological blame, the provision of choice—free agency—also confers responsibility. Indeed, it parallels the basic tenets of America's generalized
church religions; personal change is just like the decision for salvation, to
accept Jesus. Expressing an inner moral light, both are largely divorced
from environmental influences. In this way, the refusal to change behavior, on the one hand, or to accept Jesus, on the other, testifies to individual
responsibility. Bad people make bad choices, and the wicked refuse salvation. Consequently, the young woman who goes through case management and has another child out of wedlock is freely stating her defiance
of social norms. While this ostensibly provides the ideological justification for treating her harshly (family caps, time-limited welfare, the withdrawal of services, personal supervision), it also provides a basis for
social scorn. Her repregnancy endorses the immoralities and inferior
traits that the culture ascribes to poor unwed mothers and further
endorses the hardships of those who defy social norms.

Thus, failed case management refutes structural causation, in this case
that poor young women brought up without succoring families or neighborhoods and deprived of customary options are left with motherhood as
their most alluring social expression. These sorts of melodramas of blame
are at least as powerful as the most poignant and excessive soap operas
that profess the standard morality and therefore the implicit fairness of
American stratification: the poor are poor by dint of their dissolution.
Moreover, since many of these mothers were themselves born out of wedlock, the failure of case management also conveys a whiff of genetic
determinism.

Child Foster Care

Even when it is protected from the blind insights of psychotherapy, public child welfare, notably the foster care program, provides a routinely
deplorable environment for poor children, who are disproportionately

black and Hispanic. Public child welfare has an apparent goal to provide alternative homes for abused, abandoned, and neglected children. Presumably innocent of the characterological flaws that are invoked to deprive adults of generous relief, poor children without families are among the most deserving of all citizens. Public provisions for them test the sincerity of America's ceremonial civil religion. Yet the reality of the program dispels any notion that the American people will voluntarily come forward to provide surrogate families for homeless children or that they will endorse generous alternative arrangements through their government.

The seven hundred thousand foster children in care at any time during 1998 faced a Dickensian nightmare. Few adequate families volunteer to foster children; it is the common knowledge of child welfare workers that many foster parents should be in foster care themselves. Some children die in care each year, frequently murdered by their foster parents (Costin, Karger, and Stoesz 1996). Many others are routinely neglected and abused. Indeed, the psychological and physical abuse that they suffered at the hands of their natural parents often is continued by their foster parents, as if out of mockery and sadistic irony, to make them feel at home. Foster parents are routinely poor, elderly, undereducated, and socially marginal, hardly fit parents even for their own children, let alone mentors for frequently troubled youngsters. Kinship foster parents, most frequently grandmothers, are even poorer and less educated; after failing with their own children, they are now celebrated and awarded custody of their grandchildren, with frequently tragic results. Many foster parents obviously skim off a large portion of the subsidies paid to care for the children. Indeed, few foster children actually receive the whole subsidy, little as it is; typically, foster children lack adequate clothing; share cramped quarters; eat monotonous high-fat, high-carbohydrate meals. They are boarders, unentitled but envious of the affections enjoyed by natural children.

Congregate settings for foster children—orphanages—are customarily sullen places, little different than reform schools. Both give free play to predatory adolescent cultures; both are understaffed and frequently with poorly trained, inattentive workers. In spite of the debilitating and misplaced guilt of foster children that they, not their parents, are responsible for their mistreatment, both family foster care and the typical congregate home reinforce the children's damaged sense of themselves. There are very few Boys Towns and an overabundance of scandals.

In spite of the exculpations of much of the professionalized social service literature, the situation of these children has been known for decades, if not actually centuries (Lindsey 1994; Costin, Karger, and Stoesz 1996; Bremner 1970; Epstein 1999). The awful state of scholarship in child welfare documents the transition of social work from a field for well-meaning bumblers to a more pernicious deception that employs distorted research to cozen the taxpayer with the corrective myth, that is, assurances that little is enough. The preponderance of research, poorly conducted and with obvious experimenter biases, falsely testifies that minimal family reunification and preservation efforts are successful substitutes for long-term foster care (Epstein 1999; Rossi 1991).

Only a public infected with a mad greed and bitter spite could believe such woeful research. Some researchers even defend the child welfare system on grounds that it did not create the insanity and misery of its charges and therefore should not be held responsible for their restoration to normalcy. Apparently, foster care, like the domiciliary program in the Veterans Administration, has an obligation for only three squares and a flop. Those bedraggled veterans are still better off than many foster kids. The refusal to attend to these children's needs by both the public and private sectors gets past the family-value speeches of Sunday sermons and Thanksgiving feasts. Indeed, public child welfare seems simply to enact the operant values of the private sector, with its sharp neglect softened perhaps by the intervention of more compassionate elites.[7]

The death of a child in care occasions an investigatory commission that invariably hangs blame on some fault of caseworker judgment rather than the appalling inadequacy of the system itself. The commission then goes through a bland ceremony of public concern, making recommendations to decrease caseloads by a jot, revive the call for more foster parents, enrich the mix of better-trained workers, and invest in the development of a questionnaire that can separate homicidal foster parents from the safer sort of sociopath who takes in children to profit by a few hundred dollars per month. It is little wonder that few foster children grow into productive adults and that many age into unfortunate lives.

However, the deeper ritual of foster care serves to assure the public of its charitability at the same time that it denies resources to the children. Public child welfare stands for the vaunted sacredness of the American family even while it fails to provide its wards with appropriate families or warm congregate settings. On the one hand, foster care endorses the ceremony of social solidarity, but on the other it plays a more profound role by imposing the operative value of social efficiency. Foster care is a program of minimalism, designed to suppress the costs of caring for dependent children. It also reduces the potential size of the caseload by endorsing a series of bogus diversion programs, notably family preservation and family reunification, by underfunding child protective services, and by sheltering perversely behind the protection of its own inadequacies. In this last way, it need not separate children from inadequate parents who are still a tad bit more functional than the typical abusive foster parent, kin, or congregate setting. Thus it creates a cruel eligibility test for foster care that also appears to protect the American family from the Red

Riding Hood fantasy of the child-snatching caseworker: children are eligible for child welfare services only if the abuse they suffer from their natural parents is likely to be greater than the abuse they will receive from foster parents. At the end of their ordeal in foster care, usually at eighteen years of age, they rush from the cold arms of public protection with little education, training, or money, no home, no job, but with a poor sense of themselves as social beings and with a crackling anger for their years of emotional deprivation.

While the public child welfare system appears to endorse the ceremonial civil religion of the United States, in fact it sustains the tenets of the operative civil religion through a series of corrective myths applied to a recipient group containing a disproportionate number of racial and ethnic minorities. These myths, centering on the adequacy of the current arrangements of parsimony, are propagated by the social service literature itself. Indeed, without starting off in thrall to the corrective fallacy, no reasonably analytic reviewer could possibly take the research seriously, let alone permit it the vanity of scientific credibility. Yet the rituals of disinterest, science, higher learning, compassion, and helping—the hallmarks of the modern professions of the personal social services—are understood as composing the role of a secular priest in sustaining public belief better than as an Enlightenment commitment to rational social policy or even to American notions of decency.

Entertainment

Social welfare services, even when they provide a concrete benefit, are ritualized entertainments of America's civil religion. Humans may be little more than clever apes, but if consciousness has any meaning, then it is worth commenting on the large number of people who do not benefit from the ceremonies of their culture. Indeed, the ceremonial civil religion is practiced to justify the operative values of Americans, subscribing to republican and democratic ideals but also to the necessity for socially efficient welfare programs. All would be well if social welfare provisions realized a good portion of their goals. Unfortunately, they do not, and the modern social sciences have fallen to the temptations of prestige and profession to defend social efficiency through the construction of corrective myths.

These corrective myths—beliefs that thin, inexpensive social welfare provisions can remedy grievous social and personal problems—largely dramatize an extreme form of individual responsibility that is the core of conservative ideology. The rituals of social efficiency performed by social welfare programs promote social integration, but it seems at the expense of many. The culture has made a profound decision to preserve its Pecksniffian social and economic differences in denial of generosity and forgiveness. The nation has typically embraced conservative ideologies, refusing the claims of the less fortunate for substantive relief even while increasing a formal commitment to procedural equality. American prefer ences, that is, the tenets of the nation's operative civil religion, represent the triumph of Romantic influences over Enlightenment impulses. While the Enlightenment provides the sacred texts of the nation's ceremonial civil religion, Romantic thought—the rejuvenation of mysticism— inspires the spectral proofs that actually determine American decision making.

Notes

1. Molly Orshanskyset the poverty line at three times the minimally adequate food budget. The recent National Academy of Science survey noted a much greater multiplier and argues for a higher minimum.

2. At the beginning of 2000, every state was running a TANF surplus due to continuing high levels of employment that seem to have greatly reduced program rolls. Under the TANF rules, the states have great flexibility over their block grants, yet they have not chosen to increase benefits.

3. A bit of creative financing through the private sector might have actually produced a profit. If a private charity agreed to contribute, say, $10 million to the state (perhaps for road construction so as to keep the bookkeeping honest), the state could then have shifted $10 million to welfare, which would produce another $40 million in federal AFDC payments. The $50 million in total expenditures, turning over more than once throughout the year and therefore being taxed (property and sales at least) more than once, would produce a bonanza of revenues for the state, out of which it would contract back with the charity for the services that it intended to provide with its initial $10 million while adding a small good-faith bonus. The charity would in turn reserve some of the contract, adding it to another $10 million, this time earmarked perhaps to restore the governor's mansion. In such a manner, all private philanthropy in the state, such as it is, could be quickly quadrupled. No Ponzi scheme ever had such an opportunity to become legitimate. Moreover, with a no-show position here and there in the charity's staffing patterns to accelerate its capacity for public contributions (along with an obliging accountant), the poor of Mississippi would become some of the world's best fed and best cared for, and, with the profits of the scheme reinvested in education, some of the wisest among the world's needy. In such a way, Mississippi, the nation's metaphor for the depraved in American history, could have purchased a noble modern calling, and fittingly, from its point of view, with funds from the hated federal government. Alas, the metaphor is reality, and the state cleaves tightly to its plantation heritage.

4. Edin (1991) probably underestimated the illegal incomes. Moreover, the great amount of apparent work performed by welfare recipients supports notions of their being able-bodied at the same time that it contradicts notions of their

being lazy or work aversive or harboring distinct subcultural values. These are probably many of the people absorbed into the current tight labor market of the nation's unprecedented economic expansion. The situation beckons to an enlarged notion of the labor force with the implication of blending the Unemployment Insurance program with TANF, if not eliminating TANF altogether in deference to some sort of guaranteed national minimum for everyone or mostly everyone. However, the social distinctions, if not the racial and ethnic ones, among the different recipient groups of the insurances and assistance programs has provided a sufficient barrier to a serious assault on categorical assistance and generosity itself.

5. All serious drama requires that the actors be paid. Indeed, poor people would do well to seek unionization.

6. Blaming the witch instead of the bewitched would be a true sign of an advanced society if the witches were more often the powerful and the corrupt or if witchcraft trials were ever conducted to establish freedom. The unfortunate association of witchcraft trials with scapegoating, mass hysteria, intolerance, and the base motives of political factionalism discredits a promising social form. The United States would be a far more decent society today if, instead of Goody Proctor and Alger Hiss, the mobs had pondered the fates of Cotton Mather and Joe McCarthy.

7. It is telling that some of the lobbies for children, notably the Children's Defense Fund, enjoy congressional and White House influence way beyond their actual popularity among the public. In spite of imitating an Ivy League reunion and a board meeting of an art museum, the decennial White House Conference on Youth, for all its patrician bombast and portentous moralizing, is a better advocate for children than the general public. Goodwin's (1997) "clubwomen" were far in advance of popular opinion in pushing for mothers' pensions. Then again, the elites never seem to demand very much, staying in line with the comfortable acquiescence of the Child Welfare League more than with the needs of dependent children for normalcy.

Chapter 6

Two Romances:
The Enlightenment
and the Anti-Enlightenment

It would be inaccurate to trace forward the defining conventions of eighteenth- and nineteenth-century thought to contemporary political ideologies as though modern liberals sprung whole from the critical freedoms of the Enlightenment and conservatives from the mysticism of the Romantic era. For one, modern conservatives chart their intellectual lineage back to the Enlightenment, particularly Adam Smith. On the other side, modern liberals take much from Romantic heroism, particularly the drama of man ascendant against society. Still, contemporary social policy decision making in the United States formally justifies itself with allusions to the Enlightenment and more materially with the quantitative evidence provided by the social or human sciences, elaborations of the eighteenth century's generalized "science of man" that began as distinct disciplines in the nineteenth century and reached considerable sophistication, but rarely great profundity, during the latter half of the twentieth century.

The festival religion of the United States appears to take inspiration from the Enlightenment's preference for deism; it acknowledges God but displaces active celestial intervention with a natural system of hopeful regularity favoring American convenience. However, unlike the Enlightenment's "religion without miracles, priestly hierarchies, ritual, divine saviors, original sin, chosen people, and providential history" (Gay 1966, 373), the American civil religion has simply secularized these churchly forms for the congregate benefits of patriotism. Moreover, the operative civil religion and the psychic core of American preferences draw from the wild inventiveness, unchained to any objective reality, of the Romantic reaction to the Enlightenment. Social welfare decision making in the United States and probably in human society generally remains a Romantic process, relying largely on intuition, revelation, superstition, and tradition, that is largely devoid of the substance of rationality particularly in matters of welfare policy. Indeed, contemporary policy making in the

United States is actually hostile to objectivity and coherence, threading its choices through the mute preferences of presiding group interests but cloaking its absolute idealism in the raiment of rational science. While conforming to the ceremonies of Enlightenment republicanism, social welfare policy making actually subverts scientific rationality by enacting the profoundly Romantic superstitions of the culture—its adamant beliefs in extreme individuality, in heroic dominance, and in the determinative power of collective subjectivity.

To paraphrase the historian Peter Gay (1966), as the Enlightenment saw it, the world was, and had always been, divided between ascetic, superstitious enemies of progress, and people who affirmed life, knowledge, and generosity: between mythmakers and realists; priests and philosophers; believers and skeptics. This conflict between two patterns of life, of thought, and of feeling divided historical periods internally; it also divided them from one another. Each era had a dominant *intellectual* style, with either reason or superstition in control. The Enlightenment philosophers insisted that this dominance was merely the temporary ascendancy of one combatant over the other: few periods in history were without their mix of reason and superstition. In this way, while the different moods are philosophically incompatible, they are always reconciled politically.

Indeed, the Age of Reason was not a reasonable age, culminating as it did in the bloodbath of the French Revolution and succoring its own spectacular variety and number of superstitions, cults, and myths. On the other hand, the Romantic era made considerable material progress, nurturing major scientific developments, notably evolutionary biology, and the social sciences while it was hospitable to advances in humanistic democracy, particularly expanded voting franchises and the demise of slavery.

Enlightenment philosophy itself was as superstitious as any other. The eighteenth century was certainly no tribute to rationality or popular government. To the contrary, its quaint notion of benevolent despotism justified antidemocratic rule and elite control of social policy making. Except in one regard and notwithstanding an arrogant self-assurance of their own rationality and reason, the philosophes created a vision as mythical as any before it.[1] The grand exception was science and the institutions of rational discovery—freedom, skepticism, and the autonomy of the intellect. However, science is founded on pragmatic grounds rather than any deduction of truth; moreover, neither science nor the scientific community itself has yet to provide a compelling template for society and social choice. Science has prevailed because it has inspired an enormous number of gratifying technologies; its mastery of the environment, however incomplete, is still breathtaking. Nevertheless, the other core beliefs of the Enlightenment, notably its quaint and mystical assurance that liberty would create a natural, "spontaneous order" of great civic value (e.g., Adam Smith's tutelary unseen hand) and its hostility to received tradition and mysticism, such as the "metaphysics of hope," are religious totems in their maturity more than rational, demonstrable institutions of social organization.

As the philosophes observed, reason and unreason (science and myth; objective knowledge and tradition; fact and faith) are constant companions of social organization. In this sense, then, the Enlightenment as protoscience and Romantic thought as subjective validation remain two styles of thought, two visions of society, two very different types of justification for social choice with very different consequences and contingencies. Even if philosophic perspectives follow historical imperatives, they are at least the banners and forums for the consideration of social policy. They may also have some determinative effect on the form of government and the substance of policy that a society chooses.

The justifications for contemporary American policy bathe in Enlightenment ideals, notably social progress through science, sanctioning decisions on grounds of rational information to advance hallowed social goals—freedom, the public good, and republicanism. Yet, in fact, rational information rarely exists, and even less frequently relative to social welfare problems and solutions. Rather, the Enlightenment injunction for rational analysis has been compromised through the social sciences in creation of corrective myths—the cunning and disingenuous utopianism of social efficiency—that justify the unreasoned, Romantic demands of American culture, its political conveniences.

The false practice of the "science of man"—the obedience of social sciences to the myths of contemporary culture—has replaced the "infamy" of religious superstition. The autonomy of the contemporary intellect is compromised by a facile assurance that rational expertise dictates social policy; the contemporary social scientist relieves the public's fear of ignorance and acquiesces its awe for higher reason with assurances that its policy choices are rational and wise, however imperfectly so. Indeed, science becomes a religion of revelation and tradition, in the process losing its respect for objective truth. The assumption, of course, is that the Enlightenment had things right and that the application of rationality to culture is possible both theoretically and practically while also appropriate for the improvement of the human experience, that is, progress.

Natural science seems to have proven its value pragmatically in ways that the philosophes never anticipated, with utilitarian and democratizing consequences that many of them would have found aesthetically and socially repugnant. Yet apart from the mood of science, Enlightenment thought abides a number of paradoxes, mystifications, political assumptions, and factional conveniences that have come to constitute the defining charter for a particular form of society and government: the liberal, widely enfranchised republic. Rationality, by providing a corrective for unwise policy in the form of empirical science, was central to this formulation. Science provided the actual ability to reject metaphysics, to ground human experience in a knowable world, and, most important, to control that world for humane purposes. Science, as the antithesis of superstition, was the core curriculum through which the philosophes hoped to educate the new citizen and achieve progressive social reform. Not coincidentally, science was also the engine of the new era—the industrial revolution—that married Enlightenment thought to its most important constituency, the emerging middle class and ultimately to the masses themselves. Indeed, Romantic thought is frequently phrased as the anti-Enlightenment, recognizing both a critique of the philosophic ambiguities of the Enlightenment and the reaction of traditional power to the novel politics of the masses that emerged from the industrial revolution.

The Enlightenment Myth

The spirit of the Enlightenment, more than the reality of its debatable influence over politics and society in its time, has suffused American policy discussions for as long as there has been a republic. The Enlightenment's authority, however, is mythic rather than real, conveying through the hallowed voices of the Western patriarchs, their sacred texts, revelations of original intent, and a series of founding legends, support for a variety of America's celebrated traditions. The Enlightenment myth, customarily shorn of its true intellectual or social meaning, inspires the ceremonial civil religion of the United States; it is the source of the touchstones and continuities with transcendent communal verities, as well as the language itself of contemporary social dialectics. Presumably, American policy is rationally chosen on grounds of sufficient, credible evidence; if not purely rational, then it is at least reasonable in the sense of a felicitous compromise between the impulse toward rationity and human conditions; the effects of policy are monitored; implemented policies, especially those that are long accepted, promote freedom and good citizenship; moreover, policy is hopeful, if not actually optimistic, grounding its assumptions in an upbeat view of man's essential nature. And always, American choices further social and human progress: two steps forward, if regrettably and occasionally, one step back. America believes that it succeeded as the most prominent proof of Enlightenment values, "the program of the Enlightenment in practice" (Gay 1969, 557).

Yet at its core, the spirit of the Enlightenment, but for science, is as mystical as the metaphysical and religious doctrines it sought to supplant. Both the hidden hand that so animated its bourgeois side and the humanism that inspired its heroic ideals are intuitive, the revelations and inspirations, perhaps, of dreams, travel, intellectual novelty, unknowable childhood traumas, and even true but unevaluated insight. This split between the mundane practicalities of industrialization and the demands of the human soul for expression, status, and protection—the conflict among economic, political, and social rights—has persisted as the unresolved tension between market liberalism and social liberalism, classical liberalism and modern liberalism (Berlin 1969). But for the constancy of its faith in the wise restraints of an objective reality (positivism), Enlightenment is as utopian as Romanticism; their moral, social, and political imperatives are based on basic simplifying assumptions of society and man that are customarily not amenable to empirical verification or even to a common adjudicating rule of rationality. Choice is inevitably political and temperamental, historic, and biographical.

Enlightenment thought is based on a number of assumptions and preferences that have long been issues of unsettled debate, particularly the extent of freedom consistent with a well-functioning, productive nation and the causes of social happiness and distress (progress, social problems, societal change, individual success and failure, etc.). Moreover, it is not certain that these basic controversies can ever be settled except partially, temporarily, and occasionally by an overwhelming political consensus rather than rationally through the application of science to society. In this way, riding a crest of unprecedented economic bounty, internal harmony, military might, and insulation from the devastations of war on native soil, American culture since the Second World War seems to offer the world a near-universally admired instance of the good life, at least given the common depravities, tyrannies, insufficiencies, and inequities of human culture. But the actuality of American society—the reasons for its prosperity, the nature of its apparent freedom, and even the true meaning of its success (the tally of its benefits and their costs)—and the ability and wisdom of replicating it by other peoples in far different circumstances are not so clear. The Enlightenment never succeeded in deriving from either the nature of the universe, man, or some utilitarian principle the tenets of its universalist credo: "the autonomy of man, the secularization of knowledge and thought, the natural goodness and perfectibility of human nature, and belief in reason and experience, science and progress" (Anchor 1967, 70).

The Enlightenment did, however, pose a new faith in these tenets that has informed the charter of modern democracies: "dedication to human reason, science, and education as the best means of building a society of free men on earth; . . . suspicions of religion, hostile to tradition, and resentful of any authority based on custom or faith alone" (Anchor 1967, ix). Gay (1966) summarizes the spirit of the Enlightenment similarly: "the supremacy of philosophy and the autonomy of man; the superiority of eclecticism to dogma, of intelligent ignorance to grandiose rationalism, and of practical moral reflection to theoretical speculation" (303). In a word, the goal of the Enlightenment was progress. It was to be realized through the practice of rationality applied to both man and society—to the exercise of free will and to the institutions of society. Gay's summary and quotation from Condorcet can stand as a general statement of the spirit of the Enlightenment:[2]

> Moral, political and above all social science will progress and point the way to happiness: the colonies will be freed, the slaves will be emancipated, women will at last become the equals of men, barbarous nations will civilize themselves. . . . Men will grow more beneficent, just, and virtuous; family life will be happier; war will become obsolete; the arts and literature will participate in the general renaissance. It is such contemplation, the contemplation of man the master, freed from the tyrannies of accident and superstition alike, that "presents to the philosopher a spectacle which consoles him for the errors, the crimes, the injustices with which the world is still sullied, and whose victim he often is" (Gay 1969, 120, quoting Condorcet).

The Paradox of Social Cause and Social Reform

How, though, to achieve progress? In its rejection of fatalism—certainly a major achievement in justifying the modern role for the citizen in civil society—the Enlightenment customarily failed to isolate social cause. Typically, the philosophes argued for both the power of society's institutions and the autonomy of man in determining social outcomes: both conditions—supportive institutions and freedom of will—seemed to be necessary. However, the philosophes failed to recognize or simply ignored any contradiction between structural and personal explanations. If man determines his fate largely in spite of social conditions, then each person is responsible for his or her station in life, implying that social policy is a relatively futile instrument of progress except as an exhortation and stimulus to personal effort. On the other hand, if social conditions beyond the individual citizen's control circumscribe human achievement, then social policy becomes the requisite tool to manipulate social institutions. In this case, the state, by implication in a centralized and powerful form, becomes the vehicle of social policy. Yet if motivation and circumstances both profoundly contribute to social outcomes, then the conditions of their influence and their relative importance need to be determined in order to develop policy. The rational determination of influence, let alone clarification of the possibilities, eluded the philosophes both in principle and in fact. Indeed, the Enlightenment's nascent science of man, that importantly redeemed human destiny from divine will, and eventually the descendent social sciences were chartered by this very practical task to identify the causes of social outcomes in order to take specific steps toward a better society.

In part the indecisiveness of the philosophes resulted from their snob-bery and condescension that were congruent with their self-serving faith in "enlightened absolutism," as well as in the monarchs themselves. The philosophes were no strangers to court and prided themselves on their usefulness to power. With the notable exception of Rousseau, for the most part the philosophes were not addressing the masses (even the mass of the literate, which was a small minority at the time) either directly as audience or through the possibility of a broad-based democracy as the general beneficiaries of an Enlightened program. Rather, they were often attempting to impose a self-certified belief in an undefined reason—a new learning, a higher nobility, redefined virtue—upon a mindless mass of illiterate, unthinking, impulsive, childish humanity. While they thought that slavery was unjust, they did not consider the African to be fully human, nor did they uniformly extend compassion, let alone a sense of human equality, to the landless agricultural laborers or to workers in factories and mines. They saw the lower orders as naturally inferior, hop-ing at best to teach them useful occupations but rarely extending full intellectual and social standing to any but a very small number, a tiny natural nobility, exquisitely trained and customarily members of the priv-ileged classes, including the aristocracy itself. In fact, nineteenth-century social Darwinism and earlier less explicit forms of rigid genetic determi-nation fed easily and quickly off the philosophes' stringent hierarchies of individual capacity.

An enormous amount of their dialectics was concerned with the form of dictatorial rule—the king or the aristocrats—rather than the possibility of a broadly democratic franchise, again with Rousseau as a notable exception. In this regard, modern America is a leap of political intention past the plans and expectations of its founding fathers, who created a republic in the Enlightenment's image of restricted rule that excluded from full citizenship blacks, Native Americans, women, and the poor. For the philosophes, even an open "society still preserved fences that only a few could leap, and still condemned the majority to hopeless indigence and permanent exclusion from the political public" (Gay 1969, 518). Voltaire defined the majority as "two-footed animals who live in a horri-ble condition approximating the state of nature, with hardly enough to live on . . . barely aware that they are miserable, living and dying practi-cally without knowing it." (Gay 1969, 4). In the next century, Marx, the great liberator of the proletariat, had little patience or faith in the lumpen, who may well have accounted for the majority of society; at least in this sense of ascribed inferiority, quick judgment, and easy dismissal, he was truly a man of the Enlightenment.

In their ambivalence toward cause, the philosophes constantly empha-sized the assumption that insight and correct thinking preceded social change, and by extension that the individual's free choices determined social outcomes. The philosophes were loath to accept any mechanistic explanation of social change that reduced the "disciplined aggression" of critical intellect in furthering "reason, humanity, and industriousness" (Gay 1966, 183; 1969, 51). Indeed, they insisted on the virtues of self-love, "the project of grounding virtue in interest" that ultimately expressed itself as utilitarianism (Hulliung 1994, 35). In tribute to industrialization and the "glorification" of its elites—"merchants, industrialists, bankers, attorneys, physicians, men of letters, respectable shopkeepers, and *rentiers*," in short, the bourgeoisie—the Enlightenment cherished the modern virtue of industriousness and self-control, implying the delay of pleasure, savings, and the restraint of passion "for the sake of some higher and more enduring satisfaction" (Gay 1969, 49, 45, 46). Charity and humanity—"succoring"—remained voluntary, and public morals "were acquiring the status of a practical virtue," with fashion turning away from pleasure in public hangings or torture (Gay 1969, 36).

The philosophes nurtured a fierce critique of political and social institutions—notably monarchy, aristocracy, and the Catholic Church, and not just the ancient order in France but also in England, Italy, Scotland, Spain, and to a lesser extent in the German states and Austria—that restricted power and policy making to an elite few who often inherited their mandates. Taking heart from intuition, a more precise sense of injustice and corruption, and, importantly, the growing wealth and influence of the bourgeoisie, particularly the merchant classes, the philosophes developed a series of structural reforms for politics and government, the law, and education.

"It became possible, and even stylish, to seek the causes of drunkenness and crime in social circumstances and to explain poverty neither as a divine dispensation nor as a just punishment for laziness but as a stroke of misfortune or a failure of society" (Gay 1969, 37). In this spirit, the Enlightenment advanced representative government but, again except for Rousseau, not broadly popular government. The philosophes also pressed policies for more humane criminal codes and a variety of schemes for public education that occasionally contained provisions for universal public education (following Condorcet) and vocational preparation. More frequently, their designs for public education followed from their general contempt for the masses, transmitting a desire for an orderly public of docile citizens; mass education was intended to impose simple rules of conduct for public virtue and good citizenship. In this manner, the Enlightenment's program for education made both structural and individualistic assumptions.

Perhaps there is some charm in excusing the general failure of the Enlightenment's program as realistic utopianism, a good attempt at difficult, humanistic goals. Yet neither in their programs for individual betterment nor in their proposals for the structural reform of the law, education, and politics did the philosophes make the socially efficient assumptions of many Romantics nor create instances of the corrective myth, unless their fictions of the American experience fit this bill.[3] Still, the most excessive of these exaggerations—Tocqueville's *Democracy in America*—can easily be taken as a notorious Romantic instance of imagination over memory (the propaganda of individualism and the author's "confirmation bias") more than as an extension of the Enlightenment impulse. The Enlightenment's realization of the difficulty of human change and of the tentativeness of reason in compromising between ration and passion—the absence still of good information—inspired a minimalist social welfare agenda, hardly the revolutionary fervor of subsequent centuries. The modesty of the philosophes' expectations for their program was proportional to its influence. The diffusion of Enlightenment ideas was restricted, and "only in England, the Dutch Netherlands, and France was there as yet an adequate social foundation . . . to ensure that [Enlightenment ideas] would extend beyond the circles of government and nobility to influence public life" (Woloch 1982, 270). Moreover, the actual adoption of the program was even more circumscribed and temporary, notably in France.

The philosophes' enthusiasm for two largely incompatible explanations of social conditions—free will and institutional determination—failed to reconcile the trade-offs and contradictions between the two except to argue explicitly that both were needed. Bacon's fierce conviction that "every man has his fortunes in his own hands," the theme of Franklin's sermonizing and Edwards's Puritanism, is obviously false without some recognition of the contributions of social conditions to human achievement (Gay 1969, 8). The Enlightenment's avoidance of choosing between individual and institutional explanations of social outcomes did not impede the Romantics, and certainly never Nietzsche, who obviously agreed even more with Bacon than Bacon probably would have liked. The philosophes rejected the predetermination of social outcomes; yet, inspired by the successes of Newton and Liebniz in quantifying portions of the physical world, they grandly insisted that nature was knowable through natural science, and similarly that society was perfectible through social science. Both tasks, but especially the reform of social institutions, entailed a rejection of fatalism and passivity in favor of proactive and thoughtful citizens who acted in a free society, exercising their critical capacities to pursue the social good. At least, the social good (the general will) would be produced either intentionally (for Rousseau) or unintentionally (for Adam Smith) through greater individual autonomy. Yet the programs of the philosophes customarily assumed, and without much discussion, that the reform of social structures and freely chosen individual behaviors were compatible causes and not subsumed within each other. Yet even while insisting on the possibility of rationally understanding nature and society, the philosophes maintained a great faith in mystical causation, particularly by attempting to justify the "spontaneous" benefits of freedom.

The Mysticism of Spontaneous Order

The Enlightenment justified its reforms with the assumptions of freedom: first and foremost that progress required freedom but also that the natural goodness of man or at least his capacity for social harmony would emerge in an open, minimally controlled society; that some sense of equality was necessary in society to maintain freedom; that both law and government should be instituted to protect freedom. The invisible purposiveness of the marketplace is the exemplary instance of the Enlightenment's basic faith in spontaneous order, the most meritorious expression of freedom. Yet spontaneous order, the contribution notably of the Scottish Enlightenment, is essentially "antirationalist" mysticism rather than evidence of the Enlightenment's commitment to reason, let alone science. The fervor of the Enlightenment to improve upon oppressive rule inspired arguments for minimalist government that overwhelmed its very commitment to rationality and reason, pressing analysis back to metaphysics—the choice of first principles from intuition and surmise that were convenient to political commitments rather than assertions about social reality that were empirically true.

Smith was a tortured moralist who wrote compellingly about human suffering and usually instrumentally about freedom. He is not the clairvoyant saint of conservative hagiography whose derivation of moral theory and social welfare justifies an indulgent freedom for commerce, a nearly limitless personal freedom, and even the mood of anarchy, if not its substance. His works are models not of consistency, clarity, and rationality but of compassion, developed by a cautious traditionalist who summarized and systematized prevailing economic theories. Indeed, his most striking claim to collegiality as a philosophe is his humanitarianism, not his rationality. *The Theory of Moral Sentiments*, anticipating the 1776 publication of *The Wealth of Nations* by seventeen years, is a tract on human folly so profound that it doubts the capacity of human reason to make planful social progress. Rather, Smith's argument is predicated on the assumption that "the social arrangements under which we live are of such a high order of complexity that they invariably take their form not from deliberate calculation, but as the unintended consequences of countless individual actions, many of which may be the result of instinct or habit" (Hamowy 1987, 3).

Moral Sentiments preaches that the common good ("the order of the world, and the perfection and happiness of human nature") is secured as the unintended consequence of the individual's pursuit of self-interest;

thus personal morality should not necessarily be confused with either (Smith [1759] 1994, 239). Smith elaborates a role for two moral verities— justice and regard for others—that is not utilitarian; personal morality does not necessarily protect and advance society, system maintenance, social continuity, or political tranquillity. In this way, collectivities can be both more and less than the sum of their separate units: bricks are not microcosms of buildings. Because of man's necessary, seemingly inherent ignorance and, very importantly for Smith, a judicious self-restraint that is the quintessential moral quality, collective man (government) should not interfere with the multitudinous decisions of men out of which the wisest and most beneficent social institutions emerge:

> But though man is thus employed to alter that distribution of things which natural events would make, if left to themselves; though like the gods of the poets he is perpetually interposing, by extraordinary mens, in favour of virtue and in opposition to vice, and, like them, endeavours to turn away the arrow that is aimed at the head of the righteous . . .; yet he is by no means able to render the fortune of either quite suitable to his own senti- ments and wishes. The natural course of things cannot be entirely con- trolled by the impotent endeavours of man. (Smith [1759] 1994, 239)

The invisible hand of spontaneous order makes unnecessary, and even harmful, the artificial controls of government. The famous quotation itself has been an eloquent page in the speeches of marketplace survival- ists who claim that their greatest pleasures lie in the wealth and benefits they create for their workers, customers, and fellow citizens, and the free- dom that they engender for the society itself:

> The rich only select from the heap what is most precious and agreeable. They consume little more than the poor; and in spite of their natural selfish- ness and rapacity, though they mean only their own conveniency, though the sole end which they propose from the labours of all the thousands whom they employ be the gratification of their own vain and insatiable desires, they divide with the poor the produce of all their improvements. They are led by an invisible hand to make nearly the same distribution of the necessaries of life which would have been made had the earth been divided into equal portions among all its inhabitants; and thus, without intending it, without knowing it, advance the interest of the society, and afford means to the multiplication of the species. (Smith [1759] 1994, 264–65)

Yet in more than two hundred years of subsequent economic analysis, these distributive assumptions have never been proven, nor were they apparent during Smith's era or before. It is also notable that in spite of the world's then leading empiricist (Hume) living around the corner from him and the commitment of the Enlightenment to proofs from nature, Smith felt no compunction to test his propositions about natural distributions. His use of history was more illustrative than analytic. Indeed, for Smith the issue of proof was frequently not empirical but metaphysical and expository. Yet the role of government remains attractive, and with good reason (suspicion of commercial conspiracy and motive generally), while America has always had a "governmental habit" even in its most freewheeling days (Hughes 1977). Yet Smith is not simply arguing that public benefits result from unsavory private motives such as when invention is the occasional product of rapacity and esurience; rather, he defines greed, vanity, and power as the engine of industriousness, innovation, and therefore progress. Smith is embracing the more difficult proposition that the distribution of benefits and wealth created by freedom is actually harmed by collective decision making, notably through government, and that this harm reduces national wealth. The excesses of *Moral Sentiments*, partially corrected in *The Wealth of Nations* with caustic commentary on the monopolistic motives of the business sector, are passionate arguments for freedom that induce a reluctant momentum for the prerogatives of wealth as necessary for social and economic progress (not salvation). Yet the quality of the argument, its ability to transcend ideology and intuition, is not improved by its noble aims; after all, there is hardly a philosopher who ever sought the destruction of the species or at least who said so.

Smith's argument fails pointedly as an expression of the vaunted rationality of the Enlightenment. He posits a convenient nature of man; his argument requires the presence of material human capacities that emerge through freedom, or he is left with the very untenable prospect of something being created from nothing at all. But the immanence of justice and of regard, let alone competitiveness, the motive to dominate, and self-restraint are all conjectural and contrived; they are never located in the anatomy of the body, the physics of the world, or the sociology of culture. They are the nonscientific, immaterial, soul-like and spiritual characteristics of a God-given nature of man—a series of suppositions and rhetorical inventions that are endlessly compliant with the requirements of social debate. In fact, much of Smith's argument, even adjusting for the literary conventions of the time, proceeds from ex cathedra pronouncements that defy any sort of objective proof, even in principle: "[O]ur regard to the will of the Deity ought to be the supreme rule of our existence" ([1759] 1994, 241); "God, the great avenger of injustice, is a motive capable of restraining the most headstrong passions" (241); "[B]etween one permanent situation and another [referring to poverty and wealth], there was, with regard to real happiness, no essential difference" (209); "The reward which Nature bestows upon good behaviour under misfortune is thus exactly proportioned to the degree of that good behaviour"

(207); "Though in the present state of society this misfortune [the fall from riches to poverty] can seldom happen without some misconduct, and some very considerable misconduct, too, in the sufferer, yet he is almost always so much pitied, that he is scarce ever allowed to fall into the lowest state of poverty" (202).

The Wealth of Nations is the more compelling and sophisticated work, in part because Smith dropped some of his sermonizing and piety, but mainly because he addressed the most important instance of spontaneous order, its economic expression, and with panache and a thoroughgoing concern for the losers in the marketplace.[4] Quite explicitly, Smith argued that the least amount of intrusion into a free market, by either government or the private connivings of businesspeople to achieve monopoly control, produced the greatest amount of wealth and consequently the greatest social benefit (this again despite his conflation of happiness with wealth). The individual's pursuit of private interests spontaneously generates both wealth and social tranquillity through the mystical coordination of unknowable forces.

Yet unlike his previous argument in Moral Sentiments or in his earlier lectures, in The Wealth of Nations Smith acknowledges a growing respect for the protections and material benefits of government and the need for an elaborate system of taxes. In fact, with each passing publication and the progress of the different editions of The Wealth of Nations, Smith propounded an ever-enlarged role for government (Canaan 1994). In the final, fifth edition, Smith outlines government roles not only in national defense and the maintenance of public order but also in "public works and public institutions," including public education. Nevertheless, Smith maintains his consistent argument for the minimalist state, ever substituting charitable donations and market fees for public revenues while restricting historical commitments of the state, notably for clergy, church activities, and state-chartered corporations (e.g., Hudson Bay Company and East India Company).

Smith's roles for civil government, as well as for the taxes it requires, are frank and large intrusions into the market, but he does not specify the explicit conditions under which the general injunction for laissez-faire can be breached apart from a vague sense of utility. He justifies the growing role for government—indeed, he even appears to enlarge some of the public responsibilities, notably for education and perhaps public works, that contemporary governments had shouldered—as a result of the evolution from tribal hunter societies to industrial nations on grounds that "the acquisition of valuable and extensive property . . . necessarily requires the establishment of civil government" (Smith [1776] 1995, 767).[5] This unfortunate device of inventing historical evidence of genetic social development has been a near substitute for metaphysics that was given immense play among the Romantics, who were simply continuing an authentic Enlightenment tradition. Still, Smith clearly fears government even while he maintains a regard for its many roles. But he even more abhors the undue influence of the private sector, notably monopoly and privilege, that gets worked into public sinecures for commerce, the church, and aristocracy. In the end, it may be judicious to interpret Smith's fears generally as a concern with discretionary power and not simply as a historically bounded preference to dissolve the remnants of mercantilism.

Yet for all of Smith's humanitarianism, his program was still constrained both by the rigid caste assumptions of his time and by the characteristic snobbery and condescension of the philosophes. While he proposed general education, he restricted its depth because

> though the common people cannot, in any civilized society, be so well instructed as people of some rank and fortune, the most essential parts of education, however, to read, write, and account, can be acquired at so early a period of life, that the greater part even of those who are to be bred to the lowest occupations, have time to acquire them before they can be employed in those occupations. For a very small expence [sic] the public can facilitate, can encourage, and can even impose upon almost the whole body of the people, the necessity of acquiring those most essential parts of education. (Smith [1776] 1994, 842, 844)

This was still a step toward greater democracy of concern amid the indifference of the times to the plight of common people. In part it reflected Smith's sympathy for those who suffered the drumming monotony of factory work and its alienating consequences. He had absolute faith in the apparently democratic conviction that "the natural effort of every individual to better his own condition . . . is alone and without any assistance, not only capable of carrying on the society to wealth and prosperity, but of surmounting a hundred impertinent obstructions with which the folly of human laws too often incumbers its operations" ([1776] 1994, 581). However, he did not have a commensurate faith that democratic effort would have equalizing effects, nor that it should. Indeed, the free market and liberty generally were devices to sort the citizenry into appropriate categories of social and even moral worth.

In his consideration of the role of religion and the church in the life of the lower classes, Smith disparages any lofty expectations for their social progress, even through universal education. He quotes Hume's argument for paying clerics a comfortable wage "to bribe their indolence" and assure, in the logic of restricted competition, that they do little to stir up popular resentments ([1776] 1994, 848, 850).[6] His program for limiting the "disagreeably rigorous and unsocial" moralism of the "little sects" also related to general education, but again with a clear separation of the possibilities by class. "The middling or more than middling rank and fortune" were apparently to benefit from professional training and university education with exposure to science and philosophy, basically the program of the Enlightenment. The rest of society was to be saved from "enthusiasm and superstition" by callous manipulations: the "frequency and gaiety of public diversions," "small premiums and little badges of distinction," "military exercises," and other expressions of condescension and disregard for the capacities of common people (842–46).[7]

Smith's balancing of public responsibility with what he saw as the wisdom of both minimalist government and dispersed power was driven by his antagonism to mercantilism, by a variety of assumptions about the ability of the different classes of society and the proper conditions of society, and of course by a mystical reverence for the redemptive beneficence of spontaneous order that made his policies practicable. After all, he lacked specific evidence that contemporary society fell short of the best of all possible worlds, and therefore he was obliged to draw inferences about what might be from a very imperfect, indeed a largely contrived, view of a reality that was yet to be. Thus in spite of an often compelling skepticism, his arguments remain largely polemical, political, and finally irrational, relying on growing perceptions of social and economic abuses to press for reform, that is, "the recovery of nerve" (Gay 1969).

Apparently, within Smith's evolutionary scheme different invisible hands are as specialized in guiding different types of culture as industrial workers in a factory.[8] Consequently, the circumstances of nature and culture gain importance as Smith acknowledges their centrality early in *The Wealth of Nations*, but he does not pursue the possibilities for planning and management, that is, instrumental rationality. He *prefers* spontaneous order because he *doubts* the possibilities of reason except in pursuing a very narrow sense of personal advantage. Thus again in spite of Smith's elegant, erudite, and trenchant illustrations, the core of his argument remains antirationalist, dependent on an untestable, inscrutable, and divine force.

Yet he cannot be faulted for ignoring either the impossibility of experimental validation or data that were impossible to collect. However, his argument is developed as a polemic, admittedly subtle, and does not parallel the empirical requirements of even nonexperimental science such as evolutionary theory. On the one hand, he does not propound testable notions as such, and on the other he fails to specify utilitarian criteria that would provide a goal for the instrumentality of economic and social policy. Rather, Smith elaborates his initial assumptions of spontaneous order in the manner of a metaphysical argument but illustrated with specific references to the economic world. While the invisible hand may be a "literary embellishment" following Letwin, spontaneous order remains the core structure of his argument, not simply a metaphor of exposition.

Spontaneous order assumes that individuals have almost no control over social institutions and, more important, should not try to extend their ignorance to control them. Because of both an inherently limited intellect and the inevitable moral imperfections of the powerful, the results of "calculation" and control are inevitably counterproductive. Thus, spontaneous order as social policy—laissez-faire—plays havoc with social cause and individual responsibility; if the individual has no control over social institutions, then he bears no blame for his misfortune, poverty, or even laziness. Smith's assumption of free will is obviously contradicted by his frequent comments about the influence of culture over human motivation. Indeed, culture itself may be the grandest of all spontaneous orders, keeping people clothed in public, orderly in crowds, and communicative through language. The utilitarian issue (the influence of public expenditures on national wealth) and the ethical issue (the obligation for relief) are not as neatly separated as Smith would wish, and his cavalier assignment of final justice to God and the afterlife (at least in *Moral Sentiments*) is not closely argued in terms of its implications for political and social tranquillity.

Moreover, the assumption that wealth and happiness are coextensive is explicitly rejected by Smith in *Moral Sentiments*, where he observes that contentment does not increase with wealth (262). Rather, man perpetually pursues the illusion of happiness through wealth. "And it is well that nature imposes upon us in this manner. It is this deception which rouses and keeps in continual motion the industry of mankind" (263), and therefore the wealth of nations as well as social order. Yet again, motivation is not a condition of society for Smith but rather an inherent quality of man (analogous to the Romantics' instincts) that is harnessed by freedom to the production of wealth. Yet by subsuming the importance of morality (justice and regard for others) to utility (production of wealth), Smith defers individual responsibility, and therefore welfare, to collective institutional responsibility—the conditions necessary to maximize wealth. In his later lectures on law as well as in *The Wealth of Nations*, Smith seemed to define government's role in protecting justice almost entirely in terms of assuring "the secure and peaceable possession" of property (Hamowy 1987, 16; Smith [1776] 1994, bk. 1). The assumption that justice emerges spontaneously from numerous individual actions motivated by "self-love," argued by both Hume and Smith, may be "one of the boldest moves in the history of the philosophy of law," but it lacks the satisfying support of factual proof, recommending in the end only the wisdom of picking one's parents carefully before being born into a free market or an unregulated society (Homowy, 11, quoting Haakonssen).

Spontaneous order comes along with spontaneous problems. As social complexity may be beyond human reason, so, too, is spontaneous order as a principle; this may perhaps explain the recourse to metaphysics in its justification. Smith's *Moral Sentiments* makes little claim as an epistemological advance of rationality, instead relying on a commonsense explication (Franklin's style of argument by aphorism), as well as the constant appeal to the reader's experience and reason; Kant, pointedly referencing Hume, defined common sense as "defiance without insight." Moreover, tradition and freedom are frequently antithetical. Individual responsibility would seem to be undercut by institutions beyond the individual's control. Thus, a nihilistic neuroticism—one of the many crises of modernity that predated modernity—is created between individual responsibility for market success and recognition that those adversely affected may not be responsible. Smith's clearly God-centered Christianity—the Creator of man's nature, notably his sense of justice, and the designer of the universe and its laws—would seem to be a necessary assumption of his natural order. Indeed, God is a professional and intellectual convenience, even a theoretical construct for Smith as much as one of his many convictions.

In addition, the moral fatalism of spontaneous order implies that because social forces are uncontrollable, "we are impotent to improve the social arrangements in which we find ourselves . . . [thus militating] against any program of comprehensive reform" (Hamowy 1987, 35). Hamowy suggests that the Scottish Enlightenment was "unaware of the full import of this implication," that is, the inadvertent restriction on *all* government action. Yet the commitments of the Scottish Enlightenment lay in justifying both tradition and individual freedom, notwithstanding the frequent contradiction between the two.

Conservatives have subsequently taken far greater comfort from spontaneous order in preserving the intuitive value of market success than Smith probably intended. Laissez-faire has always remained a questionable hypothesis of economics as much as it has been the rallying cry of the commercially successful. Certainly Smith's consistent sympathy for the poor (at least his conception of the deserving poor, who are industrious but unfortunate), even absent much faith in their moral or intellectual capacities, may explain some of the complex meanders from his own strict minimalism in order to accommodate his charities and humanitarian impulses. Smith's gradual enlargement of government over the course of his writing is made in the spirit of a moral tract that is improved as sensibilities change and not as better evidence is adduced. The enormous superstructure of intuited assumptions that sustain Smith's theory contradicts the spirit of science, underscoring the extent to which the Enlightenment is better understood as ideology than philosophy. While the philosophes may not have replaced Christianity with their own version, they did furnish industrialization—the engine of modernity—with a compatible, if secular, faith.

The Reforms of Liberty

The program of laissez-faire became increasingly plausible and largely after the eighteenth century not because Smith proved its value but because of growing discontent with the apparent inefficiencies of mercantilism and the tyrannies of government control. The reforms of liberty were carried politically by an increasingly powerful bourgeoisie, particularly its urban components, for social standing and economic elbow room. Smith's theories transformed reality—the rapacity and the indifference of industrial and commercial elites to the social harms of the factory system, mass production, mechanization, and urbanization—into myth, the sanctimonious anodyne of public virtue that justified business's new social position, political dominance, and special pleadings for less regulation and lower taxes.

The French Revolution signaled the emergence of the bourgeoisie as a political force in Europe, even though land as a productive factor continued to dominate both industry and commerce until well into the nineteenth century. Factory owners, merchants, financiers, and other large entrepreneurs came to dominate society as industrialization and its consequences became the overwhelming factors in social change. Smith's specific theories of laissez-faire, along with spontaneous order more generally and the Enlightenment impulse itself, legitimized their ascendancy (Doyle 1978). Whatever the intentions of the philosophes, the appropriation and implementation of their ideas were acts of political convenience and certainly not reasonable, coordinated, planned, intended, or coherent steps into the future.

Rather than the cause of any great change in civilization, Enlightenment thought may be more profitably understood as the fortuitous ideological consequence of the demand for material plenty and the growing influence of the industrial and commercial elites in satisfying those appetites. Mass democracy may be one of the side effects, a spontaneous emission, of industrialization. In no important sense was the Enlightenment a tribute to reason, forbearance, and control; the history of the Enlightenment, as well as its own intellectual shortcomings, mocks its pretentious loftiness.

It is worth reemphasizing that industrialization and the subsequent democratization of the marketplace, rather than Enlightened insight, were the principal reasons for the propagation of science, the culture of science and freedom, and the broader political democratization of expression (Osborne 1970; Deane 1979). The torrent of seventeenth- and eighteenth-century bleeding over the possibilities of objective, systematic truth and the regularities of nature and the nineteenth century's fantastic desire to overturn physics with literature, poetry, and self-invention were simply the ideological concomitants of fundamental cultural changes. Those changes were largely impelled by technological innovation and not the ethereal will of man. As the emergent cheerleader for industrialization's consequences, the Enlightenment authorized the displacement of previous elites, providing Romantic thought with an attentive constituency for the reactionary's comforts: a sense of beleaguerment and righteous grievance, tradition's virtues, the transcendence of imagination over mere reality, and, most powerfully, a hunger for restored status.[9]

The Enlightenment in America

Neither the colonies nor the new republic ever fully embraced Enlightenment ideals; early America came closest to the Enlightenment program in its still imperfect Constitution. America distorted the themes of the European Enlightenment—broadly conceived as empiricism and science, democracy, freedom, humanitarianism, and progress—in support of its pietistic religion and preoccupation with policy and government. Indeed, freedom was never universally intended but may have been simply the metaphor of Enlightenment universalism that was compatible with public discourse and colonial envy of the imagined cosmopolitanism of the motherland. Severe abridgments surrounded the early republic's franchise, excluding blacks and slaves, Native Americans, women, and the poor, while considerable suspicion attended Catholics and many immigrants. Still, in a letter to the colonies' governors, Washington in 1783 wrote, "At this auspicious period, the United States came into existence as a Nation, and if their Citizens should not be completely free and happy, the fault will be entirely their own" (Koch 1965, 24). As in Europe, the Enlightenment was less a fact of politics than an elegant point of view, perhaps more valuable as self-deception than even propaganda.

The numerous scholarly attempts to fashion Jonathan Edwards as providing a "rationalized theism" that opened the American Enlightenment[10]—a reconciliation of the religious with the enlightened—is based largely on his early philosophic musings, unpublished during his lifetime. However, Edwards, the author of "Sinners in the Hands of an Angry God" and a major figure in the first Great Awakening of the 1740s, had clearly rejected any rational or even rationalistic logic in terrifying sinners to repentance and salvation through the threats of confronting an unknowable, unpredictable, and very short-tempered God; the imagination that could reconcile predestination with free will made no concession to scientific proof. If there was any mood of the Enlightenment in Edwards, it was attributed and incidental:

> All wicked Men's Pains and Contrivance they use to escape Hell, while they continue to reject Christ, and so remain wicked Men, don't secure 'em from Hell one Moment. Almost every natural Man that hears of Hell, flatters himself that he shall escape it; he depends upon himself for his own Security; he flatters himself in what he has done, in what he is now doing, or what he intends to do. . . . But the foolish children of Men miserably delude themselves in their own Schemes, and in their Confidence in their

own Strength and Wisdom. . . . Till [Man] believes in Christ, God is under no manner of Obligation to keep him a Moment from eternal Destruction. So that thus it is, that natural Men are held in the Hand of God over the Pit of Hell; they have deceived the fiery Pit, and are already sentenced to it; and God is dreadfully provoked, his anger is as great towards them as to those that are actually suffering the Execution of the fierceness of his Wrath in Hell, and they have done nothing in the least to appease or abate that anger, neither is God in the least bound by any Promise to hold 'em up one moment; the Devil is waiting for them, Hell is gaping for them, the Flames gather about them. . . . In short they have no refuge, nothing to take hold of, all that preserves them every Moment is the meer arbitrary Will, and uncovenanted unobliged Forbearance of an incensed God. (Edwards 1741, 9, 11–12)

Whatever his philosophic agreements with Locke over materialism, Edwards was a stone-hard, doctrinaire theologian whose tenets of life were founded on the metaphysics of faith and grace. He encumbered science and knowledge with the limitations of divine sanction. Edwards was "highly resolved not to let science itself, as a mere description of phenomena, take the place of philosophy or theology of nature" (Yarborough in Shuffleton 1993, quoting Perry Ellis). His apparent humanism—all good things for all good men—was a very flimsy sort of credential for elevation as a philosophe.

Rather than the cleric as scientist, Edwards epitomized the practice of superstition and dogma that taunted the European Enlightenment. Instead of "a strategic movement toward" a "rational religion" and an Enlightened method for "Puritans to analyze the rhetoric of God's conversations with us," Edwards seems simply to be accommodating to the inoffensive portions of deeply antagonistic doctrine in order to deliver his revivalist enthusiasms with a timely, pertinent, and directed forcefulness. Edwards's Calvinism is the compelling political force circumscribing the American Enlightenment. While Franklin's aphoristic ideals may popularize the Enlightenment in America, continuing as inspiration for the nation's ceremonial civil religion, the reality of Edwards's unreality has been the persistent, characteristic, and compelling fact of American choice—the profound rejection of rationality as science in social decision making. The lineage that stretches back from Jonathan Edwards to Cotton Mather and the incidents at Salem recommends itself poorly as an impetus toward Enlightenment.

The American Enlightenment quickly conceded ground to American Romanticism. As May 1976 characterizes the evolution of the Enlightenment in America, it emphasized the later revolutionary and didactic phases more than its earlier moderate and skeptical phases. The moderate Enlightenment of rationality, science, Locke, and Newton and the skeptical Enlightenment of Voltaire, Hume, and Holbach were profound challenges to America's Puritan commitments. Rather, the Revolutionary Enlightenment of Rousseau and Paine—"the possibility of constructing a new heaven and earth out of destruction of the old"—became routinized during the first quarter of the eighteenth century as the didactic Enlightenment of progress, perversely detailed by Adam Smith but clearly not Hume. Indeed, the Enlightenment's defining assault on established authority was submerged in the fervor of the New World's utopianism and religious revivalism. The American Romantic period opened as the declining stages—revolution and its routinization—of its brief encounter with Enlightenment. Cultural myth was more the fact of American society than rational skepticism; American exceptionalism prevailed over humanitarianism.

The pillars of the American Enlightenment sustain a borrowed style of European novelty—intellectual mimicry diluted by three thousand miles of ocean—more than the substance of intellectual or philosophic depth. Mysticism, common sense, intuition, and always the devices of religious knowledge (scripture, revelation, epiphany, introspection, and faith) constitute the archaeology of America's belief in its civil religions. The announced deference of Adams, Franklin, Madison, Hamilton, and even Jefferson, as well as Edwards, was paid to rationality and science as devices for reaffirming the truth of their experience and convictions rather than checks on their perceptions. Even the pragmatic details of governance were worked out within the confines of Christianity and a secular ideology edited for popular tastes, notably by Paine and by the authors of *The Federalist Papers*, that customarily stayed close to its Puritan roots. Indeed, the Enlightenment in America sustains Becker's sense of the European Enlightenment that it shifted ideology more than it created any great social innovation, except for science itself (Becker 1932). Excessive modesty, let alone cautionary self-doubt and strategic skepticism, were not sins of the new republic.

When it came down to a governing constitution, the founding fathers genuflected before reason but assumed that progress would occur by reining in the passions. Factional compromise, largely voluntary—wide permission for Lindblom's mutual adjustment—and the restraint of power by separating its exercise into mutually limiting institutions were the innovations of American political decision making that also defined the nation's near-total abandonment in practice of any reliance on reason, let alone rationality. The constitutional provisions were pragmatic adjustments to the problem of developing a defensible and coherent nation out of thirteen colonies insistent on their independence. The priority need for political compromise over humanitarian goals does not fulfill the scenario of the optimists of the American experience such as Tocqueville and Hartz. In this manner, Koch's conclusion that at its best (as represented by the founding fathers) the American character sustains an "open-minded, experimental temper" ignores the frequently cruel and exclusionary pragmatism of American adjustment (Koch 1965, 31–32).

The fact that no royal or aristocratic bloodline was established in the United States as in Europe,[11] was not for want of trying. Because of an open season, more or less, for social mobility and land at the frontiers of the New World and the difficulty of cementing a permanent ruling class, power remained relatively fluid. The United States entered its industrial age without the baggage and friction of feudal remnants—masses of credulous, impoverished agricultural workers; stultifying rules of land use and commerce written into law and tradition; and a beholden and obedient merchant class. However, freedom from these impediments was a tribute not to a hallowed American soul but to the good fortunes of a "forest primeval."

The tradition that casts the founding fathers as prophets and saints and the early republic as paradise regained ignores the likelihood that the nation's pluralism and tolerance, such as they have been, grew out of the amorality of historical circumstances and not superior virtue. The early republic (and continuing for more than 150 years) was anything but tolerant and inclusive. Writing their founding opinions in treatises, letters, books, legislation, and commentary, the American philosophes gave little hint that they envisioned a greatly expanded electorate or a central government that would assure more than procedural protections for liberty and justice, and this latter to but a fraction of the society. Equality remained inherent and divine, not yet sociological. The myth of the experimental character of America was imposed on it by European utopianism that slowly worked its way into the nation's own folklore; the pragmatic adjustment of American politicians was not infused with the neutrality, distance, or love of learning of the scientist. Indeed, the political adjustments of the early republic were made to assure political coherence and often at the expense of every other vaunted Enlightenment goal, notably including rationality, decency, and social progress. Koch's epigram might be amended to better recognize America's active political theme: at its best the nation prevented mayhem by ruling elites and mobs; at its worst it has condoned slavery, racism, prejudice, grave unwarranted inequalities, mindless industrial waste, hunger, industrial plutocracy, and ignorance. Not coincidentally, the founding fathers abided these problems with masterful, Enlightened equanimity, while a fear of popular rule probably was as strong as their suspicions of traditional power. The American constitution is itself the statement of a bitter pessimism toward human nature, the predatory instincts of man in society.

Jefferson was not quite expounding Koch's "new American culture" but rather expanding a political franchise sufficient to purchase a new nation's defense. Jefferson seems to be a very reluctant democrat, constantly qualifying his impulses toward the universal with more mundane, pragmatic considerations of nationhood and security. The colonies and early republic did not have Europe's luxury of a large standing army conscripted from an impoverished peasantry and depressed urban population and grateful to escape the grind of agriculture and the terrors of unemployment. The republic's defense was predicated on a militia whose martial will reflected the stake of the citizen in his freehold, employment, and sense of future prosperity. Indeed, the incongruity of the slaveholding squire and the early democrat is somewhat repaired by Jefferson's concession to inspire people to defend the new nation. Jefferson argued in *Notes on the State of Virginia* for expanding the political franchise granted by the constitution of Virginia to those "who pay and fight for its support" (Koch 1965, 384).

While this clearly expands the electorate beyond "one man in ten," a restricted size that Jefferson indicts as accounting for England's corruption of public administration, it is far short of anything approaching universal inclusion. While Jefferson often stated in one form or another that "the influence over government must be shared among *all* the people," his subsequent sentences invariably restrict, probably out of fear of the masses, the sharing to a greatly pared and specific diminution of "all" (Koch 1965, 389). In this case, he means only "an extension of that right to such numbers as would bid defiance to the means of corruption" (389). The universality of the Declaration of Independence was severely localized and circumscribed in the Constitution, just as Jefferson's love of mankind and his sense of universal entitlement were greatly restrained by personal inhibitions, pragmatism, self-interest, and tradition. Rationality and humanitarianism were more terms of approbation than calls to action.

Jefferson's notion of public education, again spelled out in *Notes on the State of Virginia*, parallels Adam Smith's, except it was neither as generous nor as open to merit. Indeed, his plans for public education were largely extensions of his sense of "the people," which was quite limited by the condescending suspicions, if not the actual hostilities, of the philosophes generally. Broad education was intended to teach the "first elements of morality" in preparation for later "religious enquiries" when the student matures. "As their judgments advance in strength, [the curriculum] may teach them how to work out their own greatest happiness, by shewing them that it does not depend on the condition of life in which chance has placed them, but is always the result of good conscience, good health, occupation, and freedom in all just pursuits" (Koch 1965, 388). The second stage of education, the grammar school, provided instruction in languages, largely Latin and Greek, as "an instrument for the attainment of science," but not science itself, which was intended only for "those whom either the wealth of their parents or the adoption of the state shall destine to higher degrees of learning," that is, for the scholarship student: "youths of genius from among the classes of the poor" (388, 389). Adam Smith's intentions for public education included broader and deeper instruction of the masses and provided consistent public support well beyond tuition for the few aspiring but poor young geniuses.

As with the other American philosophes, Adams's frequent references to science and rationality in politics did not constitute a nascent political science or even a respect for empiricism in policy making. Adams never detailed a method or even a mood of science except to deflate its pretensions to objective truth with his own epiphanies, a failing that continues to debilitate contemporary political science. The American founding fathers were less men of letters than the European philosophes but far more directly involved in fundamental politics. In this way, much of Adams's energy was expended in promoting the separation of powers rather than in deriving any sort of rational explanation for the novel design. His primary work, the multivolume *Defence of the Constitutions of the Government of the United States of America,* develops support for the innovations of the American government from the traditional authorities and doctrines of recognized classical and contemporary sources of wisdom on government. However, it fails to develop even protoscientific grounds for their wisdom. Adams uses "science" in the common meaning of a learned discipline, an area of systematic inquiry that is rigorous. Of course, a more sophisticated empiricism was impossible, since controlled experimentation with culture was then, as now, impossible, while history offered colonial America few examples of republican democracy for even a comparative or reconstructive approach. Yet Adams approaches his task dogmatically, relying on traditional, sacred texts and ancient prophets, rather than with the Enlightenment attitude of prudent skepticism.

Adams's "divine science of politics" and his "science of legislation" were ploys of polemics, a manner in which they most frequently continue to be employed; they are terms of self-certification. Indeed, for Adams, science is more morality, and occasionally even a synonym for republican government (*Defence,* Koch 1965, 255), than objective fact derived from a series of root assumptions about man in society. In the spirit of the times, he was much taken with Newton's mechanics and assumed that "governments [are] enacted on the simple principles of nature" and that "nations move by unalterable laws" of nature that rational inquiry would uncover (258, 266). Yet democracy, always limited in the manner of his contemporaries, was not an empirical question but a moral commitment. While he acknowledged the "natural authority of the people alone," he also feared their transitory, emotional injustices and sought to restrict popular rule through the contrivances of constitutional government, even going so far as to make a convenient evidentiary assumption that the citizens' "virtues have been the effect of the well-ordered constitution, rather than the cause" (267). But there is little evidence that "the people" referred to the broad masses; unlike Jefferson, Adams seemed pleased with England's small electorate and failed to press for wider voting rights in the United States.

Going back to the founding fathers for guidance in modern affairs is either cunning or cowardice, for these men had little, if any, vision of an industrialized future of mass equality, nor even much taste for it. Within their own world they were consumed with the difficulty of negotiating a workable alliance among thirteen disparate colonies sufficient to guard their fragile independence. However comfortable and proud the United States feels in its democratic institutions, the philosopher-statesmen of the early republic made few claims to actual science in justifying the nation's institutions; Koch's stretch to find a rudimentary political science in Adams's polemics—"a searching would-be 'science' of politics"—is tribute only to her desire to construct halos for the American prophets of the republic and reverence for their revealed words (Koch1965, 45). Still, Adams has purchased the nation's affections for all time with his deep faith in popular (although certainly not universal) experience and sovereignty, the corruption of power, and the fickleness of intellectual elites: "Democracy, simple democracy, never had a patron among men of letters. . . . Monarchies and aristocracies pay well and applaud liberally" (*Defence*, Koch 1965, 257). Nevertheless, these are deeply ideological conclusions, well-phrased but tendentious summaries of felt experience— perhaps also barbs aimed at the French philosophes, notably Voltaire—setting the theater for nationalistic myths; they are not timeless empirical truths.

Even more so with Franklin than with other figures of the American Enlightenment and its Revolution, the confusion of the grand statement of universal aspiration with the politically expedient creates a special sincerity—a deeply emotional moralizing—for the nation's assurance of its own exceptionalism. Franklin was an unusually talented man whose achievements provide propagandistic historians with the excuses for Romantic nationalism and a secular religion of patriotism. This "Newton" of the eighteenth century "provided the symbolism for his country's progress from subservient colonial status to independent creation of nationhood." While Koch and countless others mean this approvingly, the legend of Benjamin Franklin, despite his own rare modesty, has been contrived for civic emulation—pluck and luck, the myth of the poor immigrant (in his case from Boston to Philadelphia) who succeeds through hard work, the just deserts of virtue—and, above all else, a morality play of the quintessential American character: inventive, intelligent, disciplined, modest, crafty, industrious, and, of course, successful and revered. While Franklin wrote shelves of civic sermons on personal virtue, he also acknowledged, as did Adams, the institutional require- ments for society's progress. Yet Franklin has been appropriated from any contextual complexity as the edifying apotheosis of the American. Benjamin Franklin, George Washington, Daniel Boone, Johnny Apple- seed, and others have become euhemeristic myths of the American cre- ation that convert fallible humans in complex and specific situations into the gods of nationhood, the anointed avatars of sanctified values.

The myths and legends of a national Eden obscure the coercions of rule, making power appear endearing, familiar and even frumpy, protec- tive, and accessible rather than arbitrary, self-serving, and indifferent to its external consequences. The American myth, central to its civil religion, conveys the ineffable comfort of an inevitably beneficial order created miraculously and capable of transforming sin and base motives into social virtue, the adventitious glory conferred on America by God's exceptional regard for her extraordinary people and mission. Thus the descent of the modern American state appears as a consequence of human will, foresight, tutelage, and even divine intent. Myth and super- stition dispel the dread that the nation is the product of opportunism, fac- tional preference, and unforeseen social, economic, political, and environmental good fortune: the unknown and unknowable, tradition, preference, mood, and impulse rather than ration or even reason.

The American Enlightenment lacked its European sources' concern with "scientific, aesthetic and historical theorizing," instead focusing on politics and religion, and in characteristic fashion largely capitulating to the mystical and subjective. Hofstadter's buoyant sense of the Enlighten- ment in American thought—"empirical and pragmatic liberalism shaped the American spirit, along with a healthy dose of Adam Smith"—might profitably take counsel from his own documentation of the culture's per- sistent and profound anti-intellectualism (in Shuffleton, 1993, 212). Spirit itself, like the invisible hand, is a wonderful vagueness, not easily dis- missed as metaphor, to explain the reversion to the irrational in a pinch. But still allowing for the literary in factual writing, American choices of policy and their emotional precursors have customarily been less empiri- cal than pragmatic, if that. Moreover, America's vaunted political prag- matism, then and now, has rarely been the principled, reasoned discipline that the philosophes intended to either transcend or transform ignorant self-interest into a public good. Notwithstanding America's Enlighten- ment pronouncements on science, freedom, democracy, and progress in the manner of Edwards's citation of biblical Scripture to gain legitimacy, "On the whole, various forms of Protestant Christianity served the emo- tional needs of most Americans better" (Shuffleton, 1993, 27). The enthu- siasms of common people, in America as in Europe, were stylistically repugnant to the philosophes, providing reason to restrict broad political participation to an educated elite, although expanded from the extraordinarily narrow confines of a hereditary aristocracy.

America has long emphasized pietism and respect for institutional authority that emphasizes the political and irrational. It still does, and profoundly so, to define its protectiveness of factional preferences even in contradiction of Enlightenment ideals, and to promulgate in politics the enthusiastic style of religious revivalism, with its implied injunction to abide authority if not actually orthodoxy. As May (1976) concludes:

> Yet despite all nuances and divisions in this conflict [between Enlightenment thought and Protestantism] as in so many, the time came when moderates and compromisers were finally forced to take a stand on one side or the other. When this happened, in about 1800, most Americans came out on the side of Protestant Christianity, in however battered or eroded a form. This is, I think, a major fact of American history, and not only of American intellectual history. (xv)

This Puritan habit of "revelation, tradition, or illumination" (May 1976, xiv), together with an abiding faith in the spontaneous benefits of freedom (if not actually neglect), may constitute the customary American preference for minimalist reform and then usually for procedural change over any sort of substantive provision. The franchise has been broadened but usually without any compensation for prior inequalities or steps to achieve parity. Socially mandated thinking of one type or another, but typically including a generous respect for Adam Smith, has been a more important influence on social policy than the actual conditions of life. The philosophes in Europe as well as in America justified their proposals with sophisticated assumptions about the workings of society but without even reasonable evidence and none that was even remotely rational. Indeed, so free were they of rigor or of system to reliably describe their vaunted reality (nature), that Enlightenment programs are probably more inkblot-test projections of the intellectuals' own subjective needs than reasonable summations of historical necessity.

Perhaps the failures of the philosophes (to implement their program and to resolve the philosophic and intellectual flaws of their logic) and the narrow parochialism of the American Enlightenment might all be excused in historicist terms by insisting on the Enlightenment spirit's special relationship to its own time—the confines of place that necessitated the failure of the Enlightenment spirit to dominate the political choices of its own times. After all, the Puritans of the Revolutionary period were consumed with the tasks of governance and salvation to the exclusion of deeper concern with science, aesthetics, and even general social progress. But this makes excuses for obvious limitations without true explanation while emphasizing the relativity of the Enlightenment's ideas and isolating its legacy from later social circumstances. This inevitable limitation on the interpretation of any historical event may indeed be very appropriate, judicious restraint and a tribute to rational caution. But it also underscores the degree to which Enlightenment thought lacks its very own requirement of rationality and the extent of the philosophes' complacency with polemics and ideology. The Romantic period actually made a virtue of this defect.

The Romance of the Anti-Enlightenment

The Romantic reaction to the Enlightenment repudiated its central pillars (science, empiricism, rationality), substituting the transcendent will of man for the regularities of nature or, better said, reality. Romantic thought generally elaborates the philosophy of absolute idealism, which traces from Kant's critique of Hume to Fichte, Hegel, and Neitzsche, among quite a few others, notably including the twentieth century's existentialists and the postmodernists. Romantic thought, liberated from the typical constraints of nature, came to glorify a heroic role for man in society, the ability of the human imagination and will to transform, transcend, and transvalue culture as well as the ill-conceived reality of the Enlightenment. The German absolute idealists, particularly in constructing a self-defined role for social man that emphasized an extreme individualism of "freely willing agents," anticipated the operative civil religion of the United States and therefore the emotive grounds for its social welfare choices. In rejecting the Enlightenment enterprise, the Romantics sanctified the possibilities of freedom; whether or not the will is a satisfying intellectual protagonist of reality and reason, it has long been its victor in social decision making.

Romantic thought is not coextensive with absolute idealism; indeed, Goethe was contemptuous of the "shallow subjectivity of the [R]omantics" (Lowith 1964, 6). Yet the most compelling characteristic of both Romanticism and its inspiring philosophy is still the repudiation of conventional rationality and the acceptance of some novel definition of human contingencies that are the products of will: "[U]ltimate philosophical commitments are made, in the last analysis, on temperamental rather than evidential grounds" (Aiken 1956, 55). The rejection of rational proof tolerates as plausible realities a variety of individual and group enthusiasms for the subjective, the sublime, the evanescent, the ephemeral, the imagined, the hoped for, and ultimately the convenient: Nietzsche's heroic "overcoming," Hegel's teleological determinism of history and his faith in the Absolute, Fichte's absolute I (the self-positing subject) and ultimately his chauvinism, along with the contrived, belletristic, self-serving, improbable conversion of desires into social imperatives. Romanticism freed of the discipline of objectivity, however elusive, has been the vehicle of ideology but in the end a better descriptor of American social welfare decision making than the Enlightenment's skepticism, hope for reason, and disciplined check on impulsiveness.

Raising man the poet and mythmaker above man the scientist and rational social animal, the Romantics also rejected the intellectual mood of the Enlightenment. At its core, Romanticism gives permission to impose faith on perception and in this regard resurrects metaphysics, scorned by the Enlightenment (no matter how often practiced). Thus the Romantic freedoms justify reactionary conservatism as well as revolution. If there are only ideas, then there is no external authority to adjudicate between competitive ideologies, and then the fact of power itself, as both Nietzsche and Marx appreciated, comes to settle disputes. The philosophy of absolute idealism has given birth to a Romantic sentiment whose emotive logic has taken on great political force, particularly in cultures freed from traditional institutions, imbued at the start with a notion of broad democratic freedoms, and hubristic with the faith that they have willfully constructed themselves. Romanticism insisted on the infinite complexity of life and the human experience, rejecting the necessary reductionism of science. Thus, as Saiedi (1993) points out:

Belief in the limitations of sociological reason led the Romantics to reject the French Revolution and the idea of holistic social engineering. Karl Popper's criticism of holistic social engineering (radical politics) is based upon the same epistemological assumptions. In both cases, the non-rationalistic epistemology leads to a defense of the status quo (142).

Still, it was not simply science that provoked the Romantics but the broader notion of criticism—science in its profoundest sense as divorced from any obligation to fill the vacuum of discredited belief and faith. Thus, the Romantics characterized the Enlightenment as a destructive force and affirmed in their multitude of fancies the value of the imagination either to discover the imperatives for tradition or, far less often, to construct a novel revolutionary future. The rejection of Newtonian mechanics as the apt metaphor for society and man, the sense of life as ineffable, and a fear of directed change, are associated commonly in Romantic thought with the "necessity of moral cohesion for the maintenance of social order"—the functionalism of sociological theory that is at heart conservative, justifying "political legitimacy, monarchy, and civil religion" (the last as Rousseau would have it, an actual religion with all the adornments of ritual and mystification) (Saiedi 1993, 143).

Yet it obviously need not be so: Marx transformed Hegel's historical justification of the Prussian monarchy into a manifesto for radical social revolution, and innumerable irrationalists propose world revolutions in politics and human consciousness on revealed, intuited, dogmatic, or sublime grounds. Nevertheless, the Romantic imagination has long provided both emotional and political succor for displaced elites as well as the powerful, as reaction citing the many unintended harms of rationally intended policies and as orthodoxy invoking the prudence of cultural continuity, that is, the value of presiding institutions. In this way, the Enlightenment gave emerging industrial elites a sanction to pursue wealth and social position. while the Romantics provided them comfort in their victories (along with the traditional elites they displaced). Yet too much should not be made of the distinctions between the two eras in intellectual politics or mood, since both indulged the habit of simply assuming the value of their central principles.[12] Nevertheless, a polar difference, an immense and defining gulf, separates the scientific mind of skepticism and criticism, on the one hand, from the Romantic sensibility that "rejects any fundamental distinction between the spiritual and the sensory, the mental, and the material levels of being," on the other (Saiedi 1993, 69).

Thus, the epistemological question (What is knowledge, and how is it created?) becomes the telling divide between Enlightenment and Romantic thought: the standing, probity, and utility of science versus the irrational substitutes that remain philosophically ambiguous. The Romantic enterprise was initiated by Kant's rejection of empiricism. Kant argued that the world cannot be known except through the senses, that there is no objective reality as Hume proposed, that reality itself cannot be known, although it probably exists as a systematic entity. While only ideas formed about the world through the senses have any standing as knowledge, Kant did not argue for a labile imagination that constitutes the artifacts of the world by ideas. He accepted the notion that people do not walk through walls or will their immortality; the regularity of nature and the possibility of intellectual coherence based on its predictable ordering are central to his system. While ideas may be the only human reality, mind is not, and although objective reality—"things in themselves"—may exist, it lies beyond the human capacity to know and is probably irrelevant to the human condition. "The function of [human] understanding is rather to legislate the rules of inquiry by which the brute facts of sense may come to live together in a civil society of law-abiding objects" (Aiken 1956, 33). Thus science becomes both possible and desirable.

Problems arise for Kant where the usefulness of fundamental a priori principles that are not derived from experience (as Hume would have it) is applied "to suppositious entities that lie entirely beyond the range of possible experience. In doing so we lose our logical bearings, and are left with imponderable antithetical claims whose validity is equally doubtful" (Aiken 1956, 35). In this way, the cause of the universe is unknowable, as are dimensions beyond the four perceived by the senses; both cannot be proven empirically, that is, through the senses. Kant's world is made knowable through synthetic a priori principles such as cause, time, and space that allow for the coherence of experience. Hume argued that because knowledge was fundamentally based on the experience of an objective reality, metaphysics was untenable. Kant's argument that empiricism was untenable still preserved the role of natural science and explicitly rejected metaphysics as irrelevant for dealing with the world of unknowable noumena. Yet Kant's rejection of empiricism actually reaccredited metaphysics, preparing respectable philosophical grounds for the subsequent Romantic cultivation of their alternative epistemologies. Moreover, Kant never rejected God or the soul, two targets of Enlightenment skepticism, but rather attempted to prove their necessity by positing their existence through his novel entity of practical reason. Pure reason, that is, science, existed to explain the natural world, while practical reason existed to understand the rules of human behavior, that is, morality. The categorical imperative, a principle analogous to the golden rule, dictates what people ought to do.

Fichte marched Kant's logic into absolute idealism by dropping the notion of things in themselves, thereby closing any duality in the methods of developing knowledge about nature and knowledge about morality. He rejected the province of pure reason (science) even in the realm of phenomena (knowable nature). In place of the possibility of science—objectivity or even intersubjectivity—Fichte proposed an extreme form of subjectivity, the self-positing subject. All that exists for Fichte (in contrast to all that is knowable for Kant) and the Romantics generally are ideas that are given reality by the "self-positing subject," the "absolute I" that allows for self-consciousness (existence) and thus self-determination (morality).[13]

Kant and philosophers generally have been fascinated with the crisis of personal responsibility created by the principle of sufficient reason, the basic rational condition of science. The Romantics were defined by their response to this challenge.[14] If all events are determined by prior causes, then personal responsibility—free will, freedom—cannot exist, since the individual is merely blown by the winds of circumstance like any other object at the mercy of previously existing conditions, even probabilistic ones that are both sufficient and necessary to account for all consequences. Kant's solution, the principle of the categorical imperative that defined the universal criteria of moral obligation, was very different than Fichte's absolute I, developed as a metaphysic of the human will.

> Furthermore, to be free in the deepest sense was said to require a self-determination, not only of one's particular deeds, but of the general principles according to which one lives one's life. It was primarily here—in the subject's adoption of its highest practical principles—that Fichte attempted to show that self-positing was necessary for practical subjectivity [self-determination]. He envisioned one's self-determined norms as arising only

from an activity in which the subject enters into uniquely "subjective" relation to itself, insofar as it reflects upon its essential nature and in the process
constitutes its identity. (Neuhouser 1990, 168)

It is not that Fichte's theory was successful philosophy; as Neuhouser
(1990) argues, the self-positing I and the not-I (subject and object),
"although philosophically provocative, are almost certainly incapable of
being carried out" (68). Rather, Fichte's theory and absolute idealism generally have inspired immensely pervasive ideology. Quite apparently,
this process of self-reflection, and largely as Fichte intended, left a fundamental legacy to psychotherapy as well as to the subjective epistemologies, notably Freud's introspection, existential psychology, and
twentieth-century phenomenology. Absolute idealism implies that freedom is achieved through self-reflection, undergirding the moral effect, if
not the actual intentions, of psychotherapy that shifts the burden
of responsibility for individual behavior from social conditions to the
shoulders of the individual, the subject. Psychotherapy thus becomes a
process of morality to affix blame far more than simply an explanation of
human behavior. As political ideology, absolute idealism in the garb of
self-reflection and the active choices of human will mandates a social policy to create self-consciousness through social welfare programs that contain large components of counseling and psychotherapy. As a concrete
program to determine personal culpability, the relatively inexpensive
opportunities for self-reflection and personal awareness offered by psychotherapy supplant an expensive redistributive strategy to equalize
material conditions. Self-consciousness trumps fiscally ambitious programs, especially when the effectiveness of alternative strategies implies
only symbolic representation, not material outcomes.

Hegel extended Fichte's absolute idealism to a generalized historical
ideology, creating out of the self-positing reality of subjectivity a controlling principle of society—the World-Spirit, the Absolute—a dominating
ethic for social choice. He transformed Fichte's personal mysticism into
the great ethical force of a political, collective ether of the universe. From
the introduction to *The Philosophy of History:*

Reason is the Sovereign of the World . . . proved by speculative cognition
. . . that by which and in which all reality has its being and subsistence. . . .
(83) Yet it is this very plan [of Providence] which is supposed to be con-
cealed from our view: which it is deemed presumption, even to wish to recognize. . . . (85)
    History belongs to the realm of Spirit. . . . (87) The essence, of Spirit, is
Freedom. . . . (88) Spirit is self-contained existence. Now this is Freedom
exactly. For if I am dependent, my being is referred to something else which

I am not. . . . . This self-contained existence of Spirit is none other than self-consciousness—consciousness of one's own being.(89)
. . . Nature· a hidden, most profoundly hidden, unconscious instinct: and the whole process of History (as already observed), is directed to rendering this unconscious impulse a conscious one. Thus appearing in the form of merely natural existence, natural will—that which has been called the subjective side—physical craving, instinct, passion, private interest, as also opinion and subjective conception—spontaneously present themselves at the very commencement. This vast congeries of volitions, interests and activities, constitute the instruments and means of the World-Spirit for attainingits object . . . contemplating itself in concrete actuality. (Aiken 1956, 96)

The similarity of the World-Spirit to Smith's invisible hand is hardly coincidental, but no part of Hegel's idealism (or any part of Romanticism) is offered up for trial before an empirical judge. Hegel's subjective "reason" is the antithesis of Hume's empirical reason or Kant's pure reason. Indeed, Hegel consciously retreated to the protections of metaphysics, perhaps motivated to restore society to a satisfying traditionalism hallowed by time and implicit collective consent. He quite clearly conceived of the state as the vehicle for the World-Spirit; its evolved institutions assured that "the interest of its citizens is one with the common interest of the State," an element in the understanding of what is appropriate. While Marx rejected the sanctity of established institutions, his identification of the proletariat as the inevitable revolutionary force relied greatly on Hegel's teleological theory of history and its mystical evolutionary development. In the end, then, for Hegel and for the Romantics generally, humans exercise their freedom through self-consciousness to accept the unknowable righteousness of history; because historical development, guided by the World-Spirit (or some other substitute for collective behavior, including mystical invocations of "culture") has been implanted into man's nature by God, it *must* be moral. Burke, in building the conservative reaction to liberalism on the experience of the French Revolution, was like a tabloid reporter repeating a few sordid details of transitory, corrupted human existence. Hegel wrote for all time, confident that when he "speaks of spirit," he is sure "that it also speaks through him" (Lowith 1964, 9).

Nietzsche was openly, explicitly, and specifically hostile to the pillars of the Enlightenment, rejecting hopefulness, faith in reason, and humanitarianism while giving a broad legitimacy, indeed an obligation, to the philosophes' contempt for the common man. "What Nietzsche really opposed, so it is argued, is the do-good ethics of service and the false humility and charity which are enshrined as the Christian virtues" (Aiken 1956, 206). He turned away from the spontaneous morality of received wisdom and back to the individual in heroic isolation from

society's institutions as the central force in historical change and morality. His sneers at the "herd" were expressed notably as contempt for utilitarianism: *"pleasure* and *pain* . . . are foreground modes of thought and
naiveties [sic] which anyone conscious of *creative* powers and an artist's
conscience will look down on with derision, although not without pity"
(Nietzsche 1968, 154–55, emphasis in original). In contrast, he held an
overriding faith in the superior human, creative for sure and probably
also political, and the "fundamental will of the spirit" expressed as an
instinctual "will to power" (160). The will to power, the central concept
in his thought, was similar to the variety of forms of self-consciousness
in idealist philosophy that created existence. In spite of being attributed
to instinct, Nietzsche interpreted the will to power as the expression and
realization of freedom and thus being, that is, human existence.

Unlike Marx, Nietzsche put no faith in Hegelian historical dialectics,
particularly the inevitability of progress toward social improvement.
Paradoxically or perhaps quite understandably, Nietzsche could live with
a slew of posited instincts to explain human behavior, but he shrugged
his narrow aesthenic shoulders at Hegel's theory of immanent historical
causation. Indeed, Nietzsche's nihilism (the "uniformitarianism" of
democracy, utilitarianism, and other expressions of the popular will;
"nothing is true [but] everything is permitted") has had an immense
influence on modern aesthetes and the art of self-pity. Nihilism attributed
the modern mood of alienation to tendentious, beholden rationality (science), more socialized to power than culturally independent. Nihilism
despaired of the possibility of social autonomy, accepting "the essential
precariousness of the life of reason, and the innumerable symbolic masks
that unreason can wear" (Aiken 1956, 204). Power was self-determination; nihilism was to be conquered by the superior individual who by his
will to power redefines constricting social norms.[15] Nietzsche's "eternal
recurrence," the remolding of social institutions through the superhuman
will to power, implies the customary metaphysical excuse of spontaneous
order, the mystical assumption that the superhuman's efforts are both
moral and for the benefit of mankind.

Nietzsche's depreciation of democracy as the means by which weak
individuals bind creative and powerful ones—the slave mentality that he
frequently attributes snidely to Jews—is a consequence of his assumptions; democracy's deficiency is necessarily true, not amenable to falsification by mere facts that have a very questionable empirical standing.
Thus, self-transcendence leaves no room for the exculpations of institutional determination; self-definition is the manner in which humanity's
aristocrats through discipline and insight transcend their "animal heritage of reflexive, instinctual response and their social heritage of routine,
herdlike conformity" (Aiken 1965, 211). Finally, the "self-conquest of
nihilism in which the 'victor and vanquished' are one . . . in eternal recur-

rence" transforms society, providing salvation and immortality for the super human but without any need for God's presiding will (Lowith 1964, 193, 194)

The common distinction between Nietzsche's literary merits and the more profound philosophies of Hegel and Fichte may not be all that important (Aiken 1956, 202). None of them offered testable or knowable propositions about rationality, history, morality, or nature. The philosophers claimed the internal consistency of their arguments but, more important in the end, and despite their aversion to utilitarianism, played to the satisfactions of their audience, and notably political elites. The absolute idealists consistently applied to the development of their thought systems the very subjectivity (a sensitivity to political will) upon which they depended.

Whatever the philosophic limitations of absolute idealism, the Romantic spirit appropriated its attack on rationality to nurture cults of the irrational. The Romantic fallacy harbors the solipsism that people invent themselves in one fashion or another and the quality of their self-invention has proportionate influence on culture and politics. This extreme hubris is also the buried source of the extreme individualism of American social welfare policy, social efficiency and its corrective myths, and the passion for holding people responsible for their own circumstances. Heroic self-invention, the grandiosity of power, animal superiority, the transcendent and transvalued, the reality of the imagination define the Romantic mind in rejection of science and all its leveling commitment to proof.

Conclusion

The justification for contemporary social decision making in the United States is phrased in the Enlightenment's universality and humanitarianism, but its true parentage is Romantic. That is, the ceremonial religion of the nation is a liturgy of Enlightenment rhetoric, but actual policy making reflects Romantic assumptions. In neither case are the goals rational, knowingly useful, or even instrumental in pursuing explicit ends, a tribute to the nihilistic critique of society rather than to the prescription that it need be that way.

Neither philosophes nor Romantics ever troubled themselves deeply with anatomy or autopsy; the self-certified savants of wisdom and insight refused to bow before mundane reality or to dim their brilliance with the problematic unpredictability of people and their cultures. Empiricism was a useful goal, and Newton's mechanics a valuable metaphor for the Enlightenment, but they never became operative, disciplining principles of social inquiry or policy. On their part, the Romantics simply rejected objectivity and scientific rationality by hiding behind the insuperable barrier of humanity's limited senses. The Age of Reason did not have much, while the Age of Ideology paradoxically constructed its illusions alongside of the natural sciences in spite of the Romantic hostility to rationality. The recurrent influence of Romanticism itself probably had little to do with social development but much to do with apologia for power. In spite of the universal cliché of his eponym, Marx was a curiously imperfect prophet misidentifying the locations and timing of his revolution, the revolutionaries, and the outcomes of social change; Nietzsche, the perfect anticollectivist, came closer to predicting the crises of modernity but offered only the wildest, most fanciful resolution, the "boyish blasphemy" of Marvel Comics heroism (Aiken 1956, 202).

Even as autopsy failed to disclose the anatomical reality of Enlightened and Romantic elements—mind, nerve, the I, the non-I, the will to power, the public will, the will, instinct, the nature of man—the integrity of their philosophic systems was incessantly repaired with an infinite regression to other untestable postulates: an unknowable nature, divine intent, divine neglect, divine wisdom, invisible hands and other hidden body parts, and the endless immaterial devices of the spirit and the spiritual. Few ever improved upon Jonathan Edwards's inventive faith in an inscrutable God. It is not that empirical proof was devalued, disproven, or denigrated; it simply was not decisive for the poetic imaginations of two centuries that cherished the "indispensability of the sacred" (Gay's phrase) and labored mightily to create it. If Kant was transitional, then neither the Enlightened departure lounge nor any Romantic port of call along the way bothered with bon voyage toasts, welcoming committees, or hospitality wagons for his caution and modesty or his sense of pure reason as tentative and pragmatic. He is probably best appreciated as climate, a literary breeze between the hurricanes of eighteenth-century ideologues and the tornadoes of nineteenth-century fabulists. The realities of life and society—human mechanics—were mere details of grander metaphysical projects, which not by accident were grander ideological ones as well.

Kant's definition of the Enlightenment—"have courage to use your own reason"—was surely sincere, but his essay was probably written tongue in cheek, intended as parody and tease (Kant 1963, 3).[16] The wry humor, perhaps self-mocking, was well earned by the political ineffectiveness of the Enlightenment program. The philosophes on both sides of the Atlantic experienced as little encouragement to submit their theories to systematic objective judgment as did the Romantics for theirs. Indeed, the American Enlightenment concentrated on nation building, not humanitarianism or rationality.

Except for science, Enlightenment and Romantic thought were both romances, even sentimentalities. That "the philosophes fashioned their materials from the most varied sources" (Gay 1964, 209) does not mean that they came up with a substitute for superstition and faith. Indeed, they did not. Gay oversimplifies Becker's argument that the philosophes simply substituted a modern form of Christianity—"the Protestant and Jansenist tradition"—for an outdated one. Yet Becker's broader point credits the philosophes with reframing church religion as secular religion and transcendent spirituality as political fervor; the Enlightenment created "the new religion of humanity," essentially a civil religion for republican politics, that "lived on, inspiring, in the new world and the old, many lesser revolutions" than the French Revolution (Becker 1932, 158). Unfortunately, the philosophes and Gay as well imagined that their program was the product of reason, not mere metaphysical and political invention.

> [T]he eighteenth-century religion of humanity accompanied and sustained the political and social revolution which was gradually accomplished, with whatever concessions in theory, with whatever compromises in practice, during the hundred years that followed the taking of the Bastille. The concessions and the compromises were indeed many and flagrant (Gay 1996).

If Becker is perhaps too insistent for Gay on the religious derivation of Enlightenment ideas, Becker has still identified the mythopoetic political core in its ideas, that is, the very culturally dependent nihilism and perhaps even millenarianism that the philosophes chastised in others. Even Adam Smith, arguably the first great economic systematizer, created little more than an elaborate manifesto, a political program to replace the ideology of mercantilism with a more compliant faith.

In spite of their pretensions to rationality, the philosophes were denied its tools. After all, natural science was then still an immature communal endeavor, and the human sciences were barely in prototype. Yet the force of Becker's reminder is that the philosophes failed even in the mood of rationality; they were fervid ideologues, which is frequently obscured by subsequent historians, including Gay, who share the Enlightenment's emotional commitments and insist that the philosophes were geniuses who transcended their times—mortal men, perhaps, but the best sort, genuine heroes. In fact, the history of the sciences converts the specific ideological point of cultural service into a timeless thesis: the natural sciences came to fruition not as social policy but serendipitously in pragmatic service to technological ambitions while the human sciences largely went the way of all social flesh, obedient to power and without much respect for the autonomy of the human intellect.

Schwarzmantel (1998) repeats the common concession to ideology "as a necessary part of the process of politics" (187). Yet only ignorance is inevitable, and belief is beggared by the difficulty of developing credible information; social theory remains incomplete and rarely amenable to confirmation. The descriptive plausibility of the absolute idealists—

Hegel's unknowable collectivity of the World-Spirit—and the faith in mankind of the happy, upbeat, Enlightened humanists do not in any sense endorse the prescriptive necessity of any generalization. Theory and ideology, even before descending to harsh dogmatism, are separated by mood: the tolerance for ambiguity and the willingness to find out; the strength to pause before judgment and acknowledge uncertainty; the humility to submit propositions about the world to worldly, objective tests. While even Lite-ideology is an understandable response to the embarrassment of ignorance, a society is defined by the extent of its demands for superstition and unquestioning belief, its unwillingness to systematically test it suppositions.

In this sense, both Enlightenment and Romantic thought were ideologically formed, even apart from the thoroughly political epochs to which they corresponded. Their profoundest sages rarely conceded ignorance and constantly asserted their poetic effusions and free-willed inventions as abiding transcendent truths. Yet both ages are mistakenly characterized as embracing any form of reason or rational insight and better understood as impelled, if not actually formed, by a variety of uncontrolled and unanticipated social forces: the Enlightenment floated on industrialization and Romanticism, a deeply reactionary and bad-tempered epoch, gave luster to displaced elites and the aggrieved but also and more commonly to those whose will to power had prevailed. As power promiscuously draws its sanction from any obliging source, the Romantic impulse toward self-invention—the rejection of any sort of objectivity or even intersubjectivity—explains much about the popular denial in the United States of its diversion from Enlightenment goals. Indeed, America's smug and sublimely self-centered politics animates its social welfare choices, legitimizing the indifference, if not the actual cruelty, of its policies. The unique blend of Enlightenment and Romantic ideology in the United States places universal and humanistic values at the center of the national ethos while cultivating a supremely individualistic, even Puritan, pietism divorced from any grounding in the reality of social conditions, social policy, and their effects. The imperative of the Romantic license has distorted the practice of the human sciences and the rational mechanisms for informing public debate. Scientism, the fountainhead of cultural superstition for modern times, has displaced churched religion as the reigning source of ethical authority.

Notes

1. Philosophe is taken generally to refer to the Enlightenment intellectuals rather than simply to those in France.

2. It can also stand as a quick summation of Montesquieu (*Spirit of the Laws*), Hume (*Enquiry Concerning Human Understanding . . .*), La Mettrie (*Man a Machine*),

Diderot (*Letter on the Blind*), Rousseau (*First Discourse* and *Social Contract*), and many, many others.

3 Still, many utopian assumptions define *Emile, The Wealth of Nations, Spirit of the Law*, as well as the rest of the Enlightenment canon, not least of all Franklin's endless and tedious aphorisms for personal change. Moreover, popular superstitions, cults, and religious enthusiasms were as common in the eighteenth century as ever before or after (Kelly 1972). The eighteenth century was labeled the Age of Reason in either mockery or hope but certainly not as a description of its politics or style.

4. Commercial conservatives have appropriated Smith's concern with poverty, transforming it into a moat around the influence of business and businessmen. If American wealth and its ideological organs shared Smith's compassion for poverty, there would be little fuss over social legitimacy. This comment addresses Cato Institute, Heritage Foundation, Chambers of Commerce, American Bankers Association, and so forth, notably including the current generation of congressional leadership.

5. It would even seem plausible speculation to anticipate Smith's support for a truly extensive government role as industrialization eventually creates the gargantuan plenty, economic complexity, market power, and social problems of contemporary America. The gradual necessity of a welfare state with regulatory controls over immensely powerful commercial organizations (that some would argue rival the sovereignty of the state itself) seems implicit in Smith, an extension that would supersede his commitment to free enterprise. It is quite consistent with Smith's mood to envision his support for antitrust legislation as a public work "for facilitating the commerce of the society" ([1776] 1994, 779); indeed, his questioning of the "exclusive privileges" of regulated companies constituted a withdrawal of public sanction for monopoly (791–818). Yet Smith failed to acknowledge the possibility that his goals for defense and justice may have been incompatible with minimalist government. He had no evidence at all of any industrial state in which minimalism had been prudent nor of any primitive society in which a salubrious state of nature existed. Indeed, Smith frequently ignored or dismissed out of hand disconfirming arguments and data, e.g., his attitude toward governance in China ([1776] 1994, 186–87). Smith as the prototypical economist or the great assimilator "is not to deny that Smith's arguments rest on gaps and errors" (Letwin 1963, 224). But those gaps and errors are no more dismissible now; modern economics, for all its theoretical and practical elegance, still faces a profound ideological critique on grounds of its severe experimental limitations and careerist compromises. The political serviceability of Smith's work and the adaptive sensitivities of Manpower Demonstration Research Corporations's experiments are one and the same except that Smith may have had a more creditable concern with issues of poverty (adjusting here and there for the historical problem of context) and a greater ability to acknowledge his debts to the quaint embellishments of natural law theory.

6. Perhaps Hume was trying to emulate Voltaire's caustic wit; perhaps he meant it literally, for he had little use for the clergy or their pulpits. Still, bribes for indolence are hilarious justification for the Peter Principle and many universities.

7. By and large, the Enlightenment, but for Rousseau and a few relatively minor voices, hoped to democratize the small middle classes, at most, maintaining a fatalism toward the huge numbers in the lower orders. Notwithstanding laissez-faire, Smith seems to have wanted government to do more than many, coming in the end to a conclusion, admittedly limited, of public responsibility: "any deficiencies in the revenue of institutions beneficial to the whole society must be made up by general contribution," that is, general tax revenues ([1776] 1994, 878).

8. It is curious that Smith placed so much weight on specialization as the source of industrial productivity—the entire first book of *The Wealth of Nations*. Even at that time it was obvious that mechanization and not human specialization was at the heart of the industrial revolution.

9. This assumption of the causal importance of technological innovation to societal change has been vigorously challenged by the absolute idealists at the center of Romanticism. They, along with Venturi, Gay, and many other historians of ideas, prefer to grant a greater independence to historical actors by posing epiphany, invention, intellectual climate, planning, utopianism, and even rational preference as major grounds for shaping history. The historians, in their program of scholarship although not explicitly in their intellectual commitments, embody the Romantic enterprise. In appreciation of the philosophes, Gay, as one example, heroicizes them as the Romantics' independently willing agents; his Enlightenment sensibilities are delivered in grand Romantic style. In his own way, Becker challenged these notions with the possibility that the philosophes and their ideas were profoundly inconsequential except as ideologues, simply refurbishing the eighteenth century with convenient and even familiar faith. Yet the influences of technology can be separated from the independent will of man at least in principal, even while a certain arbitrariness defines any choice of historical cause. However, it is important to recognize that the issues of inevitability or control; spontaneous order or planned adoption; unintended or intended consequences; foolishness or prudence are probably not testable in fact. These questions elude definitive historical analysis and *must* remain unresolved: the past is not amenable to experimentation, while prospective experiments are severely limited, if not actually made impossible, by the constraints of cost, method, ethics, and law. The question of political control is inevitably polemical, and the historical literature, for all its erudition and depth, might profitably recognize its inherent capriciousness and ignorance in pressing for the influence of particular causes. The notion of man as an independent let alone reasonable entity may well constitute the Romantic core of the Enlightenment that undercuts its commitment to rationality.

10. Bynack's essay in Shuffleton (1993), as well as Oberg and Stout (1993) and even Chai (1998) to some extent.

11. But then again what are the Rockefellers, the Kennedys, the Vanderbilts, and the other industrial bluebloods if not hereditary aristocrats?

12. In this way, absent of course graphic signs of divine intent, both types of thought are at once positivistic and metaphysical, but their rules for adjudicating knowledge are quite different.

13. Neuhouser (1990) claims that there is general agreement that the absolute I is the concept most central to Fichte's theory. However, there is something extraordinary and even bizarre when "once we venture beyond this most general claim, consensus among interpreters of Fichte essentially ceases. This is evidenced not only by the lack of any generally accepted, comprehensive interpretation of Fichte's thought but also by the fact that there is widespread disagreement over the most elementary aspects of his principal doctrines, including that of the self-positing subject (Neuhouser1990, 315." This impenetrability permits Neuhouser to summarize Fichte's project as a "theory of subjectivity" and Martin to insist that Fichte was working out the "objectivity or the referential character of consciousness." But given the tendency of writers to mimic their subjects—in this case, Fichte's novel meaning, grammar, words, and logic—both may have been referring to the same thing, even while each claims that Fichte's philosophy failed. More to the point, the disagreement over meaning is a general characteristic of Romantic notions, notably referring to the postmodernists and other irrationalists and their hooded, obscure, seemingly intentional vagueness that encourages readers to perform a broad participatory role in their philosophies, as though they were fingerpainting with ideas or creating an installation of subjectivity from the material of the irrational.

14. Sufficient reason, in the sense that Neuhouser employs it, refers to hard determinism. Yet the soft determinist point of view—that responsibility exists to the extent to which human behavior is malleable—probably reduces, among other things, to the empirical task of discovering the conditions of malleability; this is essentially a rational project. However, the absolute idealists' rejection of science also rejects this perspective, substituting at least in the case of Fichte and Nietzsche self-invention (self-consciousness and self-determination) as a guiding principle that lies beyond empirical verification. In failing to credibly evaluate social welfare policies—a question of fact, yet also a result of a kidnapped will—the social sciences appear to be embracing in practice a irrationalist perspective that is self-defeating if their defining project is science but immensely fulfilling if their task is myth.

15. At least for Nietzsche, the masculine pronoun is always intended to have a masculine referent. "To blunder over the fundamental problem of 'man and woman,' to deny here the most abysmal antagonism and the necessity of an eternally hostile tension, perhaps to dream here of equal rights, equal education, equal claims and duties: this is a *typical* sign of shallow-mindedness, and a thinker who has proved himself to be shallow on this dangerous point—shallow of instinct!—may be regarded as suspect in general, more, as betrayed, as found out: he will probably be too 'short' for all the fundamental questions of life, those of life in the future too, incapable of *any* depth" (Nietzsche 1973, 166, emphasis in

original). This "transvaluation of values . . . explicitly renounces the whole under-lying ethics of service upon which socialism and liberalism rest" (Aiken 1956, 208).

16. If he were serious in speaking only about freedom to criticize religion, then the essay would most likely have been, in his typical fashion, as dense and heavy as German black forest cake. Kant wrote specifically about the freedom to criticize religion, but he probably really intended to press a broader sympathy for civil freedom in general. From his *Critique of Pure Reason:* "Our age is, in especial degree, the age of criticism, and to criticism everything must submit." This is probably his real attitude toward criticism and freedom, but he dared not push it politically. Criticism apparently did not extend to Frederick, his protector. Pruss-ian universities operated under a very rare and special grant of freedom, with the proviso that ideas within the academy would not be exported for political pur-poses. In "What Is Enlightenment?" Kant the Subtle maybe getting back a bit of his own, but ever so cautiously. By the way, he did not translate Horace's *sapere aude* as the more common "dare to know" but chose in his characteristically leaden style a far more ponderous and pretentious phrase. Then again, this bril-liant visionary may have intended to irritate posterity—preemptive revenge.

Chapter 7

Science, Limited Science, and Scientism

The Enlightenment and the Romantic period both furnished contemporary social dialectics with ideology rather than any sort of acultural, transcendent truth. The philosophes and the absolute idealists, let alone the earnestly Romantic, preferred evocative social faiths to scientific theories. They did not defer to empirical validation but looked inward to self-evident truth and an ineffable reason or outward to mute, obedient history. Each epoch was confident and profoundly so of its correctness, skeptical only of opponents while providing few demonstrations of critical methods. Their moods were intellectually arrogant, not modest; they all had profound moral insights, instructive far more than questioning. While the Enlightenment framed itself in rejection of metaphysics and dogma, it ironically relied on those very tools—intuition, revelation, and, of course, convenience. Abjuring rationality altogether, the Romantics embraced all that the Enlightenment rejected, including, most notably, the probity of received values.

Science stands apart from these ideological traditions however much its practice, particularly in the social sciences, has been debased by transitory fashion and the functional demands of culture for continuity and maintenance. To some degree, the centrality of technology to modern culture has protected the communality and independence of the natural sciences. In contrast, the course of the social sciences has followed the directed lines of political preference more closely than the inspiration of Newton, becoming in the end a scientism of rationality—its parody and ritual form—particularly relative to social welfare decision making.

Science is rationality, "systematic knowledge of the true causes of particular things" (Smith 1997, 16). Its forms of inquiry, practice, mood, and most important communality are the unique philosophic legacies of the past few centuries. Even acknowledging constant nihilistic influences (culture's inevitable demands), science still offers the only reliable alternative to ideology, superstition, and tradition as a source of social authority.

Science's assumptions of rationality—the regularity of nature and the ability to discover it—have demonstrated a pragmatic ability to identify causes through replicable, prospective demonstrations of mastery. Science has prevailed because it has conferred power; it has crowded out alchemy because it has indeed been able to transform lead into gold. Producing the rare triumphs over dogma, natural science in particular and largely through its technological prowess has seemed to act independently of the intuitive myths of Enlightenment and Romantic thought. Unfortunately, the social sciences have more often created the scientism of cultural belief, its myths, and the evidence for faith that accompanies social choice.

The social sciences came into prominence on the coattails of the natural sciences, whose luster brightened the appeal of rationality as the source of all wisdom, including the social, the political, the psychological, the economic, and the anthropological, together with their applied, derivative expressions (Smith 1997). Thus, the social sciences drew their status not from their own achievements but from the technological and commercial success of the natural sciences. The ceremony of rationality, but absent the tangible forms and products of scientific inquiry, became the source of a new symbolism of power and prestige, performing the functions of priest, wizard, shaman, elder, poet, fabulist, and, not least of all, entertainer in authorizing cultural values. The criticism of the social sciences emerges as their specific, operationalized, replicable, and very constrained defining essence yields to the intuitive and largely superstitious demands of culture for dramas of cohesion, coherence, socialization, and legitimacy. Paradoxically, if not perversely, the failure of the social sciences to conduct rational social inquiry (the development of empirical theory; the application of scientific method to social problems; the evaluation of social institutions and policies) may actually explain their political and social popularity.

Too many histories of social science, but also natural science, have been written from the intellectual's perspective as heroic adventures in discovery rather than as pragmatic and practical steps to achieve common goals. Personal curiosity, the compelling riddles of nature, the noble structures of the scientific community, the brilliance of discovery, and the struggle for reliability and truth dominate the pages even while the demands of culture dominate scientific practice. The worst of the reconciliations of scientific heroism with cultural force have taken inspiration from Thomas Kuhn. They confound sociological consensus with scientific consensus, equating the diversity of scientific fields as though each scholarly field's freedom to select its own methods and to call them scientific conferred an equality of rational credibility on their subsequent "truths." Taking one step further into absolute idealism, the consensus itself becomes the scientific truth. The very idea of consensus is at first glance not improbable, since the conventions of scientists do indeed constitute the canons of proof, and thus scientific criteria are in fact social. However, the value of the chosen criteria of proof to reliably explain phenomena is far less debatable. The social sciences have yet to engineer any solution to a social problem; no social institution has been modeled as successfully as a plane or a car; the causes of social problems have not been decisively identified in the manner of the causes of a variety of diseases; and, of great moment, social policies have not been evaluated with the neutrality, probity, precision, or credibility that physics, chemistry, biology, and engineering bring to their defining inquiries.

The natural scientists' ideas and artifacts have been appropriated by culture for its own ends, not for theirs. Even more customary, culture appropriates the scientific community itself. The quiet pause of academic freedom does not assure that scientific innovation will command any integrity of use. The appropriations fail to confer the stature of scientific credibility no matter how universal the social consensus. The faith that most people place in the effectiveness of psychotherapy, Head Start, welfare, training programs, nutrition programs, the unworthiness of the poor, the power of education, personal responsibility, genetic determination, and the rest does not make it so. However, the fecklessness of the social will as social engineer does not deny the possibility of material placebo effects, only the possibility of creating them through consensus.

> Philosophers have a reputation for playing with words . . ., one of the most fruitful ways to study the history of intellectual culture. The choice of a word may be very significant in the human sciences, as it may reinforce, legitimate or even bring into existence one rather than another view of life. (Smith 1997, 15)

Semantic confusion seems to be offered in apology or substitution for the observation that "the historical record indicates that none of the methods adopted by the human [e.g., social] sciences nor any of the knowledge generated succeeds in commanding universal assent." Therefore, the human sciences are not "so much about uncovering the truths of human nature as about adventures of human expression of such power that they have acquired the status of truths" (Smith 1997, 15). However, without frank demands for tangible results and the rigors of objective experimentation, the heroic, eternal pursuit of the golden fleece belongs in the fields of literature and public relations, not science. Children who parade around in their parents' clothes blowing kazoos have not acquired adult capacities or status. The repeated confusion of the rational function of science with its social function, its production function with its ceremonies, is more than simply linguistic; it aspires to confer on social belief and civil faith the rational authority of scientifically validated theory.[1] It is not that "scientific knowledge (in this case, clinical psychology) correlates in revealing ways with the cultural and political upheavals that scored" the twentieth century (Smith 1997, 17). Rather, the field of clinical psychology acquiesced the times *without* making a notable scientific contribution. Indeed, psychotherapy and psychoanalysis are full-blooded pseudosciences, alternative medicines because their methods of validation are alternative to the canons of experimental science.

By employing the terms of consensus—"universal assent"—as though the differences between scientific proof and demotic preference were insubstantial, the distortion of meaning also slyly ignores the immaturity of the social sciences. The debilitating pitfalls of the social sciences cannot be so easily masked and excused by including their ideological flexibility ("diversity" for Smith) within the roundhouse of science, admitted for devotion, cherished for weakness. Yet in spite of the sometime agreement of beholden and loyal souls, the failure of rational proof creates the central challenge to the social sciences, keeping open the question of whether a necessarily limited application of rationality to human affairs can be both practical and pragmatic.

The social sciences are limited in achieving true rationality, first by an inability to define the criteria of rational goals but second by the difficulty of proving instrumental value, the pragmatic relationship of defined means to defined ends. In the absence of any ability to prove the highest good or the defining considerations of life and the universe, custom and politics dictate the goals to be pursued instrumentally by the social sciences. The practical ability of a science of man to describe the pragmatic value of social policy was the most modest hope of the Enlightenment and surely one of the most unfulfilled of the many promises of contemporary social science. Yet, further, the ability to measure the instrumental value of social policy in achieving its goals also evaluates the predictive value of social theory that justified policy in the first place. Without these tests, theory slides into polemics. Biased and corrupted tests of outcomes intentionally degrade theory into ideology, and social science becomes mythopoetic, performing the mindlessly obedient ceremonies that it initially sought to supplant with independent, rational authority.

The pragmatic value of the social sciences is further limited by the inability to either identify or test some notion of initial cause. At best they can theorize about proximate cause or sustaining cause, or revert to a less immediate cause on the basis of some sort of posited theory of the middle range (following Robert Merton) that itself is conditioned by cultural and political attitudes to social problems. Thus, a problem solution that is ignorant of true cause substitutes for more profound theory. Still, it would have been perfectly acceptable to reduce poverty, social distance, and the effects of racial discrimination through the variety of Great Society programs without actually identifying and handling the wellsprings of social inequality if the programs had succeeded. However, their actual effects are still not known reliably because they were not credibly measured, and the problems they addressed still persist. The same has been routinely true of subsequent policy initiatives. Therefore, any sense of the effects of social policy remains as ideological as the motives of the social sciences in undermining rational tests of social welfare programs. "The status of truth" elegantly references the institutional negotiation between the social sciences and political forces that compromises the objectivity, let alone neutrality, of social inquiry (Smith 1997, 14).

Furthermore, the common challenges of social research impose practical limitations on the ability to test pragmatic relationships. Sample size, randomization, instrumentation, measurement, and the rest have been discussed in the social sciences with numbing precision and impressive depth. Yet the practical constraints on social research—notably resources but also important legal and ethical considerations—also reflect social preferences, in particular the will to find out. What initially appears to be a limitation of inquiry on grounds of cost slowly confesses both political and professional motives; researchers themselves hide bias behind imperfect method in winsome accommodation to prevailing cultural myths.

Theoretically, the pragmatic and practical utility of the social sciences constructs a bulwark against Romanticism. However, if a limited practice of rationality is impossible for social policy, then the society is largely stuck with the insights and preferences of Fichte and Hegel, among the rest. Absent a limited rationality, society is fated to social policies impelled by technological change, the mystical forces of historical determination, an indeterminate, collective expression of genes, and superhuman, transcendent, self-positing subjectivism. With only political preference, the step from natural science to the social sciences marks the distance from technology to propaganda, from intellectual autonomy to the pay and applause of orthodoxy.

Yet the social sciences, particularly relative to social policy, cannot conform with the rationality of the natural sciences. Goals are imposed on all social systems, while the instrumental, pragmatic role of the social sciences is constrained at a minimum by practical considerations of method, cost, legality, and ethics. Nevertheless, the social sciences are attempts at a limited practice of rationality, giving up hope for rational goals but developing an instrumental capacity for a *demonstrable* benefit, a production function of scientifically credible information. The pressing question is whether even this limited role has been achieved or can be achieved. In this sense, the failure to credibly evaluate social welfare programs deepens the chasm between the social and natural sciences that denies the possibility of instrumental rationality in the social policy-making process.

Simon's bounded rationality is a famous instance of limited rationality. In 1972, he summarized his sense of progress in rational decision making:

> [T]he decision maker today, in business, government, universities, has available to him an unprecedented collection of models and computational tools to aid him in his decision-making processes. Whatever the compromises he must make with reality in order to comprehend and cope with it, these tools make substantially more tractable the task of matching man's bounded capabilities with the difficulty of his problems. (Simon 1982b, 176)

This optimism sustains social welfare dialectics today and with largely the same models and tools (even with the addition of vastly improved computational speeds and greatly increased amounts of data). The issue, however, is whether the increased sophistication has produced better decisions, whether progress in formal, procedural rationality has had a payoff in substantive rationality, whether new means better realize old ends. Simon's hope is tested by his system's own assumptions and evidence. The possibility of limited rationality is also assessed in broader application to the question of whether the American electorate makes either substantively or procedurally rational decisions—the value of "rational choice theory" in political science.

Bounded Rationality

The 1978 Nobelist Herbert Simon developed bounded rationality in order to accommodate to the necessary and de facto limitations of applying the logic of the natural sciences to social problems and conditions. He held out little hope for synoptic or comprehensive solutions to social problems and implicitly offered bounded rationality to handle only incremental change and partial solutions (Simon 1960, 1983). In an estimable and modest way, bounded rationality competes for recognition as the Enlightenment's hope for a science of man. Bounded rationality quite insistently frames the "science of administration" (planning, implementation, and evaluation) around the subjectivity of actors in organizations; it adapts scientific discovery to the imperfections of the human actor, the compelling limitation of uncertainty (Simon 1977, xiii; 1982b, 405).

In tribute to Kant's notion that only phenomena rather than noumena (things in themselves, true objective reality) can be studied, bounded rationality accepts the determinative force of psychological man in human affairs. Bounded rationality as a theory of choice is predicated on assumptions about both individual and collective human thought. Human problem-solving processes are hierarchical and handled serially, customarily not by rational principles but by heuristics. These "rules of thumb" guide the "highly selective trial-and-error search for possible solutions"; they include means-end analysis, problem factoring, and, most important, "satisficing" (Simon 1977, 277). Satisficing is the bridge between formal thinking and human motivation and emotion. It substitutes the implicit satisfaction of decision makers for the pure or economic criteria of substantive rationality, that is, the achievement of maximal or optimal levels of outcomes. Satisficing minimizes the distinction between subjectivity and objectivity, since "most decision-making, whether individual or organizational, is concerned with the discovery and selection of satisfactory alternatives; only in exceptional cases it is concerned with the discovery and selection of optimal alternatives . . . the difference between searching a haystack to find the sharpest needle in it and searching the haystack to find a needle sharp enough to sew with" (March and Simon 1958, 193). Still, Simon never defines a tool or a principle to identify the judges who will select the criteria of satisficing.

Simon's distinctions among psychological rationality, economic and sociological rationality, and organizational rationality precede the task of validation (Simon 1982b, 405–6). Whatever the subject matter for rational analysis—the cognitive processes of choice (procedural rationality), goal maximization (substantive rationality), or the impersonal application of organizational rules to organizational ends (organizational rationality)—the problem remains to certify findings: the quality of cognition, the maximization of goals, or the consistency with which organizational rules are applied to organizational ends. Scientific discovery is both disciplined and certified by scientific proof, the tests that verify outcomes, separating true discovery from false claims. These tests evaluate scientific hypotheses; they are the core of scientific rationality and scientific authority. They determine the maturity and rational contribution of any discipline.

Yet the actual instances of the application of bounded rationality to public policy that Simon offers discredit its scientific credibility, testifying to the persistent nonrational core of social research and its inability or refusal to evaluate social institutions. The choice of heuristics is not the greatest pitfall. Rather, inadequate data and porous methodologies frustrate any research conclusion.[2] Simon (1982a) reports a study conducted in 1933 to assist California's welfare department to "most advantageously distribute its funds between operating expenses and relief payments" (15). The study varied workload for the different types of workers and measured their error rates in four field offices of the state welfare department during a four-month period. In addition, the study also evaluated the number and promptness of recipient referrals to other agencies for medical care, clothing, surplus commodities, and the like. On the strength of its findings, the study recommended workload adjustments. However, anticipating the next seventy years of welfare research, it was conducted as an unreplicated demonstration project; its sample was very limited; its data were not checked for accuracy, particularly relative to the critical issue of whether referral services were actually received; there was no follow-up; no evaluation was conducted of the implementation of the recommendations or the adequacy of the referral services. Its most sensible recommendations about staff flexibility could have been made without the research data.

"Fiscal Aspects of Metropolitan Consolidation," "Tax Incidence and Metropolitan Consolidation," and "The Incidence of a Tax on Urban Real Property" are speculative but without proving a solution to the normative problems that still bedevil microeconomics (Simon 1982a). Simon provides a number of intuitive answers to the research problems, but he does not show that they are optimal or even improvements over what exists. Indeed, competitive outcomes are valued through satisficing techniques that reduce to the customary expectations of democratic election and republican representation. Still, the rationality of America's techniques of social choice remain open to debate even while they are sacralized tenets of the nation's ceremonial civil religion.

It is notable that Simon is never able to isolate either the proximate or the initial cause of problems. Therefore, in each case in which he presses forward particular factors without experimental proof as explanations of target conditions (air quality, milk production, increased productivity, technological change, atomic energy, and so forth; the breadth and erudition of his research are astonishing), he makes crucial but untested assumptions. Moreover, the research typically ignores the unintended consequences of the postulated relationships, notably their likely external diseconomies.

Finally, Simon certifies the "power of the planner in any complicated field," citing as examples the application of operations research techniques "to problems of traffic congestion" (Simon 1982b, 55). Yet the theoretical melioration of these problems may have perversely contributed to the increased traffic congestion of recent years and the underutilization of mass transit in the United States. The solution to the problem of traffic congestion in the United States may lie in continuing traffic congestion— the fortuitous neglect of European cities—not the professionalization of traffic engineering in satisficing Americans' demand to drive to work in empty cars. It is not a small point that he admits to "a bias toward the processes of discovery rather than the processes of verification" (Simon 1977, xv).

Satisficing is little more than stakeholder analysis—deferring to the judgments of the powerful. But without attention to the efficacy of the stakeholders' wisdom, satisficing better pertains to the deeply philosophic discussions of governance than to the acta of operations research. Who should get chosen to play Solomon is both a technical, empirical question and a deeply normative one that consistently brings up the problem of conflictual goals: democratic decision making is a defining

institution in a society that cherishes the individual, not only an instrumental assumption of dubious value. In other words, the price of democracy, perhaps paid for in the coin of economic efficiency, may not be a
price at all in terms of social tranquillity.

Simon's bounded rationality may be an advance in the discussion of
rationality, even a step toward becoming rational, but it has not arrived.
To the contrary, it acknowledges the irrationality of human choice by posing a few enormously constrained possibilities for rationality in social
decision making (the unsystematized heuristics, as well as the examples
of their application). However, it decidedly avoids testing the value of
those recommendations in actual operations. Simon's voluminous publi-
cations on the role of the social sciences in society raise the issue, too, that
the principal contribution of bounded rationality, despite his intentions,
may lie in its scientistic neologisms, a techno-language for social dialectics. This novel language of satisficing, game theory, computer simula-
tion, partial solutions, and the like—the hubbub of operations research
that is perhaps effective for closed, limited, sensibly quantified systems
but visited by Simon on large, open-ended, bewildering systems—tends
to obscure the nature of social decision making by suggesting that it can
be rational, at least partially. However, this possibility is not proven or
demonstrated in Simon's own research. It is not proven or demonstrated
by other social science systems of inquiry. There are still no good evaluations of the effects of social welfare policies, and the predictive value of
social research remains as weak as its ability to identify cause even in theories of the middle range.

The sense of what the social sciences could do with good data—the
quantification of social research—does not imply that those techniques
have been fruitful with very imperfect data. Yet the premature quantification of social welfare decision making along with the thrill of linguistic
invention elevates orthodoxy to holiness, creating the symbolism of rationality through an appropriated nomenclature of science for the depressingly
consistent "satisficed" policies of the American society. Indeed, there is a
collective mystery to satisficing that could stand as the telepathic bridge
between the instinctual collectivity of man and Hegel's World-Spirit. Still,
Simon brought a wonderful humanity, even a noble solemnity, to his work.
But humanity is an ancient pretense of new learning that bested the
Enlightenment with problems that still eat at civilization.

Bounded rationality may be a socially coherent form of social decision
making. However, without better tools than satisficing and other heuristics and without assessments of its effects, it cannot achieve a true
rational form in either the psychological, economic, or organizational
sense. Its constraints and uncertainties fail to certify the contributions of a
limited rationality: there is no evidence that bounded rationality, at least
during America's enchantment with technology as fashion, produces

more than an intuitively pleasing style for principal stakeholders to shore up consent, run their organizations, and keep their positions.

Rational Choice Theory

The extensive body of rational choice theory and its application also directly test limited rationality in the social sciences, the progress it has made in more than 250 years of development as a science of man. Rational choice theory in political science is particularly relevant to social welfare policy, assessing the social decision-making process against the degree to which it achieves social goals, as well as the conformity of its tenets with democratic assumptions.[3] Rational choice theory evaluates, on the one hand, the promise of Simon's satisficing and, on the other, the progress of democratic rule itself in incorporating objective science into policy considerations.

Rational choice theory in the social sciences, but particularly in economics and political science, lies at the heart of almost every attempt to explain elections, public policy preferences and choices, consumer behavior, and social attitudes. Only the rarest study in the library of rational choice theory concludes that human behavior is inexplicable or at least unpredictable and then displays the good taste and the forbearance to marvel at its stale triviality and the momentous indeterminacy of porous methods. Most research is marred from the outset by innumerable ambiguities and design imperfections that would have dissuaded an investigator with a true dedication to science from mounting the project in the first place.

As previously noted, Page and Shapiro (1992) commend American social policy making for its rationality; Cook and Barrett (1992) insist that the American people are firmly behind the welfare state, a rational social arrangement; McCloskey and Zaller (1984) argue that the change in American public opinion marks definitive (and rational) social progress. In some form or another, survey reports usually commend the American public for its rationality, meaning both good sense in selecting goals and prudence in pursuing them. Yet those who point to the imperfections such as racial biases in the American ethos (e.g., Gilens [1999] and Teles [1998]) or who simply purport to describe public opinion (e.g., Public Agenda [1995] and Schiltz [1970]) make the profound instrumental assumption that public opinion as an aggregate of individual consideration and thought determines important social outcomes. In pressing the credibility of their findings, the authors invariably define themselves as scientists, never as ideologues or propagandists. In spite of numerous and invalidating practical pitfalls—notably response falsification— almost all opinion polls also insist that they accurately measure collective attitudes. Yet in addition to the practical and pragmatic failures of the polls as credible empirical research, rational choice theory itself fails to explain, even in principle, the nature of social decision making. Without any standing as credible science, rational choice is best interpreted as a disguise for ideology, a hermeneutic novelty commending the optimism of American exceptionalism in the tradition of Tocqueville, Hartz, and Key.

Rational choice theory (including public choice theory) is a specific instance of the broader claim that political attitudes, notably toward voting and public policy, can be scientifically understood—described explicitly and employed to predict important social behaviors. The customary definition of rationality in political science follows along with Page and Shapiro's (1992) sense of rational choice ("real, stable, mutually consistent, and sensible"), reducing scientifically demanding criteria to a commonsense rule of thumb. While the vulgarized definition fobs off bronze as gold, the more specific and debilitating difficulties arise from the practice of ambiguous science. The scientism of rational choice deflates all its pretensions to retrieve the mysterium of American democracy from the mush of Romantic self-righteousness and nationalistic grandeur, the unproven and embarrassing chauvinism of a nation in search of the mandate of heaven. Rational choice theory, intent upon explaining America's policies, in the end fails to do more than legislate them with the muted irrationality of tradition. Rational choice and its descendant research provide little evidence to dispel the disquieting possibility that America, for all its vaunted civility, wisdom, and tolerance, is frequently animated by base desires, not simply selfishness and a cruel indifference to the suffering of vulnerable citizens.

Rule (1997), for one, traces rational choice back to Hobbes and the utilitarians, especially because of its instrumental logic and its passivity toward the selection of goals. Yet the consistent distortion of definitions, the abiding tendency toward self-evident truths, the subtle antiscience of its methods, and notably the tendency to reify human subjectivity (the logic of constructing all human institutions out of human perception, that is, Simon's oxymoron of "subjective rationality") reprise absolute idealism and Romanticism as social science—the power of the self-positing, unknowable collectivities of human experience such as public opinion (and even biological exceptionalism) to explain society.

Rule's summary of the tenets of rational choice cuts past the apologetics of the theorists themselves (1997, 80–81). First, recalling Simon, rational choice theory is predicated on an a priori definition of human actions as purposive while hierarchically ordered by reasonable priority, given the information at hand. Second, it entails a process of rational calculation among alternatives that again recalls Simon's heuristics, although he quite explicitly did not define them as rational. Thus Chong (2000) assumes that "rationality is based on subjective calculations of self-interest, that individuals are motivated by both material and social goals, and that calculations of interest are contingent on the history of one's choices, including the values, identifications, and knowledge that one has acquired through socialization" (6). Finally, rational choice theory holds that social institutions, including public opinion, are constructed upon these calculations, implying that the rationality of calculation confers rationality on the end product, and even that "long-term values are more influential than self-interest in determining mass policy preferences" (Chong 2000, 6). Importantly, this graduation from individual thought to social institution and tradition provides an actual method for achieving explanations of social events from individual sources, ultimately a path from the innate human inheritance to the Hegelian World-Spirit. The issue remains, however, of whether rational choice explanations fulfill their billing and actually account for social events, that is, the degree of the theory's rationality.

Green and Shapiro (1994) draw their devastating critique of rational choice theory from a rigorous analysis of the political science literature in pivotal areas. They argue that three complex "methodological patholo-gies" undercut rational choice theory: post hoc theory development, inadequate test formulation, and the tendentious selection and interpre-tation of data. "[T]hese . . . mistakes stem from a method-driven rather than problem-driven approach to research, in which practitioners are more eager to vindicate one or another universalist model than to under-stand and explain actual political outcomes" (Green and Shapiro 1994, 33).

Post hoc analysis fails to test theory as prediction but instead amends theory to conform with findings and "cleans" data to fit theory. In such a way, rational choice reconstructions have been employed to explain con-gressional seniority systems, federal budget deficits, and the growth of third parties. Analogous to Simon's means-ends heuristic, post hoc analy-sis is a critical method of the intellectual postmortem that should lead to the development of specific hypotheses for empirical testing. Yet failing true definitive tests, post hoc explanations become the apologetics of ide-ological convenience that is personal, professional, and more often politi-cal. The typical rational choice analysis both assumes some basic self-evident proposition of rationality (e.g., the pursuit of self-interest, money, security, or pleasure) and then comes to the custom-fitted conclu-sion that it has identified the specific instances of rational goals or rational motives. In this light even the beloved functionalism of sociol-ogy—useful to explain the most mindless ploys of social institutions—fails as a testable theory; rather, it persists as ideology, a bit of post hoc wisdom with nearly infinite applicability.

Second, rational choice scholarship sidesteps definitive tests. The con-structs of the rational choice models are frequently both unobservable and unspecified. Thus, "tastes, beliefs, decision rules, and at a higher order of abstraction, equilibria, form the essential ingredients of most rational choice models." As the proportion of the model's unspecified and unmeasured abstractions increases, "it becomes increasingly difficult to establish whether a set of data confirms or disconfirms a rational choice explanation" (Green and Shapiro 1994, 39). Furthermore, criteria of success are rarely defined; indeed, Simon's satisficing seems to replace specific criteria of utility. Thus, in the absence of predictive accuracy, the value of an equilibrium model is preserved by the "hope that enough people act rationally enough of the time in their political behavior for economic theories of politics to yield descriptions, explanations, and predictions which are frequently useful approximations to the truth" (Green and Shapiro 1994, 41). But this hope for regularity in the long run is worse than the undefined "reason" of the Enlightenment; it is superstitious tenacity, the addictive rationalization of compulsive gamblers. In this way, Chong's "long-term values" act as a proxy for tradition, conceding the essential irrationality of rational choice theory.

The third complex of methodological pathology encompasses faulty processes for selecting and interpreting evidence. Evidence is "projected from theory," while the area in which the theory is tested is arbitrarily restricted to events that fit its predictions. Rational choice endorses its notions with highly selective data while ignoring disconfirming instances; "this practice [is] reminiscent of advertisements that show one brand's achievements while mentioning neither its failings nor the comparable achievements of its competitors . . . illustrations combed from the political landscape, memorable moments in history" (Green and Shapiro 1994, 43).

The three pathological complexes, together with the numerous practical pitfalls of survey research itself, cheapen the value of opinion polls in defining the influence or accuracy of the reported ethos of the United States. The failure of rational choice theory and method as science discredits an enormous library of social science's efforts to make sense of political behavior and to reduce the nation's civil religion to reported attitudes. The public's preferences remain obscure, and the thing called mass opinion, if it exists at all, is an analytic curiosity.

The alternative strategy of reading intention and attitude back into the public through their actual choices of policy remains a viable substitute and the skeptic's challenge to rational choice modeling. Interpretations from policy itself and its associated problems are far less amenable to ideological distortion than polling, but they are still an imperfect expression of rationality. The return trip from policy back to motive and intent brackets the American ethos in the material and graphic cachet of long-standing, institutionalized policies. The centuries-long denial of adequate provisions for an enormous number of dependent children gets

past scientistic hairsplitting over misreported nobility—the public's puta-
tive goodwill—to arrive at the nation's embedded cruelty and indifference
as an explanation for long-standing social and economic inequalities.

The reaction formation of the field toward Green and Shapiro's indictment beckons to a psychologist more than to a logician. Curiously, much
of the criticism of rational choice theory is also targeted against Green
and Shapiro's call for theoretical precision and measurement probity.
This class of criticism, in essence denominational feuding among established churches, a form of Counter-Reformation, misperceives rational
choice theory as true science and calls for its spiritual alternative. So, for
example, Hauptmann (1996) objects to the implicit metaphor of rational
choice in politics, the tendency to explain political behavior with economic terms in the manner of Becker's (1991) analysis of the family.

Yet if economic specifications are inadequate for political decisions,
then adequate theory construction and testing would disclose the insufficiencies and the failure of models to unravel their defining problems.
However, Hauptmann resurrects antirationality with her critique of
rational choice, ignoring any province for science in human affairs.
Rather, she wallows in the mysteries of man's inscrutability, calling forth
the spiritualism of "the citizen" in a rapture of community, commitment,
and the awesome complexities of human thought and existence. Her
sense of the citizen actually comprised the sacred core of Enlightenment
mysticism that was beatified by the American Romantics, notably Emerson and Whitman. Yet scientific analysis is still appropriate for political
behavior even if it is determined by nonrational factors such as emotionality and tradition. To leave politics, as Hauptmann and others do, within
the metaphysics of existentialism and phenomenology rejects rationality
and all that it implies. The fact of emotionality as political *cause* does not
certify the logic of absolute idealist *methods of proof;* that people love does
not mean that intense feelings are adequate for objective proof; the charm
of the human enterprise in one area does not entail its perfusion throughout. Ritual and ceremony, the unreason of superstition and tradition, may
well be the defining behaviors of social man, but they are still amenable
to pragmatic scrutiny, at least in principle.

In this way, the authors anthologized in Friedman (1995) who appear
to sustain Green and Shapiro's denunciation of rational choice theory
actually reject their call for practical and pragmatic science. Indeed,
rational choice theorists and many of their critics are simply arguing over
the best manner of imposing the illusion of rationality on human behavior, insisting that "rational choice assumptions are both self-evidently
true and unfalsifiable" (Friedman 1995, 12). They reject, usually out of
hand, the possibility that people are largely not rational or customarily
even motivated by any nontautological notion of self-interest or by altruism. Thus, Olson (1965) and other theorists who require intentions to

explain outcomes torture logic and evidence to derive some plausible grounds for the purposive rationality of political behavior.

Yet man in society may participate in and take guidance from ceremony and ritual perhaps as an aversion to reflection and thought. Ritualistic behavior may satisfy needs for group identification, status, prestige, and power that may actually be harmful in the long run either to the species or to any of its subgroups. Man as a ritualistic rather than rational being—the issue of emotionality—remains open to systematic scrutiny. Moreover, it is not a small point that intentions are immensely difficult to substantiate, not the least because they are customarily reported along with the behaviors they are supposed to explain but also because they may not be known. Macbeth had the luxury of pure, conscious motive, but few others do, while the fulfillment of ceremonial roles is not easy for a survey respondent to concede.

Many of Green and Shapiro's critics share the traditional resistance to science that defines both Romanticism and postmodernism. It is hard to assess whether Friedman's notion that theory is protected from falsification except as a Weberian ideal type is designed to sustain science or undercut it with compliant methods. Friedman (1995) insists that theory must explain facts while adding the proviso "that untheorized inexactitude or inapplicability does not falsify theory" (16). Indeed, nothing seems capable of falsifying rational choice theory for Friedman and many of his collaborators. Theory simply becomes more or less applicable while it is protected from disqualification with the assumption that "a theory cannot be falsified by a single bad prediction, or even a string of them, once we recognize that each falsification concerns only the application of the theory to a particular case, and shows merely that the theory is less than universally applicable to the real world" (Friedman 1995, 18). In this way, it remains impossible to deny the rationality of America's policy choices, since eccentric evidence along with some sort of strained definition of rationality can sustain even the most improbable, poorly examined hypothesis. Green and Shapiro are convincingly eloquent on this point. Aside from bad science itself, infinitely obedient intellectualism has become the vehicle for the many hurrah-for-America studies and the successful careers of their authors. Cultural huckstering is predicated on a pervasive wish for the world to remain unknowable—the hubris of ignorance—that unfortunately also opens the door to its being ungovernable or at least inhumane. Indeed, the immense amount of support for rational choice theory within the academy is a by-product of America's attachment to its irrational preferences.

The partisans of reasonableness and of bounded rationality share much in common. The use of principles of [standard science] . . . is dismissed in one way or another as of marginal relevance to reflective thought. Such principles [they argue] are neither explanatory nor predictive of human behavior. When these principles are construed as a system of prescriptions regulating our beliefs, values and choices, they lose touch with human capacity. Principles of [standard science] . . . do very well as systems of truths about some domain or other but they have neither descriptive nor prescriptive relevance to human behavior. (Levi 1997, 8)

The abdication of rationality is neither naive nor neutral. Rather, scientism provides the cachet of reason for America's ceremonial beliefs. Bounded rationality and rational choice theory are representative of the state of the social sciences, exposing their failure to apply a practical, pragmatic limited rationality to social problems, policies, or the policy-making process itself.

The Subversion of the Rational

The impulse of the Enlightenment toward a science of man has not bloomed in the social sciences. Pure rationality is impossible without pure rational goals, and these have defied every attempt of discovery or invention; philosophy is still an open field. Moreover, a practice of limited rationality has not borne fruit. Despite a near-universal agreement that the social sciences are properly assigned to instrumental chores—theories of the middle range, pragmatic demonstrations of the relationship between means and ends—that consensus has not inspired a credible but limited rationality. Simon's theory of bounded rationality and rational choice theory in political science, typical of the "status of truth" in the social sciences, at best stand for the protorational. Yet their steady bending to acquiesce social orthodoxy (America's civil religions) suggests that scientism rules the social sciences, especially when seen against the uniform and bleak backdrop of the social sciences' failure and refusal to credibly evaluate social welfare programs. The glow of rationality that bathes American exceptionalism also obscures with its disingenuous testimonials the persistent cruelties of American culture.

The dynamics of social policies remain largely unknown. The "causes of particular things" are not identified, largely because true experimental tests have been poorly conducted, underfunded, or distorted. The absence of a pragmatic, practical body of research denies any rational authority to social welfare decision making and negates social progress itself. In application, the social sciences have routinely subverted empirical methods and systematic tests of theory with an attachment both to ethnographic subjectivism ("memoirist reportage," as Joyce Carol Oates says) and to a contrived quantitism. The conjuring act of scientism tacitly endorses a prescriptive nihilism, the notion that culture *ought to* invade all its institutions while loosening restraints on Romanticism and its progeny, notably existentialism, postmodernism, and scientism.

The attack on science, also carried out by the social sciences themselves, is not usually mounted from a demand for greater rationality. Rather, the alternative and frequently antirationalist camp pushes to replace the contrivances of scientism with a more customary source of social authority. The attack is often as political as the functions it seeks to replace, arguing against greater rationality in policy making and for the influence of particular ideologies and traditional social institutions. In this regard, postmodernism as the reprise of Romanticism has been a prevalent know-nothing not because of any eloquence or philosophic "interest" but because it represents ideologically a very central position in the American consciousness, the tenets of the nation's operative civil religion. The scientism of the social sciences creates the proofs that authorize the superstitions of American values, minimizing disconfirming information and producing false evidence in support of compatible political choices that frequently cut against humanitarian sensibilities. The faux effectiveness of the personal social services is certainly not a beneficence for needy children.

It takes a faith in both natural law and God's plan extending far past the simple a priori assumptions of nature's regularity or H. G. Wells's secular optimism to believe that science is a humanitarian act. But it requires a true terror of reality and change, a buried sense of personal insignificance, to deny science. Objective, coherent science demands the strength to face ignorance and handle it with more than superstition and denial. Rational choice theory and bounded rationality, most insidious for claiming to be the standard form, are best understood as alternatives to both science and its requisite curiosity about the unknown. Alternative rationality, scientism, is the Trojan horse of science. It looks like a horse, and it sounds like a horse, but it does not run like a horse.[4]

Notes

1. Ravetz (1971), along with the many who have taken exception to the postmodern reading of Kuhn, clearly does not make the error. Indeed, he handles the differences among fields as a measure of scientific maturity and scientific contribution. The social problems of scientific discovery are not its strengths.

2. Perhaps, too, the methodological rationality of research needs to be humanized with an appreciation of confirmational response bias, particularly relative to the motives of the researcher considered against the challenges of allotting very scarce research moneys to competitive tasks while being conscious of the pressures for the next research contract.

3. Rational choice theory here is largely restricted to political science. A wider discussion of the failure of economics to handle social welfare issues is presented in Epstein (1997). Also see an extensive body of criticism by Rule (1997), Levi (1997), and McCloskey (1985), among many others.

4. Leo Doroucher was having a tough time with the Brooklyn Dodgers during spring training. They could not hit at all. One day, a horse said to Leo, "Hey, put me up." Well, why not, thought Leo. So the horse went up to bat, and on the first pitch smacked the ball to far right field but stood immobile at the plate. "Run, run!" yelled Leo. "Run?" replied the horse, "If I could run, I'd be at Hialeah."

Conclusion

Hiding from the Jacobins

Grafting the hidden hand onto the World-Spirit might reconcile the eighteenth- and nineteenth-century, classical liberalism with the grandest of all conservative collectivities, the individual with the state, personal ambition with social grace. The World-Spirit gives a name, purpose, and destiny to the summation of individual actions and a vehicle of dialectical conflict: a monstrous imperative through which unknown forces do the bidding of an unknown Absolute in service to unknowable ends that are nonetheless providential and disciplined and that justify the preservation of social orthodoxy. Yet in one form or another this has been the ideological assurance of both Enlightenment and Romantic thought, demanding faith and rewarding it with the comfort of religious absolutism, the engulfing conviction that all is somehow just in the arms of an enveloping destiny.

Either there is science along with its substance, mood, and communal norms or there is the perpetual mush of social decision-making and its frequent tyrannies of World-Spirit and self-positing rectitudes. Limited forms of rationality are not credible transitions between true science and human passion but marriages of convenience that birth teratomas, a tooth of reason here, an ear of sensibility there. Even if the Enlightenment did not really mean what it seemed to say, Romance kills romance. As society embraces increasingly powerful technologies such as nuclear energy and genetic engineering, the Romantic will to power may burn more than a few pathetic witches. The potential for mayhem and cruelty, for the quotidian insults of cultural denigration, is stupefying renewing the necessity of civilization, pause, humanity, and decency. Clairvoyance even with Madame Blavatsky's unique skill is a craven ploy.

Many criticisms of social science and policy already exist in some form in the literature, testifying to the openness of America's intellectual life. Unfortunately criticism remains rare, more common as contemporary fashions juxtaposed to previous ones than as vital competition within any period. But more to the point, criticism when its appears is customarily both politically and socially ineffectual. A torrent of warning and recrimination would have little effect unless delivered with a sizable political punch. The trick is to nurture a society in which the rational warrant is attended to on its own merits and not simply for its coincidence with a changing social reality.

It is perhaps too solicitous of political vanity to reach the happy judgment that contemporary democratic society has made notable social gains even while conceding that it still has a ways to go, implying as it does a moral growth that parallels the size of its economy. While this past century has certainly been the Age of Science in the West, it has unfortunately not been a scientific age. That is, science prevailed as technology but not necessarily as an enlightened mood of the culture. Wieland's 1798 comments, at the decline of the Enlightenment and after the French Revolution, require only modest adjustments for the contemporary West:

> If by Enlightenment you mean the twilight gradually brought forth by the ever progressing cultivation of the sciences, I gladly concede that, on the average, things look a little less gloomy than they did in the sixteenth century. [Yet if Enlightenment implies an ability for man] to think and act rationally and consistently [then] we shamefully flatter our age if we claim for it the smallest real advance over all earlier centuries, with the single exception perhaps, that in most European countries neither witches nor heretics are any longer being burned to the greater glory of God. (Gay 1969, 108–9)

This is not strictly true of the West in the twentieth century which seems to have perfected brutality with total, global wars, the Holocaust, ethnic cleansing, and more thorough political and religious purges than the Inquisitions and Star Chambers of earlier centuries. Still, the funeral pyres are more commonly if less dramatically authorized today by the spectral proofs of the social sciences that continue to script witches' hammers in fear that contemporary heresy may threaten political stability. The relationship between social efficiency and social denial is little different than the relationship between the *Malleus Maleficarum* and the Inquisition (Summers 1971). The whole elaborate argument of the *Malleus Maleficarum*, along with Summers' nostalgia for the Inquisition as a necessary protection against the "Bolshevism" of its time, was stitched together without a shred of credible evidence. All of the *Malleus'* certitude emerged from the fantastic imaginings of its authors and their invocation of the wisdom of the saints, notably Thomas and Augustine, in fulfilling the paranoia of Pope Innocent VIII, surely one of the most ironic christenings in history.

In the same manner and with little rational content, the social sciences' theologians contrive corrective myths in justification of the political imperatives that deny vital resources, and by extension greater social standing, to a variety of contemporary witches—social deviants of one sort or another who carry the stigma of personal responsibility for their conditions. The Inquisition, particularly its very limited reign in America, may have done less harm through its folly, cruelty, and self-deception than contemporary social policy that has abandons working people to drudgery and more than two million people to prison and that contrives the deplorable situations of foster children, the mentally ill, and those with low status and income. Both the Inquisition and contemporary social policy are forms of state sanctioned aggression. Yet any summary judgment is very elusive and the temptation to exaggerate is perhaps as great as the probability of simple error. Rogers Smith (1997) in pointing out that predatory stereotypes, the usual justification of cruel denial, have been ubiquitous in eighteenth- and nineteenth-century America seems also to suggest that they have been near exclusive determinants of American social welfare policy. This unfortunately ignores the nation's constantly expanding franchise, its enlarged sense of equality (at least until recently), and the stunningly deep and rich high culture it has shared among many of its citizens. His excellent history has been fairly criticized for its excesses.

Superstition, and not just a bashful attempt to disguise ignorance, is the pervasive and abiding authority for social policy. Indeed, the contemporary array of social services, produced through the same distorted research methodologies that create alternative medicine, are about as unsuccessful as herbal cures and about as popular as totems of belief. Alternative medicine—distant healing and prayer, innate capacities for healing trauma, the biology of love, brainwave and consciousness training for self-healing and spiritual development, and psychoneuroimmunology amplifying the more customary armory of acupuncture, chiropractic, meditation, herbalism, and so forth—competes successfully with traditional medicine, enjoying an enormous, faithful, credulous clientele.[1] The ready acceptance for alternative proofs of efficacy pervade social thought.

The reasons for splitting off classic, fulminating, bug-eyed know-nothings from the earnest provisioners of belief and policy in the social sciences—Hunt's (1999) distinctions among those who distort research for self-affirmation—are more issues of style than substance. The greatest assault on social science research comes less from the fringe of intellectual respectability and more from the accumulated and willing concessions of the researchers themselves to the dictates of social efficiency. Gardiner's (1957) list of fads and fallacies in the name of science needs to be greatly expanded beyond the crackpot impulses of American hucksterism and true belief to embrace the more pernicious forms of institutionalized belief: not just Dianetics, flying saucers, psionics machines, naturopathy, and the near-infinite and timeless number of obeisances to gullibility but also psychotherapy, family preservation, genetic determinism, drug abuse prevention, and the many other rituals of the operative American civil religion elaborated by respectable intellectual disciplines. To denigrate the margins of credulity as voodoo science misses the far more powerful influence of the mainstream scientific mystifications of social policy (Park 2000). Moody's (1975) engaging excuse that explorations of life after life are entertainment and not really science, misses the deadpan faith of his ten million readers and the degree to which alternative science has undercut the real thing as the hermeneutics of social faith.[2] The circus of American social policy is played out in the main tent, not the sideshows.

The institutionalized social services propagate the corrective myth, the core assumption of social efficiency and the political ceremony at the heart of the welfare state. The corrective myth, social efficiency and by extension the social services are largely Romantic ideals although with some roots in Enlightenment thought. However, the philosophes rarely simplified the notion of progress and change, even in their occasional preferences for universal education. By relying largely upon the myths of extreme individualism, heroically "overcoming" the rigidities of custom, socially efficient welfare programs draw inspiration from the absolute idealists of the1nineteenth century. But even here, the programs that rely upon subcultural and individual ideologies invoke an assumption of social efficiency that contradicts the Romantics. The major philosophers and theorists of both the Enlightenment and the anti-Enlightenment rarely underestimated the difficulty of social and human change. Indeed, the ethereal mysticism of the absolute idealists as well as Marx' ferocity are tributes to their sense of the near intractability of cultural mores and established political institutions.

The corrective myth promotes the fiction that social and individual problems can be identified and efficiently addressed through parsimonious interventions. This sense of efficient social engineering through objective observation and controlled experimentation realizes a euhemeristic myth in Frederick Winslow Taylor, the Paul Bunyan of political symbolism at the turn of the twentieth century (Kanigel 1997). Indeed, Taylor inspired both a generation of industrial engineers as well as their rationalistic epigones in the social sphere. At least in terms of its philosophic underpinnings and ideological symbolism, the Progressive Era in the US can be interpreted as the fruition of Romantic impulses in the garb of Enlightenment rationality—the promise that Emersonian individualism, a deep Romantic expression of mystical independence, could be realized through Enlightenment rationality in both commerce and society.

Indeed, these thoughts impelled the creation of the social sciences as methodological descendants of the "science of man." Yet in actuality the social sciences most frequently embellish America's enchantment with self-sufficiency rather than develop the earlier rudiments of structuralism or, even more basically, of objectivity. Indeed, ascriptive ideals—the persistent scapegoating of Romanticism— persists through the twentieth century. The mythopoetic mind has enthralled the scientific imagination.

Social policy and social welfare policy in particular are not the same subjects as morality and personal meaning; they call on rationality in quite different ways. Whatever the standing of the personal, social policy is necessarily instrumental and therefore amenable to rational evaluation against the ability to achieve its avowed goals—the purposes for which it was instituted—not whether those goals are themselves rational. Thus, the critique of social policy making starts with the observation that it frequently contains motives beyond its explicit instrumental purposes. In tribute to "how small a part conscious choice and realistic thinking play in human action," the policies themselves have taken on primary symbolic (political) meaning that largely displaces any social welfare production function. Indeed, politics is the process of allocating resources according to power, not justice, fairness, effectiveness, or efficiency. The political process has no faith in reason or rationality, and given the appalling deficiencies of social welfare research, it also defies a far more modest goal: "[W]hat matters is not the attainment of truth but simply the struggle to find it" (Beiser 1996, 312).

It would take more than a charitable or loyal reading of the social service literature to conclude that it is impelled by neutrality and curiosity rather than ideology and self-interest. Only the truly Romantic imagination blinded by any sense of regularity and inspired to crusade against the rigors of mundane existence—in short, the postmodern enterprise— could find civil grandeur in the social sciences' tortuous and consistent misrepresentations of the effects of both social policy and the nation's contentment with those myths. Rather than protorationality, semirationality, occasional rationality, or limited rationality, American social welfare policy, taken as a whole, constitutes overwhelming evidence that American policy making is almost entirely political, largely divorced from any consideration other than implicit group preference. Particularly in light of the nation's immense wealth, the policies themselves suggest, first, that the explicit goals of welfare are not compelling social motives but, second, that cruelty and indifference to need are often determinative values.

The nation's constant professions of Enlightenment exceptionalism suppress the raggedness of its long-standing Romantic infatuation with extreme individualism, the entrepreneurial virtues, and the illusion of self-determination: if freedom made America great, then it also beggars its claim to individual virtue, for the unseen hand that takes care of American society is guided by an invisible mind of considerable malice and cruelty. Indeed, the intensity of America's demands for comforting myths and legends and its thoroughgoing success at this task also mark the necessity to reconcile reality with perception. Postmodernism did not "decompose" sociology; objectivity, neutrality, and the autonomy of the intellect were the victims of the American will, the consensus of its people to impose a rigid, unforgiving Puritan god on the sinners it creates.

The problem of scientism did not simply begin as a reaction to technology, its displacing elites, and the special knowledge and skills of true science. Rather, there has always been a deep devotion to antiscience and pseudoscience, elaborated from mysticism, tradition, and the inertia of social status. Science and scientism are even competitive themes within the same writers, as the philosophes abundantly displayed in the tension between what they wished for and what they actually did. Even Newton pursued his mechanics within the shelter of a profoundly Christian theism. Irrationality may be an inescapable human dimension, the permanent entertainment of man in society; however, it need not so control social policy.

Lindblom's hope, if not faith, in full understanding pursued through factional research is not adequate. Understanding even as a necessarily limited or relative ideal still may require a degree of investment in descriptive and evaluative research that defies political tolerances. Critical evaluation of goal attainment needs large and constant support to build toward objective wisdom, past the cycles of ideological fashion. Unfortunately, science as a limited social process easily slips into science as compatible explanation.

> We subject our concerns to rational analysis not because we believe we will necessarily obtain knowledge thereby, but because we believe that some explanation is better than none . . . a sense of structure to our understanding of a question. From that standpoint, the final objective of any explanation is not so much the resolution of that question but rather a measure of increased awareness. (Chai 1998, 115)

It is both apt and ironic that these lines describe Jonathan Edwards and not some beleaguered social scientist. Yet the confluence of Puritanism and rationality may indeed be the wellspring of the policy sciences in America. The faith that both can be pursued is quite in keeping with an analysis of policy making as a ritual of civil religion rather than as a sincere approximation of avowed goals. Myth, particularly in its expression as failed science, also provides structure and increased awareness, conveniently without the encumbrances of objective proof. Despite the culture's refusal to look past its preferences and the imperfections of method, a limited science of social policy probably fails for its own commitments to some form of redemption.

An enormous portion of the modern social sciences, particularly in economics and political science, has fattened the American ego with assurances of its rationality. Yet the praise succeeds only by equating rationality with some political value. Simply because the decisions of the American people appear to be culturally coherent—that is, the decisions are "explained" by social preferences of one sort or another—rational choice theory and rational expectations theory commend the American system for approximating Enlightenment goals. Yet the rational enterprise in the social sciences is better understood as a form of ethnocentrism or even species-centrism than as an accurate description of policy making or as the achievement of credible information. At best the enterprise commends the American people for their mood toward rationality, if indeed it exists at all. At worst, it confuses scientific rationality with the desire to minimize the embarrassment of ignorance, creating a smug ceremony of knowing where knowledge is tenuous at best.

The difference is extraordinary between the belief that American social decision making should be rational, or at least more rational, and the insistence that it already is. Both rational choice theory in political science and rational expectations theory in economics are feeble attempts to minimize this difference by insisting that the purposive behavior of people is rational, that their attempts to maximize their preferences are efficient and wise. These self-protective theories could only be contradicted by wildly erratic, unconnected, unimaginably chaotic choices. Nevertheless, reasonable or pragmatic choice is not the equivalent of rationality. The assumption that economic man behaves rationally out of reasonable and coherent expectations of the future fails to accurately describe man in society. Economic man in vivo is an emotional, impulsive organism, imposing fierce loyalties and a blind hedonism on reality through psychological devices such as denial, projection, and, when all else fails, frank delusion that may be neither adaptive, conscious, nor wise in spite of their persistence. The fact that numerous conditions, defined as behavioral motives, but without evidence of prior existence, have been maximized against known alternatives does not certify the rationality of those motives or distinguish between their post hoc use as alibis for barely understood compulsions. In a similar manner, the most fastidiously conforming social behavior that becomes explained over decades of quantitative demography to the tenth decimal place is proof not of its wisdom but only of its endurance and regularity.

American culture has with spectacular success produced material plenty and a social system that much of the world envies as real cultural progress; for a large portion of its people, it has realized a high culture that approximates even utopian fantasies. Yet these victories emerge from the largely undirected, unplanned, and even unintended Crack of Doom of culture more than from any respect for objective, coherent social policy making in lofty pursuit of civilization or even of explicit notions of progress. The American people have had the good fortune to populate a virgin territory of unimaginable natural resources with clever, industrious, and imaginative refugees from ossified, predatory cultures and to be in place for the consumer bounty and military prowess of technological science. Yet growing social rigidity and inequality, environmental degradation, and the poverty of covetous undeveloped nations are warnings, and perhaps even threats to the persistence of Western culture in its current form.

Modern industrial civilization performs the ceremonies of science and technology to make sacred its central mystery. These ceremonies reify rationality as social choice; the magnificent but very limited achievements of science (engines, weapons, medicine, bridges, fishing rods, computers, and so forth) become convincing evidence for the rationality of society itself. Through the ritual of the scientist as modern shaman, the culture that produces science becomes scientific itself. Rational products—technology—become proof of rational society, despite the conditions of their production, their harmful side effects, or even the frequently predatory motives that inspired them in the first place and sustain their use.

For many, technological innovation, more than simply the practice of science, has driven societal change. However, this formulation of an ineluctable technology acting on society through the appetites it feeds denies the autonomy of the intellect; society fails as a conscious arbiter of its preferences, less a planner of its destiny than the automaton of its desires for better health, longer life, less toil, greater mastery of nature, intellectual creativity, and more sensual pleasure. All would be well if the seemingly unimpeachable goals of the Enlightenment were simply achieved without misadventure in creating a Hobbit-like tranquillity for man. However, progress toward nobility and technological prowess seems to be associated with fierce inequalities, competition to extermination, rigid barbarities, dehumanizing labor, disabling dreads, and the mindless sacrifice of future security, including survival, for current consumption. The unanticipated problems of pursuing a comfortable mortality may erect the very barriers to achieve it. Thus the practice of science and technology as the source of both ease and affliction seems to be a social tool, a near-material artifact of culture that stands apart from the discussion of its uses. In this sense, ideology is profitably separated from science even while one the enormous influences of culture on the practice of science are apparent. But this too makes the point since at least Western culture, frequently with the naïveté of the sorcerer's apprentice, has developed technology as the tool of social policy but, again, with little appreciation for its independence. In this sense, science has ruled as servant.

While the natural sciences fulfill the needs of technology, the social sciences seem content to justify their concessions to popular preferences. Yet the social sciences have not been the rational, critical bulwarks against uninformed enthusiasm. To the contrary, they have most commonly composed the music, colored the floats, and choreographed the victory parades for an orthodoxy that assigns people to the roles they already occupy. Yet there is nothing in the logic and capacities of the social sciences that necessitates this role; it is scripted by social preference, which presumably but not assuredly is open to debate and influence.

Science was cast by the Enlightenment as the engine of progress. Yet the enormous advance of the natural sciences has not been the occasion or inspiration for strides in social decision making. Despite their frequent statistical sophistication and an astute awareness of methodological rigor, the social sciences remain relatively primitive and immature, informing social policy forums with ideologically distorted faith in convenient causal theories far more often than providing true approximations of reality.

Knowing is not doing, and the failures of rationality in social welfare policy are not the innocent, well-meant, easily corrected errors of progressive wisdom. They are the interminable substance of politics; ascendant and successful factions act to solidify their victories through the production of convenient myth. While it need not be so, and in principle at least, more credible statements of social reality are possible, outside of the natural sciences it has been so. In social welfare policy making, science in the guise of the social sciences has become one of society's most powerful superstitions, as conservative and even reactionary in guarding established preferences as the eighteenth-century Catholic Church that incensed the philosophes. Rationality has been distorted through the policy sciences into rationalization. The Romance of wishfulness that inspired Freud to confuse imagination with memory (Voltaire's barb at Montesquieu) has swamped Simon's "bounded" reason. In spite of Enlightenment intentions and Romantic certitudes, social progress is accidental, probably uncontrollable, and often misleading, at least in part because of a failure of nerve, the unwillingness of culture to confront itself accurately. Hume insisted that "man must unmask pleasing dreams for the sake of realistic programs, fictions for the sake of reality"—a fine, noble mood phrased for marble and pigeons but routinely forsaken in the social policy-making process and typically by culture itself.

Wealth and power inspire narcotic transformations of luck into wisdom and vain convenience into rational choice. Self-deception is the worst kind; the delusion of enlightenment in the reality of romance may exact payment in social tranquillity, justice, and reason itself. Social progress, after all, implies more than wealth and power. Then again, the explosively self-aggrandizing Romantic imagination so prevalent throughout the history of human consciousness may be the spontaneous order of successful culture, the manner in which liberty is cashed in for adaptation. A fully conscious human being may be biologically impractical and unsound; self-deception may be necessary for social health; the practice of science may need to be restricted to the mastery of chores. The hierarchy of heroic man may be written into the funded genome even against the protests of biology.

A man of great democratic sensibilities, "Condorcet wrote in hiding from the Jacobins" which may in the end provide an important insight into the development of ideology (Gay 1969). The club of belief is customarily chartered by the perceptions and demands of power—the clichés of orthodoxy but also the frightful spasms of long-denied populations—and its inquisitorial intolerance for political opposition, let alone heresy. Wisdom and popularity are only occasional companions.

Notes

1. Just a few representatives drawn from the 1999 California Conference on Alternative Medicines.

2. Moody's *Life after Life* boasts sales of more than ten million copies. It is not by accident that his 1999 book is titled *The Last Laugh*.

Afterword

Despite the gracious proprieties of Amy Vanderbilt, Martha Stewart, and Emily Post, criticism need not keep a pinky in the air and apologize with a solution. The many obsessive and institutionalized attempts to braid myth into reality fail to resolve social problems in the United States. Things happen, but not because they have been planned or even intended. The best of eighteenth-century thought simply laid out a general direction with the expectation that cultural experience would flow toward inspired preferences. Even nineteenth-century writers, despite their weakness for the fantastic and quaint, customarily did the same. In this spirit, the broad outlines of an approach—a general strategy for contemporary American culture—might profitably embrace generosity, recognizing the thoroughgoing failure of social efficiency and the heartlessness of cheapening out further on the inadequate provisions of American social welfare policy. To the extent that explanations of American society start with a structure of values, such as individualism, they might also consider cruelty as an abiding characteristic of America's operative religion and apply generosity as its antidote.

Precisely because of the depth of policy ignorance, social welfare experiments are necessary to learn whether greater equality, not simply technique, can handle social problems. In addition to resources, imagination requires a political constituency and freedom from the social welfare professionals. There has rarely been a group of people so liberationist in rhetoric yet so acquiescent of social convenience. The theatrical intensities and empty reassurances of public administrators, psychotherapists, psychologists, counselors, and social workers of every posture and preference, notably including the faith-based and sublime spiritualists of the recent Republican ascendancy, should disqualify them from franchises of public trust and other opportunities to strain social meaning through their self-regard and self-interest. No professional helpers or amateur saviors should be allowed to evaluate or even measure their own services; this is a task for those who lack conviction. After enduring the penance of numbingly long statements of obligatory gratitude, the old horses who nuzzle power with their soft noses should be put out to pasture. Please, God, no more professional welfare experts with empty diplomas, mystical humanism, "practical" research, and plangent assurances that the spectral credentials of group membership, experiential epiphanies, rehearsed suffering, and self-pity are adequate substitutes for learning and achievement.

The lives of plants, fish, and celestial bodies are full of mystery and wonderment. But the stubborn refusal of social welfare policy to test its effects is directed ignorance, a mute statement of contentment with the failures of society. Insubstantial social policy will persist until inquiry can be freed from an obedience to the pieties of cultural orthodoxy. There are no adequate substitutes for social science. But a credible science of man and society is a still-distant goal demanding rededication or at least the courage to deny the fictions that it has been realized or that it is even being pursued.

References

Aiken, H. D. 1956. *The Age of Ideology*. New York: Mentor Books.

Alinsky, S. D. 1969. *Reveille for Radicals*. New York: Vintage.

American Heritage Dictionary. 1992. New York: Houghton Mifflin.

Anchor, R. 1967. *The Enlightenment Tradition*. New York: Harper and Row.

Andrews, D. A., I. Zinger, R. D. Hoge, J. Bonta, P. Gendreau, and F. T. Cullen. 1990. "Does Correctional Treatment Work? A Clinically Relevant and Psychologically Informed Meta-analysis." *Criminology* 28:419–29.

Andrews, G., and R. Harvey. 1981. "Does Psychotherapy Benefit Neurotic Patients." *Archives of General Psychiatry* 38:1203–8.

Anelauskas, V. 1999. *Discovering America as It Is*. Atlanta: Clarity Press.

Baggette, J., R. Y. Shapiro, and L. R. Jacobs. 1995. "The Polls—Poll Trends: Social Security—An Update" *Public Opinion Quarterly* 59:420–42.

Becker, C. L. 1932. *The Heavenly City of the Eighteenth-Century Philosophers*. New Haven, Conn.: Yale University Press.

Becker, E. 1973. *Denial of Death*. New York: Free Press.

Becker, G. S. 1991. *A Treatise on the Family*. Cambridge, Mass.: Harvard University Press.

Beiser, F. C. 1996. *The Sovereignty of Reason*. Princeton, N.J.: Princeton University Press.

Bellah, R. N. 1967. "Civil Religion in America." *Daedalus* 96:1–21.

———. 1975. *The Broken Covenant*. New York: Seabury Press.

Bellah, R. N., and P. E. Hammond. 1980. *Varieties of Civil Religion*. New York: Harper and Row.

Bergin, A. E. 1971. "The Evaluation of Therapeutic Outcomes." In *Handbook of Psychotherapy and Behavior Change*, ed. S. L. Garfield and A. E. Bergin. New York: Wiley.

Bergin, A. E., and M. J. Lambert. 1978. "The Evaluation of Therapeutic Outcomes." In *Handbook of Psychotherapy and Behavior Change*, 2d ed., ed. S. L. Garfield and A. E. Bergin. New York: Wiley.

Berlin, I. 1969. *Four Essays on Liberty*. New York: Oxford University Press.

Betsworth, R. G. 1990. *Social Ethics: An Examination of American Moral Tradition*. Louisville, Ky.: Westminster/John Knox Press.

Blenkner, M, M. Bloom, and S. M. Nielsen. 1971. "A Research and Demonstration Project of Protective Services." *Social Casework* 52:489–99.

Bloom, H. 1992. *The American Religion: The Emergence of the Post-Christian Nation*. New York: Simon and Schuster.

Bouchard, T. J., Jr. 1994. "Genes, Environment, and Personality." *Science* 264:1700–1701.

———. 1995. "Breaking the Last Taboo." *Contemporary Psychology* 40(5): 415–18.

Bouchard, T. J., Jr., D. T. Lykken, M. McGue, N. L. Segal, and A. Tellegen. 1990. "Sources of Human Psychological Differences: The Minnesota Study of Twins Reared Apart." *Science* 250:223–28.

Bouchard, T. J., Jr., and M. McGue. 1990. "Genetic and Rearing Environmental Influences on Adult Personality: An Analysis of Adopted Twins Reared Apart." *Journal of Personality* 58:263–92.

Bowen, G. L., and P. A. Neenan. 1993. *Research on Social Work Practice* 3:363–84.

Bremner, R. H. 1970. *Children and Youth in America*. Cambridge, Mass.: Harvard University Press.

Broad, W. J. 1991. "From Top of Their World to a Scientific Osctracism," *New York Times Current Events Edition*, March 17th, 130. New York.

Brock, T. C., M. C. Green, D. A Reich, and L. M. Evans. 1996. "The Consumer Reports Study of Psychotherapy: Invalid Is Invalid." *American Psychologist* October, 1083.

Brown, M. K. 1999. *Race, Money, and the American Welfare State*. Ithaca, N.Y.: Cornell University Press.

Casey, R. J., and J. S. Berman 1985. "The Outcome of Psychotherapy with Children." *Psychological Bulletin* 98:388–400.

Chai, L. 1998. *Jonathan Edwards and the Limits of Enlightenment Philosophy*. New York: Oxford University Press.

Chalk, R., and P. A. King. 1998. *Violence in Families: Assessing Prevention and Treatment Programs*. Washington, D.C.: National Academy Press.

Chong, D. 2000. *Rational Lives*. Chicago, Illinois: University of Chicago Press.

Citro, C. F., and R. T. Michael. 1995. *Measuring Poverty: A New Approach*. Washington, D.C.: National Academy Press.

Coleman, J. S. 1990. *Foundations of Social Theory*. Cambridge, Mass.: Harvard University Press.

Cook, F. L., and E. J. Barrett. 1992. *Support for the American Welfare State*. New York: Columbia University Press.

Costin, L., H. J. Karger, and D. Stoesz. 1996. *The Politics of Child Abuse in America*. New York: Oxford University Press.

Crane, J. 1998. *Social Programs That Work*. New York: Russell Sage Foundation.

Crews, F. 1993. "The Unknown Freud." *New York Review of Books*, November 18:55–65.

Cryns, A., K. Gorey, and G. Brice. 1989. "Long-Term Care Outcome Research as a Junction of Researcher Location: A Comparative Analysis." Paper presented at the forty-second annual society meeting of the Gerontological Society of America, Minneapolis.

Dahl, R. A., and C. E. Lindblom. [1953] 1992. *Politics, Economics, and Welfare.* New Brunswick, N.J.: Transaction Publishers.

Danziger, S. H., G. D. Sandefur, and D. H. Weinberg. 1994. *Confronting Poverty: Prescriptions for Change.* Cambridge, Mass.: Harvard University Press.

Davies, G. 1996. *From Opportunity to Entitlement: The Transformation and Decline of Great Society Liberalism.* Lawrence: University Press of Kansas.

Dawes, R. M. 1994. *House of Cards.* New York: Free Press.

Deane, P. 1979. *The First Industrial Revolution.* New York: Cambridge University Press.

Dineen, T. 1996. *Manufacturing Victims.* Montreal: Robert Davies Publishing.

Doyle, W. 1978. *The Old European Order, 1660–1800.* New York: Oxford University Press.

Dugger, C. W. 1995. "For Youth: A Guiding Hand out of Ghetto." *New York Times,* March 9:1.

Edin, K. 1991. "Surviving the Welfare System: How AFDC Recipients Make Ends Meet in Chicago." *Social Problems* 38:462–74.

Edwards, J. 1741. *Sinners in the Hands of an Angry God.* Boston: S. Kneeland and T. Green.

Elkin, I., I. T. Shea, J. T. Watkins, S. D. Imber, S. M. Sotsky, J. F. Collins, D. R. Glass, P. A. Pilkonis, W. R. Leber, J. P. Docherty, S. J. Fiester, and M. B. Parloff. 1989. "National Institute of Mental Health Treatment of Depression Collaborative Research Program." *Archives of General Psychiatry* 46:971–83.

Ellwood, D. T. 1988. *Poor Support.* New York: Basic Books.

Epstein, W. M. 1984a. "Technology and Social Work 1: The Effectiveness of Psychotherapy." *Journal of Applied Social Sciences* 8:155–75.

———. 1984b. "Technology and Social Work 2: Psychotherapy, Family Therapy and Implications for Practice." *Journal of Applied Social Sciences* 8:175–87.

———. 1992. "Professionalization of Social Work: The American Experience." *Social Science Journal* 29:153–66.

———. 1993a. *The Dilemma of American Social Welfare.* New Brunswick, N.J.: Transaction Publishers.

———. 1993b. "Randomized Controlled Trials in the Human Services." *Social Work Research and Abstracts* 29(3):3–10.

———. 1995. *The Illusion of Psychotherapy.* New Brunswick, N.J.: Transaction Publishers.

———. 1997. *Welfare in America.* Madison: University of Wisconsin Press.

———. 1999. *Children Who Could Have Been: The Legacy of Child Welfare in Wealthy America.* Madison: University of Wisconsin Press.

———. 2001. "Critical Analyses." In *Handbook of Social Work Research Methods,* ed. B. Thyer. Thousand Oaks, Calif.: Sage.

Errera, P., B. McKee, and D. C. Smith. 1967. "Length of Psychotherapy: Studies Done in a University Community Psychiatric Clinic." *Archives of General Psychiatry* 17:454–58.

Erskine, H. 1975. "The Polls: Government Role in Welfare" *Public Opinion Quarterly* 39:257–74.

Eysenck, H. F. 1952. "The Effects of Psychotherapy: An Evaluation." *Journal of Consulting Psychology* 16:319.

Eysenck, H. F., and S. Rachman. 1965. *Causes and Cures of Neuroses*. London: Routledge and Kegan Paul.

Fanshel, D., and E. Shinn. 1978. *Children in Foster Care: A Longitudinal Investigation*. New York: Columbia University Press.

Feldman, R. A., and T. E. Caplinger. 1977. "Social Work Experience and Client Behavioral Change: A Multivariate Analysis of Process and Outcome." *Journal of Social Service Research* 1:5–32.

Feldman, R. A., J. S. Wodarski, and T. E. Caplinger. 1983. *The St. Louis Conundrum*. Englewood Cliffs, N.J.: Prentice Hall.

Ferris, P. 1999. *Dr. Freud: A Life*. New York: Perseus Books Group.

Fischer, J. 1973a. "Is Casework Effective: A Review." *Social Work* 18(1):5–20

———. 1973b. "Has Mighty Casework Struck Out?" *Social Work* 18(4):107–10.

———. 1978. "Does Anything Work." *Journal of Social Service Research* 1:215–44.

———. 1981. "The Social Work Revolution." *Social Work* 26:199–209.

Frank, J. D., and J. B. Frank. 1991. *Persuasion and Healing*, 3d ed. Baltimore: Johns Hopkins University Press.

Fraser, M., E. Taylor, R. Jackson, and J. O'Jack. 1991. "Social Work and Science: Many Ways of Knowing?" *Social Work Research and Abstracts* 27(4):5–15.

Friedman, J. 1995. *The Rational Choice Controversy*. New Haven, Conn.: Yale University Press.

Gans, H. J. 1995. *The War against the Poor*. New York: Basic Books.

Gardiner, M. 1957. *Fads and Fallacies in the Name of Science*. New York: Dover.

Gay, P. 1964. *The Party of Humanity*. New York: Knopf.

———. 1966. *The Enlightenment: An Interpretation*. New York: Knopf.

———. 1969. *The Enlightenment: The Science of Freedom*. New York: Knopf.

Gerstein, D. R., and H. J. Harwood, eds. 1990. *Treating Drug Problems*. Vol. 1, *A Study of the Evolution, Effectiveness and Financing of Public and Private Drug Treatment Systems*. Washington, D.C.: National Academy Press.

Giblin, P., D. H. Sprenkle, and R. Sheehan. 1985. "Enrichment Outcome Research: A Meta-analysis of Premarital, Marital and Family Interventions." *Journal of Marital and Family Therapy* 11:257–71.

Gilens, M. 1999. *Why Americans Hate Welfare*. Chicago: University of Chicago Press.

Ginzberg, E. 1988. *Young People at Risk: Is Prevention Possible?* Boulder, Colo.: Westview Press.

Glisson, C. 1995. "The State of the Art of Social Work Research: Implications for Mental Health." *Research on Social Work Practice* 20:119–28.

Goldsmith, H. H. 1993a. "Nature-Nurture Issues in the Behavioral Genetics Context: Overcoming Barriers to Communication." In *Nature, Nurture and Psychology*, ed. R. Plomin and G. McClearn. Washington, D.C.: American Psychological Association.

———. 1993b. "Temperament: Variability in Developing Emotion Systems." In *Handbook of Emotions*, ed. M. Lewis and J. M. Haviland. New York: Guilford Press.

Goleman, D. 1995. *Emotional Intelligence*. New York: Bantam Books.

Goodin, R. E., B. Headey, R. Muffels, and H. Dirven. 1999. *The Real Worlds of Welfare Capitalism*. Cambridge: Cambridge University Press.

Goodwin, J. L. 1997. *Gender and the Politics of Welfare Reform: Mothers' Pensions in Chicago, 1911–1929*. Chicago: University of Chicago Press.

Gorey, K. M. 1996. "Effectiveness of Social Work Intervention Research: Internal versus External Evaluations." *Social Work Research* 20:119–28.

Gottschalk, L. A., R. A. Fox, and D. E. Bates. 1973. "A Study of Prediction and Outcome in a Mental Health Crisis Clinic," *American Journal of Psychiatry* 130(10):1107–11.

Green, P. G., and I. Shapiro. 1994. *Pathologies of Rational Choice Theory: The Critiques of Applications in Political Science*. New Haven, Conn.: Yale University Press.

Gross, M. L. 1978. *The Psychological Society*. New York: Random House.

Grunbaum, A. 1984. *The Foundations of Psychoanalysis*. Berkeley: University of California Press.

Hahn, A. 1994. *Evaluation of the Quantum Opportunities Program (QOP): Did the Program Work?* Waltham, Mass.: Brandeis University, Heller Graduate School, Center for Human Resources.

Hamowy, R. 1987. *The Scottish Enlightenment and the Theory of Spontaneous Order*. Carbondale, Ill.: Southern Illinois University Press.

Handler, J. 1995. *The Poverty of Welfare Reform*. New Haven, Conn.: Yale University Press.

Harris, J. R. 1995. "Where Is the Child's Environment? A Group Socialization Theory of Development." *Psychological Review* 102:458–89.

———. 1998. *The Nurture Assumption: Why Children Turn out the Way They Do*. New York: Free Press.

Hauptmann, E. 1996. *Putting Choice before Democracy*. Albany: State University of New York Press.

Hawton, H. 1952. *The Feast of Unreason*. Westport, Conn.: Greenwood Publishers.

Hearn, F. 1997. *Moral Disorder and Social Disorder*. New York: Aldine de Gruyter.

Herberg, W. 1960. *Protestant–Catholic–Jew: An Essay in American Religious Sociology*. Garden City, N.Y.: Anchor Books.

Herrnstein, R. J., and C. Murray. 1994. *The Bell Curve*. New York: Free Press.

Hirschman, A. O. 1991. *The Rhetoric of Reaction*. Cambridge, Mass.: Harvard University Press.

Howard, K. I., S. M. Kopta, and M. S. Krause. 1986. "The Dose-Effect Relationship in Psychotherapy." *American Psychologist* 41:159–64.

228

References

Hulliung, M. 1994. *The Autocritique of Enlightenment.* Cambridge, Mass.: Harvard University Press.

Hunt, M. 1999. *The New Know-Nothings.* New Brunswick, N.J.: Transaction Publishers.

Icard, L. D., R. F. Schilling, and N. El-Bassel. 1995. "Reducing HIV Infection among African Americans by Targeting the African American Family." *Social Work* 19:153–63.

Imber, S. D., P. A. Pilkonis, S. M. Sotsky, I. Elkin, J. T. Watkins, J. F. Collins, M. T. Shea, W. R. Leber, and D. R. Glass. 1990. "Mode-Specific Effects among Three Treatments for Depression." *Journal of Consulting and Clinical Psychology* 58:352–59.

Jaynes, G. D., and R. M. Williams. 1989. *A Common Destiny: Blacks and American Society.* Washington, D.C.: National Academy Press.

Jencks, C. 1992. *Rethinking Social Policy.* Cambridge, Mass.: Harvard University Press.

Kanigel, R. 1997. *The One Best Way: Frederick Winslow Taylor and the Enigma of Efficiency.* New York: Viking.

Karasu, B. 1999. "Spiritual Psychotherapy." *American Journal of Psychotherapy* 53:143–62.

Kelly, G. A. 1972 "Forms of Irrationality in the Eighteenth Century." In *Irrationalism in the Eighteenth Century,* ed. H. E. Pagliaro. Cleveland, Ohio: Case Western Reserve Press.

———. 1984. *Politics and Religious Consciousness in America.* New Brunswick, N.J.: Transaction Publishers.

Kessler, S. 1994. *Tocqueville's Civil Religion: American Christianity and the Prospects for Freedom.* Albany: State University of New York Press.

Kline, P. 1988. *Psychology Exposed or the Emperor's New Clothes.* London: Routledge.

Koch, A., ed. 1965. *The American Enlightenment.* New York: George Braziller.

Kotkin, M., C. Daviet, and J. Gurin 1996. "The *Consumer Reports* Mental Health Survey." *American Psychologist* 51:1080–82.

Kuttner, R. 1999. "Running with the Bulls." *New York Times Book Review,* February 28:20.

Lambert, M. J., and A. E. Bergin. 1994. "The Effectiveness of Psychotherapy." In *Handbook of Psychotherapy and Behaivor Change,* 4th ed., ed. A. E. Bergin and S. L. Garfield. New York: John Wiley.

Lambert, M. J., E. R. Christensen, and S. S. DeJulio 1986. "The Assessment of Psychotherapy Outcome." In *Handbook of Psychotherapy and Behavior Change,* ed. S. L. Garfield and A. E. Bergin. New York: John Wiley. p23–62.

Lambert, M. J., F. D. Weber, and J. D. Sykes 1993. "Psychotherapy versus Placebo Therapies: A Review of the Metaanalytic Literature." Poster presented at the annual Meeting of the Western Psychological Association, Phoenix, Arizona, 1993.

Landman, J. T,. and R. M. Dawes. 1982. "Psychotherapy Outcome: Smith and Glass' Conclusions Stand up under Scrutiny." *American Psychologist* 37:504–16.

LaPiere, R. T. 1954. *A Theory of Social Control.* New York: McGraw-Hill.

———. 1965. *Social Change.* New York: McGraw-Hill.

Lapinski, J. S., C. R. Riemann, R. Y. Shapiro, M. F. Stevens, and L. R. Jacobs. 1998. "Welfare State Regimes and Subjective Well-Being: A Cross-National Study." *International Journal of Public Opinion Research* 10:2–24.

Letwin, W. 1963. *The Origins of Scientific Economics.* London: Methuen.

Levi, I. 1997. *The Covenant of Reason.* New York: Cambridge University Press.

Lewontin, R. C. 1974. "The Analysis of Variance and the Analysis of Causes." *American Journal of Human Genetics* 26:400–411.

Lewis, O. 1961. *The Children of Sanchez: Autobiography of a Mexican Family.* New York: Random House.

———. 1966. *La Vida: A Puerto Rican Family in the Culture of Poverty—San Juan and New York.* New York: Random House.

Lindblom, C. E. 1959. "The Science of 'Muddling Through.'" *Public Administration Review* 19:79–88.

———. 1965. *The Intelligence of Democracy: Decision Making through Mutual Adjustment.* New York: Free Press.

Lindblom, C. E., and E. J. Woodhouse. 1993. *The Policy-Making Process.* Upper Saddle River, N.J.: Prentice Hall.

Linder, R. D., and R. V. Pierard, eds. 1978. *Twilight of the Saints: Biblical Christianity and Civil Religion in American.* Downers Grove, Ill.: InterVarsity Press.

Lindsey, D. 1994. *The Welfare of Children.* New York: Oxford University Press.

Loehlin, J. C. 1992. *Genes and Environment in Personality Development.* Newbury Park, Calif.: Sage.

Long, D., J. M. Gueron, R. G. Wood, R. Fisher, and V. Fellerath. 1996. *LEAP: Three-Year Impacts of Ohio's Welfare Initiative to Improve School Attendance among Teenage Parents.* New York: Manpower Research Demonstration Corporation.

Lowith, K. 1964. *From Hegel to Nietzsche: The Revolution in Nineteenth Century Thought.* New York: Holt, Rinehart, Winston.

Luborsky, L., B. Singer, and L. Luborsky 1975. "Comparative Studies of Psychotherapies: Is It True That 'Everybody Has Won and All Must Have Prizes'?" *Archives of General Psychiatry* 32:995–1008.

Lubove, R. 1968. *The Struggle for Social Security.* Cambridge, Mass.: Harvard University Press.

Luttwak, E. 1999. *Turbo-Capitalism: Winners and Losers in the Global Economy.* New York: HarperCollins.

Maccoby, E. E., and J. A. Martin. 1983. "Socialization in the Context of the Family: Parent-Child Interaction." In *Handbook of Child Psychology.* Vol. 4, *Socialization, Personality, and Social Development,* ed. E. M. Hetherington. New York: Wiley.

Macmillan, M. 1997. *Freud Evaluated.* Cambridge, Mass.: MIT Press.

Magen, R. H., and S. D. Rose. 1994. "Parents in Groups: Problem Solving versus Behavioral Skills Training." *Research on Social Work Practice* 4:172–91.

Manski, C. F., and I. Garfinkel. 1992. *Evaluating Manpower and Training Programs.* Cambridge, Mass.: Harvard University Press.

March, J. G., and H. A. Simon. 1958. *Organizations.* New York: Wiley.

Marquis, D. 1930. *Archie and Mehitabel.* New York: Doubleday.

Marris, P., and M. Rein. 1967. *Dilemmas of Social Reform.* New York: Atherton Press.

Martin, W. M. 1997. *Idealism and Objectivity.* Stanford, Calif.: Stanford University Press.

Martinson, R. 1974. "What Works: Questions and Answers about Prison Reform." *Public Interest* 35:22–54.

Marty, M. 1959. *The New Shape of American Religion.* New York: HarperCollins.

Marx, L. "Uncivil Respect of American Writers to Civil Religion in America." In *American Civil Religion,* ed. R. E. Richey and D. G. Jones. New York: Harper and Row.

Massey, D. S., and N. A. Denton. 1993. *American Apartheid.* Cambridge, Mass.: Harvard University Press.

Masson, J. 1988. *Against Therapy: Emotional Tyranny and the Myth of Psychological Healing.* New York: Atheneum.

May, H. F. 1976. *The Enlightenment in America.* New York: Oxford University Press.

Mayer, S. E. 1997. *What Money Can't Buy.* Cambridge, Mass.: Harvard University Press.

Mayer, W. G. 1992. *The Changing American Mind.* Ann Arbor: University of Michigan Press.

Maynard, R., W. Nicholson, and A. Rangarajan. 1993. *Breaking the Cycle of Poverty: The Effectiveness of Mandatory Services for Welfare-Dependent Teenage Parents.* Princeton, N.J.: Mathematica Policy Research.

McCloskey, D. N. 1985. *The Rhetoric of Economics.* Madison: University of Wisconsin Press.

McClosky, H., and J. Zaller. 1984. *The American Ethos: Public Attitudes toward Capitalism and Democracy.* Cambridge, Mass.: Harvard University Press.

McGue, M. 1988. "Genetic and Environmental Determinants of Information Processing and Special Mental Abilities: A Twin Analysis." In *Advances in the Psychology of Human Intelligence,* ed. R. J. Sternberg. Vol. 5. Hillsdale, N.J.: Erlbaum.

McGue, M., T. J. Bouchard Jr., W. G. Iacono, and D. T. Lykken. 1993. "Behavioral Genetics of Cognitive Ability: A Life-Span Perspective." In *Nature, Nurture and Psychology,* ed. R. Plomin and G. McClearn. Washington, D.C.: American Psychological Association.

McGue, M., and D. T. Lykken. 1992. "Genetic Influence on Risk of Divorce." *Psychological Science* 3:368–73.

Mead, L. M. 1992. *The Politics of Poverty.* New York: Basic Books.

Mead, S. E. 1977. *The Old Religion in the Brave New World: Reflections on the Relation between Christendom and the Republic.* Berkeley and Los Angeles: University of California Press.

Meinert, C. L. 1986. *Clinical Trials: Design, Conduct, and Analysis.* Oxford: Oxford University Press.

Meyer, J. W., and B. Rowan. 1978. "Institutionalized Organizations: Formal Structure as Myth and Ceremony." *American Journal of Sociology* 83:340–63.

Miller, R. C., and J. S. Berman. 1983. "The Efficacy of Cognitive Behavior Therapies: A Quantitative Review of the Research Evidence." *Psychological Bulletin* 94:39–53.

Mills, C. W. 1959. *The Sociological Imagination*. New York: Oxford University Press.

Miringoff, M., and M. Miringoff. 1999. *The Social Health of the Nation*. New York: Oxford University Press.

Mishel, L., J. Bernstein, and J. Schmitt. 1999. *The State of Working America*. Ithaca, N.Y.: Cornell University Press.

Moloney, D. P., T. J. Bouchard Jr. and N. L. Segal. 1991. "A Genetic and Environmental Analysis of the Vocational Interests of Monozygotic and Dizygotic Twins Reared Apart." *Journal of Vocational Behavior* 39:76–109.

Moody, R. 1975. *Life after Life: The Investigation of a Phenomenon—Survival of Bodily Death*. St. Simons Island, Ga.: Mockingbird Press.

———. 1999. *The Last Laugh: A New Philosophy of Near-Death Experiences, Applications, and the Paranormal*. Charlottesville, Va.: Hampton Roads.

Moos, R. H., and B. S. Moos. 1986, 1994. *Manual: Family Environment Scale*. Palo Alto, Calif.: Consulting Psychologists Press.

Murray, C. 1984. *Losing Ground*. New York: Basic Books.

Nietzsche, W. F. 1968. *The Will to Power*. New York: Vintage Press.

Neuhouser, F. 1990. *Fichte's Theory of Subjectivity*. New York: Cambridge University Press.

New York Review of Books. 1994a. "The Unknown Freud: An Exchange." February 3:34–43.

———. 1994b. "The Unknown Freud: Yet Another Exchange." April 21:66–68.

Norris, C. 1990. *What's Wrong with Postmodernism: Critical Theory and the Ends of Philosophy*. Baltimore: Johns Hopkins University Press.

Oberg, B. B., and H. S. Stout. 1993. *Benjamin Franklin, Jonathan Edwards and the Representation of American Culture*. New York: Oxford University Press.

O'Brien, C. C. 1999. "Buried Lives." *New York Review of Books* December 16:81–84.

Office of Technology Assessment. 1980. *The Implications of Cost-Effectiveness Analysis of Medical Technology. Background Paper 3: The Efficacy and Cost Effectiveness of Psychotherapy*. Washington, D.C.: United States Congress.

Olasky, M. 1992. *The Tragedy of American Compassion*. Washington, D.C.: Regnery Gateway.

Olson, R. G. 1965. *The Morality of Self-Interest*. New York: Harcourt, Brace, and World.

Orne, M. T. 1962. "On the Social Psychology of the Psychological Experiment: With Particular Reference to Demand Characteristics and Their Implications." *American Psychologist* 10:776–83.

Osborne, J. W. 1970. *The Silent Revolution*. New York: Scribner's.

Page, B. I., and R. Y. Shapiro. 1992. *The Rational Public: Fifty Years of Trends in Americans' Policy Preferences*. Chicago: University of Chicago Press.

Page, B. I., R. Y. Shapiro, and G. R. Dempsey. 1987. "What Moves Public Opinion?" *American Political Science Review* 81:23–43.

Park, L. C., and L. Covi. 1965. "Nonblind Placebo Trial." *Archives of General Psychiatry* 12:336–45.

Park, R. 2000. *Voodoo Science.* New York: Oxford University Press.

Patterson, C. H. 1984. "Empathy, Warmth, and Genuineness in Psychotherapy: A Review of Reviews." *Psychotherapy* 21:431–38.

Patterson, J. T. 1981. *America's Struggle against Poverty: 1900–1980.* Cambridge, Mass.: Harvard University Press.

Pecora, P. J., M. W. Fraser, and D. A. Haapala. 1992. "Intensive Home-Based Services: An Update from the FIT Project." *Child Welfare* 71:177–87.

Pedersen, N. L., R. Plomin, J. R. Nesselroade, and G. E. McClearn. 1992. "A Quantitative Analysis of Cognitive Abilities during the Second Half of the Life Span." *Psychological Science* 3:346–53.

Plomin, R. 1990. *Nature and Nurture: An Introduction to Human Behavioral Genetics.* Pacific Grove, Calif.: Brooks/Cole.

Plomin, R., and C. S. Bergeman. 1991. "The Nature of Nurture: Genetic Influences on 'Environment' Measures." *Behavioral and Brain Sciences* 14:373–427.

Plomin, R., H. M. Chipuer, and J. M. Neiderhiser. 1994. "Behavioral Genetic Evidence for the Importance of Nonshared Environment." In *Separate Social Worlds of Siblings: The Impact of Nonshared Environment on Development,* ed. E. M. Hetherinton, D. Reiss, and R. Plomin. Hillsdale, N.J.: Erlbaum.

Plomin, R., R. Corley, J. C. DeFries, and D. W. Fulker. 1990. "Individual Differences in Television Viewing in Early childhood: Nature as Well as Nurture." *Psychological Sciences* 1:371–77.

Polit, D. F., J. Kahn, and D. Stevens. 1985. *Final Impacts from Project Redirection.* New York: Manpower Research Demonstration Corporation.

Polit, D. F., J. C. Quint, and J. A. Riccio. 1988. *The Challenge of Serving Teenage Mothers: Lessons from Project Redirection.* New York: Manpower Research Demonstration Corporation.

Public Agenda. 1995. *The Values We Live By: What Americans Want from Welfare Reform.* New York: Public Agenda.

Quint, J. C., J. M. Bos, and D. F. Polit. 1997. *New Chance: Final Report on a Comprehensive Program for Young Mothers in Poverty and Their Children.* New York: Manpower Research Demonstration Corporation.

Rachman, S. 1971. *The Effects of Psychological Treatment.* Oxford: Perragon Press.

Raphael, D. D., D. Winch, and R. Skidelsky. 1997. *Three Great Economists.* New York: Oxford University Press.

Ravetz, J. R. 1971. *Scientific Knowledge and Its Social Problems* Oxford: Clarendon Press.

Rawlings, L. 1998. *Poverty and Income Trends: 1997.* Washington, D.C.: Center on Budget and Policy Priorities.

Reid, W. J., and C. Bailey-Dempsey. 1995. "The Effects of Monetary Incentives on School Performance." *Families in Society,* 76:331–40.

Reid, W. J., C. Bailey-Dempsey, E. Cain, T. V. Cook, and J. D. Burchard. 1994. "Cash Incentives versus Case Management: Can Money Replace Services in Preventing School Failure?" *Social Work* 18:227–36.

Reid, W. J., and P. Hanrahan. 1982. "Recent Evaluations of Social Work: Grounds for Optimism." *Social Work* 27:328–40.

Riccio, J., and Y. Hasenfeld. 1996. "Enforcing a Participation Mandate in a Welfare-to-Work Program." *Social Service Review* 70:516–42.

Richey, R. E., and D. G. Jones. 1974. *American Civil Religion.* New York: Harper and Row.

Rieff, P. 1966. *The Triumph of the Therapeutic.* New York: Harper and Row.

Rife, J. C., and J. R. Belcher. 1994. "Assisting Unemployed Older Workers to Become Reemployed: An Experimental Evaluation." *Research on Social Work Practice* 4:3–13.

Rivlin, A. 1993. *Reviving the American Dream: The Economy, the States, and the Federal Government.* Washington, D.C.: Brookings Institution.

Robinson, J. L., J. S. Reznick, J. Kagan, and R. Corley 1992. "The Heritability of Inhibited and Uninhibited Behavior: A Twin Study." *Developmental Psychology* 28:1030–37.

Rose, G., and I. M. Marshall. 1974. *Counseling and School Social Work: An Experimental Study.* London: Wiley.

Rosen, A., E. K. Proctor, and M. Staudt. 1999. "Social Work Research and the Quest for Effective Practice." *Social Work Research* 23:4–14.

Rosenhans, D. L. 1973. "On Being Sane in Insane Places." *Science* 179:249–58.

Rosenthal, R., and D. B. Rubin. 1978. "Interpersonal Expectancy Effects: The First 345 Studies." *Behavioral and Brain Sciences* 3:379–86.

Rossi, P. H. 1991. "Evaluating Family Preservation Programs: A Report to the Edna McConnell Clark Foundation." New York: Edna McConnell Clark Foundation. Mimeographed.

Rousseau, J. J. 1954. *The Social Contract.* Chicago: Henry Regnery.

Rowe, D. 1981. "Environmental and Genetic Influences on Dimensions of Perceived Parenting: A Twin Study." *Developmental Psychology* 17:203–8.

———. 1983. "A Biometrical Analysis of Perceptions of Family Environment: A Study of Twin and Singleton Sibling Kinships." *Child Development* 54: 416–23.

Rubin, A. 1985. "Practice Effectiveness: More Grounds for Optimism." *Social Work* 30:469–76.

Rule, J. B. 1997. *Theory and Progress in Social Science.* New York: Cambridge University Press.

Saiedi, N. 1993. *The Birth of Social Theory.* Lanham, Md.: University Press of America.

Salamon, L. 1999. *America's Nonprofit Sector.* New York: Foundation Center.

Santangelo, L. K. "Scientific Credibility of Social Work Research." Unpublished manuscript.

Schiltz, M. E. 1970. *Public Attitudes toward Social Security: 1935–1965.* Washington, D.C.: United States Department of Health, Education, and Welfare.

Schuerman, J. R., R. L. Rzepnicki, and J. H. Littell. 1994. *Putting Families First.* New York: Aldine de Gruyter.

Schwarzmantel, J. 1998. *The Age of Ideology: Political Ideologies from the American Revolution to Post Modern Times.* New York: New York University Press.

Segal, S. P. 1972. "Research on the Outcomes of Social Work Therapeutic Interventions: A Review of the Literature." *Journal of Health and Social Behavior* 13:3–17.

Seligman, M. E. P. 1995. "The Effectiveness of Psychotherapy: The *Consumer Reports* Study." *American Psychologist* 50:965–74.

———. 1996. "Long-Term Psychotherapy Is Highly Effective: The *Consumer Reports* Study." *Harvard Mental Health Letter* 13(1):5–9.

Shanks, A. 1995. *Civil Society, Civil Religion.* Oxford: Blackwell.

Shapiro, D. A. 1985. "Recent Applications of Meta-analyses in Clinical Research." *Clinical Psychology Review* 5:13–34.

Shapiro, D. A., and D. Shapiro. 1983. "Comparative Therapy Outcome Research: Methodological Implications of Meta-analysis." *Journal of Consulting and Clinical Psychology* 51:42–53.

Shapiro, R. Y., K. D. Patterson, and J. T. Young. [1986]. "Economic Status and Other Influences on Public Opinion toward Social Welfare Policies." Annual Meeting of the Northeastern Political Science Association, November 13–15, Boston.

Shapiro, R. Y., K. D. Patterson, J. Russell, and J. T. Young. 1987a. "The Polls: Employment and Social Welfare." *Public Opinion Quarterly* 51:268–81.

———. 1987b. "The Polls: Public Assistance." *Public Opinion Quarterly* 51:120–30.

Shapiro, R. Y., and J. T. Young. 1989. "Public Opinion and the Welfare State: The United States in Comparative Perspective." *Political Science Quarterly* 104:59–89.

Sheldon, B. 1986. "Social Work Effectiveness Experiments: Review and Implications." *British Journal of Social Work* 16:223–42.

Sherover, C. M. 1980. "Rousseau's Civil Religion." *Interpretations* May:114–22.

Shuffleton, F., ed. 1993. *The American Enlightenment.* Rochester, N.Y.: University of Rochester Press.

Silbershatz, G. 1999. "How Useful for Psychotherapists Are Randomized Controlled Experiments?" *Harvard Mental Health Letter* 16: 5–9.

Simon, H. A. 1960. *The New Science of Management Decision.* New York: Harper and Brothers.

———. 1977. *Models of Discovery.* Boston: D. Reidel.

Simon, H. A. 1982a. *Economic Analysis and Public Policy.* Vol. 1. Cambridge, Mass.: MIT Press.

———. 1982b. *Economic Analysis and Public Policy.* Vol. 2. Cambridge, Mass.: MIT Press.

———. 1983. *Reason in Human Affairs.* Stanford, Calif.: Stanford University Press.

———. 1997. *Administrative Behavior.* New York: Free Press.

Slemrod, J. 1994. *Tax Progressivity and Income Inequality.* New York: Cambridge University Press.

Smith, A. 1994 [1776]. *The Wealth of Nations.* New York: Modern Library.

———. 1966 [1759]. *Moral Sentiments.* New York: A. M. Kelley.

Smith, M. L., G. V. Glass, and T. I. Miller. 1980. *The Benefits of Psychotherapy.* Baltimore: Johns Hopkins University Press.

Smith, R. M. 1997. *Civic Ideals.* New Haven, Conn.: Yale University Press.

Smith, S. R. 1987. "That Which We Call Welfare by Any Other Name Would Smell Sweeter: An Analysis of the Impact of Question Wording on Response Patterns." *Public Opinion Quarterly* 51:75–83.

Smith, T. W., and M. Lipsky. 1993. *Nonprofits for Hire.* Cambridge, Mass.: Harvard University Press.

Social Security Administration. 1998. *Income of the Aged Chartbook, 1996.* Washington, D.C.: Social Security Administration, Office of Research, Evaluation, and Statistics.

Sokal, A. D., and J. Bricmont. 1999. *Fashionable Nonsense: Postmodern Intellectuals' Abuse of Science.* New York: St. Martin's Press.

Sotsky, S. M., D. R. Glass, T. Shea, P. A. Pilkonis, J. F. Collins, I. Elkin, J. T. Watkins, S. D. Imber, W. R. Leber, J. Moyer, and M. E. Oliveri. 1991. "Patient Predictors of Response to Psychotherapy and Pharmacotherapy: Findings in the NIMH Treatment of Depression Collaborative Research Program." *American Journal of Psychiatry* 148:997–1008.

Stassen, H. H., D. T. Lykken, and G. Bomben. 1988. "The Within-Pair EEG Similarity of Twins Reared Apart." *European Archives of Psychiatric Neurological Science* 237:244–52.

Stein, L. I., and M. A. Test. 1980. "Alternatives to Mental Hospital Treatment." *Archives of General Psychiatry* 37(April):392–412.

Strupp, H. H. and S. W. Hadley. 1979. "Specific Versus Nonspecific Factors in Psychotherapy," *Archives of General Psychiatry* 36:1125–36.

Stuart, R. B. 1973. *Trick or Treatment.* Champaign, Ill.: Research Press.

Summers, M. 1971. *The Malleus Maleficarum of Henrich Kramer and James Sprenger.* New York: Dover.

Taylor, W. L. 2000. "Keeping the Dream" *Poverty and Race* 9(1):10–11.

Teles, S. M. 1998. *Whose Welfare? AFDC and Elite Politics.* Lawrence: University Press of Kansas.

Tellegen, A., D. T. Lykken, T. J. Bouchard Jr., K. J. Wilcox, N. L. Segal, and S. Rich. 1988. "Personality Similarity in Twins Reared Apart and Together." *Journal of Personality and Social Psychology* 54:1031–39.

Thomlison, R. J. 1984. "Something Works: Evidence from Practice Effectiveness Studies." *Social Work* 29:51–56.

Tillitski, C. J. 1990. "A Meta-analysis of Estimated Effect Sizes for Group versus Individual versus Control Treatments." *International Journal of Group Psychotherapy* 40:215–24.

Titmuss, R. 1971. *The Gift Relationship: From Human Blood to Social Policy.* New York: Pantheon.

Tocqueville, Alexis de. 1969. *Democracy in America.* New York: HarperCollins.

Tripodi, T. 1984. "Trends in Research Publication: A Study of Social Work Journals from 1956 to 1980." *Social Work* 29:353–59.

Truax, C. B., and R. R. Carkhuff. 1967. *Toward Effective Counseling and Psychotherapy: Training and Practice*. Chicago: Aldine.

U.S. Census Bureau. 1999. *Historical Income and Poverty*. Series P-60. Washington, DC: Government Printing office.

United States Department of Health and Human Services. 1999. *Mental Health: A Report of the Surgeon General* Rockville, MD: U. S. Department of Health and Human Services, Subsxtance Abuse and Mental Health Services Administrationl, Center for Mental Health Services, National Institutes of Health, National Institute of Mental Health.

VanderBos, G. R. 1996. "Outcome Assessment of Psychotherapy." *American Psychologist* 51:1005–6.

Vattimo, G. 1991. *The End of Modernity*. Baltimore: Johns Hopkins University Press.

Venturi, F., 1971. *Utopia and Reform in the Enlightenment*. New York: Cambridge University Press.

Videka-Sherman, L. 1988. "Meta-analysis of Research on Social Work Practice in Mental Health." *Social Work* 33:325–38.

Ways and Means Committee, U.S. House of Representatives. 1998. *The Green Book* Washington, D.C.: Government Printing Office.

Weaver, R. K., R. Y. Shapiro, and L. R. Jacobs. 1995. "The Polls—Trends: Welfare" *Public Opinion Quarterly* 59:606–27.

Weisz, J. R., B. Weiss, M. D. Alicke, and M. L. Klotz. 1987. "Effectiveness of Psychotherapy with Children and Adolescents: A Meta-analysis for Clinicians." *Journal of Consulting and Clinical Psychology* 55:542–49.

Williams, J. P. 1952. *What Americans Believe and How They Worship*. New York: Harper Brothers.

Wilson, W. J. 1987. *The Truly Disadvantaged: The Inner City, the Underclass, and Public Policy*. Chicago: University of Chicago Press.

Woloch, I. 1982. *Eighteenth Century Europe, Tradition and Progress, 1715–1789*. New York: Norton.

Wood, K. M. 1978. "Casework Effectiveness: A New Look at the Research Evidence." *Social Work* 23:437–58.

Wootton, B. 1959. *Social Science and Social Pathology*. London: George Allen and Unwin.

Index

absolute idealism, 178–85
accountability, 65–66, 89n9, 144
Adams, John, 96
Adecedarian program, 83
administration, 2, 198
Adoption and Safe Families Act of
  1997, 116
adoption studies, 50–58
AFDC. *See* Aid to Families with
  Dependent Children
affirmative action, 7
African Americans, 117, 121, 136, 141
Aid to Families with Dependent
  Children (AFDC), xiv, xv, 2, 93, 115,
  130, 139.
  See also Temporary Assistance to
    Needy Families
alternative medicine, 196, 213
alternative visions, viii–ix, 20–22, 36,
  44n4
America:
  chosenness, 98–99, 107;
  Enlightenment in, 169–78;
  exceptionalism, xvii, 208, 214–15;
  goodness of people, 127–28;
  Romanticism, 170–71;
  welfare state, 2–5
American covenant, 97–98
American Psychological Association,
  64
anti-intellectualism, 176, 179
a priori principles, 180–81, 203, 217

authority, ix, vii, 25, 41, 85–86, 154, 177;
  scientific, vii, 12–13, 31, 78–79, 82
autopsy, 185, 186

Bacon, Francis, 159
Baggette, J., 124
Barrett, E. J., 115–16, 125
Beecher, Lyman, 103–4, 105
behavior, 141–44;
  conformity, xiii–xiv, 26, 99, 141;
  explanations, 32–35, 48–50, 131, 157;
behavioral genetics, 32–34, 48–50;
  Harris's essay and, 50–58;
  political role, 58–59
behavior modification, 75
belief, 87–88.
  See also civil religion
Bellah, R. N., 93, 94, 97–100, 104, 107
Bell Curve, The (Herrnstein and
  Murray), 34, 56
Benefits of Psychotherapy, The (BOP)
  (Smith, Glass, and Miller), 60–63
Bergeman, C. S., 54–55
Bergin, A. E., 60–61
Berlin, I., 9
best interest, 17, 19
Betsworth, R. G., 106
blame, 127–28, 141, 147, 150n6
Bloom, H., 144
BOP. *See Benefits of Psychotherapy, The*
Bouchard, T. J., 51–52, 88nn2, 4
bounded rationality, 198–202, 208

bourgeoisie, 158, 168
bulk-cargo empiricism, 87
bulletins of social progress, 81–86,
    89–90n13
Burke, Edmund, 183
Bush, George W., 110n6

Calvinism, 10–11, 94, 131, 170
capitalism, 94, 101, 113–15
case management, 144–45
cash transfer programs, 135–40
categorical imperative, 181
cause, 26–27, 196–97;
    social cause, 156–60;
    symmetry of, 92, 110n3
ceremonial civil religion. *See* civil
    religion
Chai, L., 216
Chalk, R., 81, 85–86
character, national, 109n2
characterological explanations, 5,
    119–20, 131, 145
charisma, 14, 84–85
charitable sector, 3–4, 11, 18, 22–23n1,
    23n6, 149n3
children, 137;
    child welfare system, 71–74;
    foster care, 48, 72, 127, 130, 136;
    research, 146–47
Children's Defense Fund, 150n7
Chong, D., 203–4
Christianity, 10, 100, 102, 104, 106, 167,
    176–77, 187
civic ideals, 8–12
civil religion, vii–xi, 14, 42–43, 83, 185;
    antirationality, 206–8;
    belief as need, 87–88;
    ceremonial, xiv–xvii, 15, 41, 93,
        97–102, 194;
    cohesion and, 94–96;
    as denial, 107–8;
    as ethnocentric, 104–5, 109n2;
    faith-based, 101, 110n6;
    operative, xvi–xvii, 96, 97, 102–5,
        119, 178;
    patriotism, vii, xi, 104–5, 175;
    polls and, 111–12, 127;
    psychotherapy as, 69;

Rousseau's view, 93–97;
    sanctions, 93–95, 98;
    social ethics, 105–7;
    social preferences and, 14–15, 91–92,
        119–20, 139;
    social realities and, 99–101;
    tolerance, 100–104;
    universalism, 97–99.
    See also ritual
civil rights, 97
civil society, 96
Civil War, 99
classical liberalism, 9
clinical significance, 79, 89n12
cognitive therapy, 61–62
cohesion, 94–96
Colorado Adoption Project, 55
Committee on the Assessment of
    Family Violence Interventions, 85–86
common sense, 166–67
compassion, 7, 160, 167, 189n4
competition, 25, 40, 41, 94, 162
compulsion, 102
consensus, 194–95
conservatism, 9, 131, 151.
    See also Romanticism
Constitution, 169, 172–73
Consumer Reports, 64–65
Cook, F. L., 115–16, 125
corrective myth, xi, 86–87, 148–49, 153,
    159, 214
counselors, 84–85
Crane, J., 81–83
creativity, 184
Crews, F., 67
criticism. *See* skeptical criticism
CRP (NIMH Collaborative Research
    Project), 63–64
cruelty, 87–88, 92, 103, 107, 188;
    disrespect, 139, 140, 145;
    ethos of, 108–9, 131–32;
    in poll responses, 113, 117
cultural poverty, 74
culture, 74, 121–22, 166, 217–18;
    appropriation of science, 194–96

Dahl, R. A., 37–39
Danziger, S. H., 136

Declaration of Independence, 173
decoy research, 89n9
*Defence of the Constitutions of the
Government of the United States of
America* (Smith), 174
deism, 151, 162
democracy, 32, 45n8, 101–2, 105, 155,
168, 190n7
Democracy in America (Tocqueville), 97,
159
denial, 107–8, 112, 120, 124, 127
deservingness, vii, 14, 119, 124, 127,
133n6, 146;
moral hazards argument, 136–37;
racism, 141–42
destiny, vii, 56
determinism, 181, 191n14
deviance, xv–xvi, 4–6, 136
disabled, 3, 10, 11, 125, 127, 137
distributive assumptions, 161–63
dualism, 152

Earned Income Tax Credit, 2
education, 22, 23n2;
Enlightenment views, 158, 164–65,
173–74;
interventions, 82–83
Edwards, Jonathan, 159, 169–70, 176,
186, 216
efficiency, ix, 30, 32, 47, 115;
satisficing, 200–201.
See also social efficiency
elites:
American Enlightenment, 169–78;
civil religion and, 106, 108;
Enlightenment, 157–58, 164–65;
genetics and, 33–34;
poll responses, 112, 116, 120, 131;
Romanticism and, 179–80
Emerson, Ralph Waldo, 10
emotional intelligence, 57
emotionality, 206
empiricism, 87, 174, 180–81, 193
Enlightenment, viii, xi, xvii–xviii, 9, 14,
151–52;
as Age of Reason, 152, 186, 189n3;
American, 169–78;
antirationalism, 160, 165;

Christianity, 100, 102, 104, 167,
176–77, 187;
civil religion and, 185 86;
context, 177–78;
core beliefs, 152–53;
education, view of, 158, 164–65,
173–74;
elites, 157–58, 164–65;
European, 171;
goals, 155–56, 217, 218;
government, view of, 160–65,
173–75;
metaphysics, 160, 162–64;
mysticism, 159–60, 175–76;
myths of, 154–56, 175–76;
paradoxes, 153–54, 156–60;
reforms of liberty, 167–69;
responsibility, view of, 165–67,
175–76;
science and, 152–54, 173–75, 219;
Scottish, 96, 160, 167;
security concerns, 172–73;
social cause and social reform,
156–60;
spontaneous order, 160–67;
universalism, 169, 173;
as utopian, 154–55, 158–59
environmental influences, 34–35,
51–57, 145, 156
epistemology, Romantic, 180–82
equality, 21–22, 96–97, 172.
See also elites; Enlightenment
ethics, 105–7, 166
ethnocentrism, 104–5, 109n2, 217
evaluation, viii, 5–6, 15, 20, 23–24n8,
26;
panel data, 29–30.
See also research
exceptionalism, xvii, 208, 214–15
experimental demonstrations, 6–7
explanations, 26–28, 39;
characterological, 5, 119–20, 131,
145;
genetic, 7, 27, 32–34, 48–50, 131,
157;
structural, 34–35, 44n2, 86, 114, 125;
subcultural, 5, 34–35, 44nn2, 3, 92,
119–20.

See also individualism;
     responsibility
Eysenck, H. F., 60

faith, 101, 110n6, 187, 211, 214
falsification, 202
family, 7, 48.
     See also Aid to Families with
     Dependent Children; children;
     foster care; Temporary Assistance
     to Needy Families
Family Environment Scale (FES),
     52–54, 57, 88n2
family preservation services, 71–74,
     147
fatalism, 156, 159
federal budget, 2
Federalist Papers, The, 171
FES (Moos and Moos's Family
     Environment Scale), 52–54, 57, 88n2
Fichte, Johann Gottlieb, 178, 181–82,
     191n13
Fischer, Joel, 70, 74–75, 78
Food Stamps, xvi, 2, 3, 93, 115, 125,
     130, 138
formalism, 99–100
foster care, 48, 72, 125, 127, 130, 136;
     as ritual, 145–48
Franklin, Benjamin, 159, 175–76
free agency, 97, 144, 157–58, 178
freedom, 160–61, 182;
     negative freedoms, 9, 113
French Revolution, 95–96, 168, 183,
     187
Freud, Sigmund, 67
Friedman, J., 206, 207
fruit fly research, 57

Gans, H. J., 119
Gay, Peter, 151, 152, 154, 156, 187,
     190n9
General Social Survey, 121, 133n7,
     133–34n8
genetic explanations, 7, 27, 32–34,
     48–50, 131, 157
German absolute idealists, 178–85
Gilens, M., 118–19, 124, 130
Glass, G. V., 60–63, 75

Glisson, C., 79
God, 98–99
Goethe, Johann Wolfgang von, 178
goodness, 127–28
Gorey, K. M., 78
government:
     Enlightenment view, 160–65,
        173–75;
     minimal, 160–61, 177;
     representative, 12, 158
Great Awakening, 169
Great Depression, 120
Greater Avenues for Independence
     (California), 80
Green, P. G., 204–7
group socialization theory (GST), 49,
     57–58
group work, 76

Hamowy, R., 167
Handler, J., 1
Hanrahan, P., 76, 77
Harris, J. R., 48, 50–58, 59
Hauptmann, E., 206
health care, xvii
Hearn, F., 106
Hegel, G. W. F., 178, 179, 182–83, 188
Herberg, W., 100–101, 104
heritability, 50, 88n1.
     See also behavioral genetics
Herrnstein, R. J., 34, 56
heuristics, 198–99, 203–4
Hofstadter, Richard, 176
Home Observation for the
     Measurement of the Environment
     (HOME) scale, 55
humanism, 154
human significance, 65
Hume, David, 21, 162, 164, 166–67,
     180, 183, 189n6
hypocrisy, 15, 31

idealism, 178–85
ideas, 180–81
ideology, xiv, 13, 25, 31;
     of deprivation, 4–5;
     of genetics, 33–34;
     historical, 182–83;

justification of policies, 25–26;
Romantic, 179, 182–83, 187–88;
of social welfare industry, 1–2, 14–17
ignorance, 30, 32, 57, 87–88, 187, 221
illegal income, 140, 149n4
illegitimate births, 136, 144–45
imagination, 18–21, 180
impaired capabilities, 36–37, 40
imperialism, economic, 113
income:
  illegal, 140, 149n4;
  Supplemental Security Income, 2, 3,
    11, 115, 125, 138;
  surrogates for, 48
income inequality, 2–3, 75, 92, 133n2,
    137;
  public opinion, 113, 127;
  racial inequalities, 7, 15
individualism, xii-xiii, 159, 178;
  characterological explanations,
    119–20, 131, 145;
  charismatic counselors, 84–85;
  civic ideals and, 10–11;
  as myth, 20–21, 87;
  public opinion, 113–15;
  Puritan view, 96–97, 99;
  Romantic, 178, 214–15;
  subcultural explanations, 119–20;
  trial social services and, 5, 15.
  See also responsibility, personal
industrialization, 154–55, 168–69, 180,
    188, 189n5, 190n8
industriousness, 157–58, 166
Inquisition, 212–13
institutions, xiii, 9, 34–35, 40, 83,
    165–66, 177, 183–84, 214
instrumental rationality, 28–29, 38–39,
    160, 165, 196
intellectuals, 120, 133n5, 213–14
intellectual styles, 152
intelligence, 51, 52, 56–57, 59
internal validity, 78, 80–81
interpersonal expectancy effects, 63
interpretation of data, 204, 205
IQ, 51, 52, 59

Jacobs, L. R., 124, 126
Japan, 3

Jefferson, Thomas, 100, 172–73
justice, 161, 162, 166

Kant, Immanuel, 167, 180–82, 186,
    191n16, 198
Karasu, B., 144
King, P. A., 81, 85–86
Koch, A., 171–72, 175
Kuhn, Thomas, 194

labor force participation, 30, 149–50n4
laissez-faire, 9, 166–68
Lambert, M. J., 60–61, 89n8
LaPiere, R. T., 31
leadership, 14, 17
legitimacy, 29, 31, 92
Levi, I., 207–8
Lewis, Oscar, 44n2
liberalism, 9, 94, 96, 102, 120, 151
Lindblom, C. E., 13–14, 28–29, 36–40,
    216
localism, 106–7
Loehlin, J. C., 54
long-term values, 205
lower-status groups:
  claims ignored, 30–31;
  conformity expected of, xiii–xiv, 26;
  standard of living, 2–3;
  subcultural explanations and, 34–35,
    92;
  unworthiness ascribed to, 9–10,
    14–15, 17, 35, 44n3, 137
Luborsky, L. B., 68
Lubove, R., 123

Maccoby, E. E., 49
Madison, James, 96
Malleus Maleficarum, 212
Manpower Demonstration Research
  Corporation, 71, 189n5
market, 9, 106, 107, 160–61, 163, 168
Martin, J. A., 49
Martinson, R., 75
Marty, M., 100–101
Marx, Karl, 157, 179, 183, 186, 214
May, H. F., 177
Mayer, S. E., 120–21
McCloskey, D. N., 113–14, 132n1

McGue, M., 51–52, 88n2
Mead, L. M., 82
Mead, S. E., 100, 102
measurement, 29–30, 40
media, 127, 130–31
Medicaid, 2, 3, 115
Medicare, xv, 2, 47, 115
mentally ill, 77, 138.
    See also psychotherapy
mentors, 84–85
meta-analysis, 61, 89n7
metaphysics, 160, 162–64, 179, 183
methodology, xvii, 5–8, 199;
    family preservation studies, 72–73;
    psychotherapy research, 59–69;
    randomization, 73, 80, 83–84;
    review of research, 74–81.
    See also research; theory
middle class, 136, 154, 158, 168
Miller, T. I., 60–63, 75
Mills, C. W., 19, 20
Mills, Reuben, 84
Minnesota Study of Twins (MST), 48,
    50–58, 88n3
Mississippi, 139, 149n3
modernity, 167
Moody, R., 214
Moos and Moos's Family Environment
    Scale (FES), 52–54, 57, 88n2
morality, xvii, 182;
    moral hazards argument, 136–37;
    personal, 160–61;
    poll responses, 117, 125–27
moral unworthiness, 9–10, 14, 17, 35,
    44n3, 92, 137
Moynihan,D. P., 133n5
MST. *See* Minnesota Study of Twins
Murray, Charles, 34, 43–44n1, 56, 88n4,
    136
mysticism, x–xi, 93, 98, 103, 108, 109n1,
    151;
    antirationalist, 160, 165;
    Enlightenment, 159–60, 175–76;
    psychotherapy and, 142–44;
    spontaneous order, 160–67
myth, viii, 7, 102, 216;
    American covenant, 97–98;

corrective, xi, 86–87, 148–49, 153,
    159, 214;
    as denial, 107–8, 127;
    of Enlightenment, 154–56, 158–59,
    175–76;
    equality as alternative, 21–22;
    individualism as, 20–21, 87;

narrative, 106
National Academy of Sciences (NAS),
    85–86
National Center for Research on Social
    Programs, 82
national character, 109n2
National Institutes of Mental Health
    (NIMH), 76
nationalism, 104–5, 175
nature-nurture controversy, 27, 32–33,
    48–50;
    MST data, 50–58
negative freedoms, 9, 113
Neuhouser, F., 181–82, 191n13
New Democrats, 9
Newtonian mechanics, xvii, 174, 216
New York Times, 83–84
Nietzsche, Friedrich, 159, 178, 183–86,
    191–92n15
nihilism, 14, 41, 167, 184–85
NIMH (National Institutes of Mental
    Health), 63–64, 75
nonprofit sector, 3–4, 11, 18, 22–23n1,
    23n6
Notes on the State of Virginia (Jefferson),
    173
nurture assumption, 48–50

OASDI. *See* Old Age Survivors and
    Disability Insurance
O'Brien, C. C., 100
OECD. *See* Organization for Economic
    Co-operation and Development
Old Age Assistance, 125
Old Age Insurance. *See* Social Security
Old Age Survivors and Disability
    Insurance (OASDI), xv, 2, 47
Old World religions, 100
operations research, 36–37, 201

operative civil religion. *See* civil religion
order, spontaneous, 160–67
Organization for Economic Cooperation and Development (OECD), 33
orphanages, 146

Page, B. I., 121, 128–29
panel data, 29–30
paranoia, 12
pareto optima, 28
parsimony, xi, 11, 14, 95, 99
patriotism, vii, xi, 104, 175
personal social services, xii–xvi, 7, 26, 47–48;
    bulletins of social progress, 81–86, 89–90n13;
    Putting Families First (PFF), 70–74;
    racism in, 141–42;
    review of research, 74–81;
    as rituals, 140–42;
    studies, 69–86.
    See also psychotherapy
PFF *(Putting Families First)*, 70–74
philosophes. *See* Enlightenment
philosophic liberalism, 94, 96, 102
Philosophy of History, The (Hegel), 182–83
Pierard, 106
pietism, 177, 188
placebo effects, 60–62, 68, 79, 89n8, 195
Plomin, R., 54–55, 56
political science, 202–3
politics:
    decision-making, 31–32, 35–36;
    empirical validation and, 28–29;
    rationality *vs.*, 12–14;
    of self-interest, 31, 39;
    social services and, 14–17.
    See also social decision-making process
polls, 39, 44n5, 44–45n7;
    ambivalence, 113–14;
    cleavage among groups, 121–22, 133–34n8, 134nn9, 10;
    consistency, 111–12, 116–17, 121–25, 132–33n1;

denial and, 120, 124, 127;
elites and, 112, 116, 120, 131;
flaws, 111 12, 132 33n1;
lack of rationality, 112–13, 126–32;
morality and, 117, 125–27;
philosophic attitudes, 111–12, 117, 127, 129–30;
public assistance, view of, 125–26;
rational choice theory, 202, 205;
rationality and, 112–13, 126–32;
social insurance, view of, 122–25;
stability of attitudes over time, 119–21, 129.
See also public opinion
Popper, Karl, 179
post hoc analysis, 204
postmodernism, xi, xvii, 41–42, 69, 207, 209, 215–16
poverty, 1, 4;
    cultural, 74;
    as deviance, 4–6;
    moral unworthiness and, 9–10, 14, 17, 35, 44n3, 92, 137;
    negative stereotypes of, 117–19
poverty line, 2–3, 135, 149n1
power, 39–40, 184, 219–20
pragmatism, xvii, 172, 176, 194, 196, 202–3, 206
Proctor, E. K., 78, 80
production functions, xiv–xv, 15, 26, 38–39, 47, 69–70, 143
professionalization, 18–19, 76–79, 200
Programs That Work, 6
Progressive Era, 214
propaganda, 105, 112, 130–31, 176
property, 9
Protestantism, 94, 96
psychopathology research, 74
psychotherapy, xv, 7, 16;
    accountability, 65–66, 89n9, 144;
    cognitive therapy, 61–62;
    as community, 66–67;
    for depression, 63–64;
    as harmful, 60–61;
    methodology, 59–69;
    placebo effects, 60–62, 68;
    as pseudoscience, 66–67, 195–96;
    psychoanalysis, 67;

public figures and, 142–43;
as ritual, 142–44;
satisfaction with, 64–65, 68–69, 143;
spiritual psychotherapy, 143–44;
studies, 59–69.
See also personal social services
Public Agenda, 117–19, 133n4
public discourse:
civic ideals and, 8–12;
understanding, viii–xii, 116–18,
133n4
public figures, psychotherapy and,
142–43
public opinion, 17–18, 40, 44n5,
44–45n7.
See also polls
Puritanism, 94, 96–97, 99, 131, 216;
Enlightenment, 170–71, 177
Putting Families First (PFF), 70–74

Quantum Program, 83–85

Rachman, S., 60, 62
racial issues, 7, 97, 117, 121, 136;
in personal social services, 141–42
Rand Corporation approach, 36–38
randomization, 73, 80, 83–84
rational choice theory, xvii, 38, 202–8,
210n3, 217
rationality, xi–xii, 5–8;
antirationality, 160, 165, 206–8;
bounded, 198–202, 208;
civic ideals and, 9–10;
heuristics, 198–99, 203–4;
hostility toward, 151–52, 170;
instrumental, 28–29, 38–39, 160, 165,
196;
isolated metaphors, 35–36;
limitations of, 36–38, 196–97, 202,
216;
measurement and, 29–30;
politics *vs.*, 12–14;
polls and, 112–13, 126–32;
rational choice theory, 38, 202–8,
209n3, 217;
satisficing, 199–200, 205;
science as, 193–94;

skeptical criticism, xvii-xviii,
179–80, 191n16, 211–12;
subversion of, 208–9
rationalized theism, 169
Reagan administration, 115, 116
redistributive policy, viii
reform, 156–60.
See also welfare reform
Reid, W. J., 76, 77
religion, 16, 24n11, 98–102, 177, 179;
Calvinism, influence of, 10–11, 94,
131, 170;
of democracy, 101–2;
Protestantism, 94, 96;
Puritanism, 94, 96–97, 99, 131,
170–71, 177, 216;
tolerance and, 100–102.
See also Christianity; civil religion
representative government, 12, 158
republicanism, 8–9, 14, 21, 96, 104, 114
research, 5–6, 15, 23–24n8, 39, 89n9;
authority of, 78–79, 85–86;
bias, 7, 63, 73, 81–82, 88n3,
132–33n1, 197, 209n2;
bounded rationality and, 198–202;
child welfare, 146–47;
clinical significance, 79, 89n12;
demonstration effects, 73;
Harris's essay, 50–58;
institutional bias, 78–79;
interpretation of data, 204, 205;
lack of credible information, 6–7,
28–29, 31–32, 42–43, 154, 197;
placebo effects, 60–62, 68, 79, 89n8;
post hoc analysis, 204;
professional ambitions and, 76–79;
rational choice theory and, 202–8;
self-reports, 54, 64–65, 78–79;
standards, 80–81;
test formulation, 204–5.
See also evaluation; methodology
resistance to change, viii–ix
responsibility, personal, 26–28, 92, 145,
148, 181;
Enlightenment view, 165–67,
175–76;
psychotherapy's role, 69, 141.

See also individualism
retirement, 115, 122–23
Revolutionary War, 99
ritual, xi, 93, 104, 207;
    case management as, 144–45;
    cash transfer programs as, 135–40;
    foster care as, 145–48;
    personal social services as, 140–42;
    psychotherapy as, 142–44.
    See also civil religion
Romanticism, x–xii, xvii–xviii, 9,
    18–19, 87–88, 151–52, 206;
    absolute idealism, 178–85;
    American, 170–71;
    as anti-Enlightenment, 154;
    civil religion and, 185–86;
    elites and, 179–80;
    ideology, 179, 182–83, 187–88;
    industrialization and, 168–69;
    metaphysics, 163–64, 183;
    self-consciousness, 182–84;
    self-creation, 47–48;
    will, 178, 180–82, 184, 211.
Roosevelt, Franklin D., 124
Rosen, A., 78, 80
Rossi, P. H., 85
Rousseau, Jean-Jacques, 93, 95–97, 108,
    157, 159
Rowe, D., 55
Rubin, A., 76, 77
Rule, J. B., 203
Russell Sage Foundation, 6

Saiedi, N., 179
Saint Louis Experiment, 76–77
Sandefur, G. D., 136
Santangelo, L. K., 80
satisficing, 36, 199–200, 205
Schiltz, M. E., 120
Schwarzmantel, J., 187
science, 7, 33;
    authority, vii, 12–13, 31, 78–79, 82;
    consensus, 194–96;
    cultural appropriation of, 194–96;
    Enlightenment and, 152–54, 173–75,
        219;
    as ideology, 13, 31;
    limitations of, 196–97, 202, 216;
    as rationality, 193–94;
    Romantic view, 180 81
scientism, 194, 201, 208–9, 216
    bounded rationality, 198–202, 208;
    rational choice theory, 202–8
Scottish Enlightenment, 96, 160, 167
Seattle/Denver Income Maintenance
    Experiments, 71
Segal, S. P., 74–75
self-consciousness, 182–84
self-creation, 47–48
self-deception, 127, 219
self-interest, xvi, 4, 17, 31, 39, 106;
    unintended consequences, 160–61
self-reflection, 182
self-reports, 54, 64–65, 78–79
self-selection, 29–30
Seligman, M. E. P., 64–66
sense perception, 180–81, 186
shamanism, 143
Shanks, A., 105, 106
Shapiro, R. Y., 121, 124, 126, 128–29,
    203–7
Sheldon, B., 77
Simon, Herbert, 36, 198–203
"Sinners in the Hands of an Angry
    God" (Edwards), 169–70
skeptical criticism, xvii–xviii, 179–80,
    191n16, 211–12
Smith, Adam, 9, 151, 153, 159–69, 171,
    177, 187, 190nn7, 8;
    compassion, 160, 167, 189n4;
    education, view of, 173–74
Smith, M. L., 60–63, 75
Smith, R. M., 97, 102–3, 193
social cause, 156–60
social Darwinism, 157
social decision-making process, 31–42;
    bounded rationality, 201–2;
    determinants, 39, 91, 93;
    failures, 37–38;
    instrumental rationality and, 28–29,
        38–39;
    isolated metaphors, 35–36;
    as nonrational form, 31–32;
    political convenience and, 13–14;

politics and, 39–42;
scientific model and, 13.
  See also social preferences
social efficiency, 11, 14, 21, 26–28, 96,
  136, 221
  See also efficiency
social ethics, 105–7
social insurance, xiii, 115, 122–25, 137.
  See also Social Security;
    Supplemental Security Income
socialization, xiii, 4, 49, 57–58
social preferences, xiii, 14–15, 91–92,
  139, 219;
  polls and, 119–20, 128–29
Social Programs That Work (Crane),
  81–85
social reform, 156–60
Social Science and Social Pathology, 74
social sciences, xvii–xviii, 19;
  authority, 25, 41, 49;
  limitations, 196–97, 202;
  literature, 15, 35, 40–42;
  scientism of, 194, 201.
  See also methodology; research
Social Security, 115, 130, 137;
  poll responses, 122–25, 134n10
Social Security Act, 12, 114
social service imagination, 18–21
social services. *See* personal social
  services; social insurance; social
welfare programs
social welfare industry, ix–x, 1–2, 15;
  professionalization, 18–19, 200
social welfare policy, viii;
  civil religion and, 92–93;
  as harmful to recipients, 6, 10–11;
  public understanding of, 116–18,
    133n4;
  as sanctioned by society, 14, 17,
    25–26, 31, 93–95, 98;
  spending, 2, 22–23n1, 29, 71, 86, 136.
  See also welfare reform
social welfare programs, vii–viii;
  antagonism toward, 117–19;
  benefits, 2, 3, 11, 23n7, 135, 137;
  case management, 144–45;
  case workers, 16, 19, 22n1, 140,
    199–200;

as entertainment, 141, 148–49;
  failure of, 6–7, 127, 130;
  funding, 26, 30–31;
  politics and, 14–17;
  production functions, xiv–xv, 15, 26,
    38–39, 47, 143;
  recipients, 10–11, 16–17, 118, 138;
  spending, 2, 22–23n1;
  trial periods, 5, 15.
  See also benefits; evaluation;
    personal social services; research;
    welfare reform
social workers, 16, 19, 22n1, 140,
  199–200
spontaneous order:
  distributive assumptions, 161–63;
  social institutions and, 165–66
SSI. *See* Supplemental Security Income
Staudt, M., 78, 80
Stein, L. I., 71, 76
stereotypes, 9–10, 117–19, 136, 141, 213
structural explanations, 34–35, 44n2,
  86, 114, 125
subcultural explanations, 5, 34–35,
  44nn2, 3, 92, 119–20
subjectivity, 7, 181–83, 203–4
substitution effect, 138–39
sufficient reason, 181, 191n14
superstition, 152–54, 170, 176, 186–87,
  213
Supplemental Security Income (SSI), 2,
  3, 11, 115, 125, 138
Surgeon General's report (1999), 66
surrogates, social services as, 48
surveillance, 6
symmetry of cause, 92, 110n3

TANF. *See* Temporary Assistance to
  Needy Families
taxes, 22, 163
tax policy, 92–93
Taylor, Frederick Winslow, 214
technology, 190n9, 193, 218–19
Teles, S. M., 120, 133nn4, 5
Temporary Assistance to Needy
  Families (TANF), xiv, xv, 3, 11, 139,
  149n2
Test, M. A., 71, 76

test formulation, 204–5
theology, 103–4, 169–70
theory, 188;
  of cause, 26–27;
  first branching, 28–32;
  as ideology, 25, 31;
  mix of social explanations, 35–36;
  nature of explanation, 26–28;
  nurture assumption, 48–50;
  second branching, 32–34;
  social decision-making process and,
    36–42;
  strategic choices, 26–27;
  third branching, 34–35.
  See also research
Theory of Moral Sentiments, The (Smith),
  160–63, 166–67
time-ordered consecutivity, 41
Tocqueville, Alexis de, 96–97, 159
tolerance, 97, 100–104, 113, 172
Townsend plan, 124
Treatment of Depression Collaborative
  Research Project (CRP), 63–64
trial experiments, 5, 23–24n8, 29, 42
twin studies, 48, 50–58, 88n3

uncertainty, 32, 40, 44–45n7, 57, 72
Unemployment Insurance, 115
universalism, 97–99, 169, 173
University of Chicago, 73
utility, 25, 28, 39, 165–66, 184–85

validity, internal, 78, 80–81
values, vii, xii, xiii, 16–17, 93–94.
  See also civil religion
Veterans Administration, 147
victimization, 128
Videka-Sherman, L., 77–78

violence, 81, 85–86, 146–48
Violence in Families (Chalk and King),
  81, 85–86, 89–90n13
virtue, 125, 137, 215–16
vocational training studies, 71
Voltaire, xviii, 157, 175
voting franchise, 8–9, 104, 177

War on Poverty, 12
Washington, George, 169
wealth, viii, 1, 22, 166, 219–20
Wealth of Nations, The (Smith), 160,
  162–63, 165
Weaver, R. K., 126
Weinberg, D. H., 136
welfare reform, 93, 112, 117, 137;
  illegitimate births, 136, 144–45;
  work requirements, 82–83, 118, 120,
    130, 139–40
welfare state, 2–5
White House Conference on Youth,
  150n7
Wieland, Christoph Martin, 212
will, xi, 10, 108, 166;
  free agency, 97, 144, 157–58, 178;
  Romantic view, 178, 180–82, 184, 211
Williams, J. P., 101–2, 105
Women, Infants, and Children
  Program, 83
Woodhouse, E. J., 40
Wootton, B., 74
work requirements, 82–83, 118, 120,
  130, 139–40
World-Spirit, 182–83, 188, 201, 204, 211

YAVIS syndrome, 60, 65

Zaller, J., 113–14, 132n1

About the Author

William M. Epstein teaches in the School of Social Work, University of Nevada, Las Vegas. He is the author of *Welfare in America: How Social Science Fails the Poor* and *Children Who Could Have Been: The Legacy of Child Welfare in Wealthy America* as well as other books and numerous essays on social welfare.